A Facsimile Edition
of the
Dead Sea Scrolls

VOLUME I

A Facsimile Edition
of the
Dead Sea Scrolls

VOLUME I

A Facsimile Edition
of the
Dead Sea Scrolls

Prepared with
an Introduction
and Index
by
Robert H. Eisenman
and
James M. Robinson

VOLUME I

BIBLICAL ARCHAEOLOGY SOCIETY
Washington, DC
1991

Library of Congress Number 91-058627
ISBN 1-880317-01-X (Volume I)
ISBN 1-880317-00-1 (Set)
©1991
Biblical Archaeology Society
3000 Connecticut Avenue, NW
Washington, DC 20008

*The Biblical Archaeology Society
is grateful to the
Irving I. Moskowitz Foundation
for its generous funding
of this publication.*

Table of Contents

Volume I

Volume II

Introduction

THE DEAD SEA SCROLLS, DISCOVERED IN 1947 AND THE YEARS IMMEDIATELY THEREAFTER, comprise one of the most important manuscript discoveries in the field of biblical and early Jewish and Christian studies to have been made in our century. The comparable Chester Beatty Biblical Papyri and Bodmer Papyri were published promptly after their discovery, and even the Nag Hammadi Codices, after an initial period of delay due to scholarly self-interest and Near Eastern politics, have now become fully available, whereas much of the more fragmentary parts of the Dead Sea Scrolls have remained inaccessible. Hence arrangements that initially seemed reasonable need, a generation or so later, to be supplemented by some mechanism by means of which scholars who were beginning their careers when the discoveries were made (not to speak of scholars then not yet born) can gain full access to them before their careers have been completed. It is under this higher claim of the academic community and society at large that the present edition has been initiated.

A Facsimile Edition of the Dead Sea Scrolls makes use of a photographic archive of largely unpublished fragments collected in what is now the Rockefeller Museum in Jerusalem. Since the bulk of the photographs go back to the early years, they neither reflect the joins and placements, nor the deterioration and loss, which may have taken place subsequent to photography. The painstaking work involved in such preparation of the fragments as had taken place up to that time is often quite indiscernible, since the original state in which the fragments were discovered is not documented for comparison. Given the absence of any accompanying notes, identifications can only be fully appreciated once the texts are edited and it has been ascertained to what extent fragments have been placed side by side in the photographs because they actually belong together, and to what extent their position is more random. The work had not been completed at the time the photographs were made, and indeed has no doubt in many cases still not been completed, in that the critical edition itself has not been completed. Users of this *Facsimile Edition* should hence understand that the photographs do not represent the definitive work of those who have had access to them over the years but have not felt ready for various reasons themselves to publish them, nor do they in any way represent our own work.

This *Facsimile Edition* publishes the photographs as they are, since verification by the originals is not possible. New research seeking to effect further identifications and placements on the basis of the photographs alone would have been very difficult and would have delayed considerably the appearance of this edition. Attempts to join one fragment with another are best left to the work of the academic community as a whole, beginning here with the raw data on which such work can go forward.

Included in this *Facsimile Edition* are photographs of manuscript material from caves in the Khirbet Qumran region, especially Cave IV, as well as material discovered at other locations, including Wadi Murabba'at, Wadi Daliyeh and Naḥal Ḥever. These materials are all included in this photographic archive and are generally associated by the public with the Dead Sea Scrolls among the manuscript discoveries of the Judaean Desert.

An Index is appended to this Introduction, supplying for each of the plates the numeration on the photographs themselves. An unpublished and restricted "Catalog of the Dead Sea Scrolls" prepared in Israel a decade ago, listing many of these photographs by their numbers and even identifying some so listed, is out of date, inexact and incomplete, though it is circulating informally. In practice it is of limited usefulness, especially since the fragments themselves are often no longer located where they are shown on these photographs. Yet, given the paucity of available information, even such a tool should at least be mentioned. However, a new and improved Inventory has already begun to appear, though beginning with the already-published materials. There the contents of each photograph, listed by its number, are itemized, and publication information is provided. Once the fascicles containing the unpublished material become available, this Inventory can be correlated with the Index so as to identify, to the extent known from previous scholarship, the contents of each plate of this *Facsimile Edition*.

This edition is intended to bring into the public domain an archive that consists especially (but not exclusively) of unpublished materials. Duplicates of plates photographed more than once, and sometimes at different times with different contents or arrangements, have been included, though photographs of material other than manuscripts are omitted. Skipped numerals in the sequence of the photographs do not necessarily indicate lacunae in the archive. Because the Catalog itself bypasses many numbers, the existence of photographs corresponding to such numbers is from case to case an open question. On the other hand, a large quantity of numbered photographs whose numbers were skipped in the original Catalog are included here.

The availability of this *Facsimile Edition* should of course not be used as a still further reason for delay in making the originals in the Rockefeller Museum fully available under appropriate conservation procedures to the scholarly community. For critical editions prepared on the basis of this *Facsimile Edition* will at best be provisional publications (as indeed are all *editiones principes*). They will be subject to subsequent verification and the improvement of obscure readings on the basis of the originals, when the current situation with its restrictions is overcome.

Robert H. Eisenman, one of the principal voices calling for the immediate publication of a facsimile edition of unpublished Dead Sea Scrolls and the exponent of a theory of his own of Qumran origins, and James M. Robinson, known for leadership in the publication of *The Facsimile Edition of the Nag Hammadi Codices*, were engaged not only to help prepare this edition, but also to provide an Introduction and Index. We ourselves make no claim to credit for the preliminary scholarly work reflected by the photographs in the archive, such as the selection of which fragments should be on a given plate or how they would be arranged on the plate, nor for the actual photography itself. We were merely enlisted in and have cooperated with the effort to implement the right of the academic community to obtain access to this important material without further delay.

In view of our relations to California State University, Long Beach, and to the Institute for Antiquity and Christianity of Claremont Graduate School, and our proximity to a sister institution in Claremont, the Ancient Biblical Manuscript Center, it should be explicitly stated that though we are not privy to the source of these photographs, we are satisfied that they do not come from the University or the Institute, since they have no such photographs, nor from the Center, since the restrictions under which it does have such photographs have not permitted their use for this purpose.[1]

5 JUNE 1991

ROBERT H. EISENMAN
CHAIR, RELIGIOUS STUDIES DEPARTMENT
CALIFORNIA STATE UNIVERSITY, LONG BEACH
LONG BEACH, CALIFORNIA

JAMES M. ROBINSON
CHAIR, RELIGION FACULTY
CLAREMONT GRADUATE SCHOOL
CLAREMONT, CALIFORNIA

---

[1] There should now [8 October 1991] be added: . . . nor from the Huntington Library, which in the best tradition of academic freedom made its microfilms of the Dead Sea Scrolls available on 22 September 1991, after this edition had already gone to press.

Publisher's Foreword

THIS IS THE SECOND PRINTING OF THIS HISTORIC SET OF BOOKS. THE FIRST PRINTING WAS the culmination of a process that made the long-unpublished texts from Qumran Cave 4 accessible to all. The first step in this process was the publication on September 4, 1991, of the first fascicle of *A Preliminary Edition of the Unpublished Dead Sea Scrolls—The Hebrew and Aramaic Texts from Cave Four*, by Ben Zion Wacholder and Martin G. Abegg (Washington, DC: Biblical Archaeology Society, 1991). The first fascicle consisted of transcripts generated by a computer from a concordance prepared by Joseph Fitzmyer, Raymond Brown and William Oxtoby. (J. Teixidor also worked on the concordance, but only on non-Cave 4 transcripts.) The concordance was prepared in the late 1950s, shortly after the members of the official editing team made the original transcriptions of the texts of the scroll fragments. (The transcripts in the first fascicle were principally those originally transcribed by J. T. Milik.) Wacholder and Abegg did not simply recreate the transcripts, however; they made a number of suggestions for improvements in the readings.

The next step in making the Cave 4 texts more accessible was the announcement on September 21, 1991, by the Huntington Library of San Marino, California, that it would make its microfilm of the original texts available to scholars either at the library or by interlibrary loan.

The final step was the publication on November 19, 1991, of the first printing of this two-volume set of photographs prepared by Robert H. Eisenman and James M. Robinson.

This final step made the texts easily available to all. The battle of the scrolls was, for all practical purposes, over. A time of controversy and confrontation was succeeded by a time of cooperation and reconciliation. At the annual meeting of the Society of Biblical Literature held in Kansas City on November 23–26, 1991, a statement was adopted recommending that anyone who owns or controls ancient written materials "should allow all scholars to have access to them." Helmut Koester,

SBL president, announced that both the official editing team and the Israel Antiquities Authority had agreed to cooperate with the new policy embodied in the SBL resolution.

Since then, the Israel Antiquities Authority has demonstrated its willingness to work together, and for that I am indeed grateful. I believe a new day has dawned in the history of the Dead Sea Scrolls — a day when scholars will collaborate in the study of these ancient texts, a time that will see a burgeoning of Dead Sea Scroll research, a period that will bring a deeper understanding of Second Temple Judaism, early Christianity and rabbinic Judaism.

Since the publication of the first printing of these photographs, several of the depositaries of photographs, with the blessing of the Israel Antiquities Authority, are making individual photographs available to scholars. We are advised that the Israel Antiquities Authority itself is preparing its own microfiche edition of the texts for distribution to everyone who wishes to purchase a copy. These are welcome developments. In addition, the official editing team has substantially expanded the number of scholars who are working under its auspices to complete the official publications. This expansion in most cases preceded or coincided with the publication developments described above and is likewise to be applauded. Now, we understand, all of the texts have been assigned for publication. The publication process is proceeding apace. We can no doubt expect other publications and translations. Then scholars can begin the equally difficult task of assessing the meaning and significance of the texts.

It is not only a welcome time. It is an exciting time. The Biblical Archaeology Society, the publisher of these volumes, is pleased to be a cooperative partner in these efforts.

MARCH 1992
WASHINGTON, D.C.

HERSHEL SHANKS
PRESIDENT
BIBLICAL ARCHAEOLOGY SOCIETY

Index

Plate No.	PAM* No.	Plate No.	PAM No.	Plate No.	PAM No.	Plate No.	PAM No.	Plate No.	PAM No.
1	40.068	58	40.595	115	40.965	172	41.164	230	41.289
2A–B	40.074	59	40.596	116	40.966	173	41.165		
3	40.077	60	40.597	117	40.967	174	41.166	231	41.290
4A–B	40.132			118	40.968	175	41.167	232	41.291
5	40.171	61	40.598	119	40.969	176	41.168	233	41.292
6	40.217	62	40.599			177	41.170	234	41.293
7	40.218	63	40.600	120	40.970	178	41.171	235	41.294
8	40.219	64	40.601	121	40.971	179	41.172	236	41.295
9	40.220	65	40.602	122	40.972	180	41.173	237	41.296
10	40.221	66	40.604	123	40.973			238	41.297
		67	40.605	124	40.974	181	41.174	239	41.298
11	40.222	68	40.606	125	40.975	182	41.175	240	41.299
12	40.223	69	40.607	126	40.976	183	41.176		
13	40.239	70	40.609	127	40.977	184	41.177	241	41.300
14	40.240			128	40.978	185	41.178	242	41.301
15	40.282	71	40.610	129	40.979	186	41.179	243	41.302
16	40.284	72	40.611	130	40.980	187	41.181	244	41.303
17	40.289	73	40.612			188	41.182	245	41.306
18	40.290	74	40.613	131	40.981	189	41.183	246	41.310
19A	40.292	75	40.614	132	40.982	190	41.184	247	41.311
19B	40.338	76	40.615	133	40.983			248	41.312
		77	40.617	134	40.984	191	41.185	249	41.313
20	40.341	78	40.618	135	40.985	192	41.186	250	41.314
21	40.342	79	40.619	136	40.986	193	41.187		
22	40.559	80	40.620	137	40.987	194	41.188	251	41.317
23	40.560			138	40.988	195	41.189	252	41.321
24	40.561	81	40.621	139	40.989	196	41.190	253	41.324
25	40.562	82	40.622			197	41.191	254	41.346
26	40.563	83	40.624	140	40.990	198	41.192	255	41.347
27	40.564	84	40.625	141	40.991	199	41.193	256	41.348
28	40.565	85	40.626	142	40.993	200	41.194	257	41.349
29	40.566	86	40.627	143	40.994			258	41.350
30	40.567	87	40.628	144	40.995	201	41.195	259	41.351
		88	40.629	145	40.996	202	41.196	260	41.352
31	40.568	89	40.630	146	41.138	203	41.197		
32	40.569	90	40.631	147	41.139	204	41.198	261	41.353
33	40.570			148	41.140	205	41.199	262	41.363
34	40.571	91	40.632	149	41.141	206	41.200	263	41.366
35	40.572	92	40.633	150	41.142	207	41.201	264	41.367
36	40.573	93	40.634			208	41.202	265	41.368
37	40.574	94	40.635	151	41.143	209	41.203	266	41.371
38	40.575	95	40.636	152	41.144	210	41.204	267	41.372
39	40.576	96	40.637	153	41.145			268	41.373
40	40.577	97	40.638	154	41.146	211	41.205	269	41.374
		98	40.642	155	41.147	212	41.207	270	41.375
41	40.578	99	40.643	156	41.148	213	41.208		
42	40.579	100	40.644	157	41.149	214	41.209	271	41.386
43	40.580			158	41.150	215	41.210	272	41.387
44	40.581	101	40.645	159	41.151	216	41.211	273	41.388
45	40.582	102	40.646	160	41.152	217	41.213	274	41.389
46	40.583	103	40.647			218	41.276	275	41.390
47	40.584	104	40.648	161	41.153	219	41.277	276	41.391
48	40.585	105	40.649	162	41.154	220	41.278	277	41.400
49	40.586	106	40.659	163	41.155			278	41.401
50	40.587	107	40.660	164	41.156	221	41.279	279	41.402
		108	40.661	165	41.157	222	41.280	280	41.403
51	40.588	109	40.662	166	41.158	223	41.281		
52	40.589	110	40.663	167	41.159	224	41.282	281	41.404
53	40.590			168	41.160	225	41.283	282	41.405
54	40.591	111	40.666	169	41.161	226	41.284	283	41.407
55	40.592	112	40.962	170	41.162	227	41.286	284	41.408
56	40.593	113	40.963			228	41.287	285	41.409
57	40.594	114	40.964	171	41.163	229	41.288	286	41.411

*Palestine Archaeological Museum, now the Rockefeller Museum

Plate No.	PAM No.	Plate No.	PAM No.	Plate No.	PAM No.	Plate No.	PAM No.	Plate No.	PAM No.
287	41.412	343	41.519	401	41.700	459	41.821	516	41.931
288	41.422	344	41.520	402	41.701	460	41.822	517	41.932
289	41.423	345	41.563	403	41.702			518	41.933
290	41.425	346	41.564	404	41.703	461	41.823	519	41.938
		347	41.565	405	41.704	462	41.824	520	41.939
291	41.426	348	41.566	406	41.705	463	41.825		
292	41.427	349	41.586	407	41.706	464	41.826	521	41.940
293	41.435	350	41.587	408	41.707	465	41.827	522	41.941
294	41.436			409	41.708	466	41.833	523	41.942
295	41.437	351	41.588	410	41.709	467	41.843	524	41.944
296	41.438	352	41.589			468	41.844	525	41.945
297	41.439	353	41.591	411	41.710	469	41.845	526	41.946
298	41.440	354	41.593	412	41.712	470	41.849	527	41.947
299	41.441	355	41.594	413	41.713			528	41.948
300	41.442	356	41.595	414	41.714	471	41.850	529	41.949
		357	41.636	415	41.715	472	41.851	530	41.951
301	41.443	358	41.637	416	41.718	473	41.852		
302	41.444	359	41.638	417	41.720	474	41.853	531	41.952
303	41.450	360	41.639	418	41.742	475	41.854	532	41.954
304	41.451			419	41.743	476	41.855	533	41.955
305	41.452	361	41.640	420	41.744	477	41.856	534	41.956
306	41.453	362	41.641			478	41.857	535	41.964
307	41.454	363	41.642	421	41.759	479	41.858	536	41.965
308	41.455	364	41.643	422	41.760	480	41.859	537	41.966
309	41.456	365	41.644	423	41.761			538	41.967
310	41.457	366	41.645	424	41.762	481	41.860	539	41.972
		367	41.646	425	41.763	482	41.861	540	41.973
311	41.458	368	41.647	426	41.764	483	41.862		
312	41.459	369	41.648	427	41.765	484	41.863	541	41.974
313	41.460	370	41.649	428	41.766	485	41.864	542	41.975
314	41.461			429	41.767	486	41.865	543	41.976
315	41.462	371	41.650	430	41.768	487	41.866	544	41.978
316	41.463	372	41.656			488	41.867	545	41.979
317	41.464	373	41.657	431	41.769	489	41.868	546	41.980
318	41.465	374	41.658	432	41.770	490	41.869	547	41.981
319	41.466	375	41.659	433	41.771			548	41.983
320	41.467	376	41.660	434	41.772	491	41.886	549	41.984
		377	41.661	435	41.773	492	41.887	550	41.985
321	41.468	378	41.662	436	41.774	493	41.888		
322	41.477	379	41.663	437	41.775	494	41.889	551	41.986
323	41.478	380	41.664	438	41.776	495	41.890	552	41.987
324	41.479			439	41.777	496	41.891	553	41.988
325	41.481	381	41.665	440	41.778	497	41.892	554	41.989
326	41.482	382	41.666			498	41.893	555	41.990
327	41.483	383	41.675	441	41.779	499	41.894	556	41.991
328	41.499	384	41.676	442	41.780	500	41.895	557	41.992
329	41.502	385	41.677	443	41.781			558	41.993
330	41.503	386	41.678	444	41.782	501	41.903	559	41.995
		387	41.679	445	41.783	502	41.904	560	41.996
331	41.504	388	41.684	446	41.784	503	41.905		
332	41.505	389	41.686	447	41.785	504	41.906	561	41.997
333	41.506	390	41.687	448	41.786	505	41.907	562	41.998
334A	41.507			449	41.787	506	41.908	563	41.999
334B	41.508	391	41.690	450	41.788	507	41.909	564	42.000
335	41.509	392	41.690A			508	41.910	565	42.001
336	41.512	393	41.692	451	41.789	509	41.911	566	42.002
337	41.513	394	41.693	452	41.790	510	41.913	567	42.003
338	41.514	395	41.694	453	41.791			568	42.004
339	41.515	396	41.695	454	41.792	511	41.914	569	42.005
340	41.516	397	41.696	455	41.798	512	41.915	570	42.006
		398	41.697	456	41.799	513	41.916		
341	41.517	399	41.698	457	41.816	514	41.917	571	42.007
342	41.518	400	41.699	458	41.820	515	41.918	572	42.008

Plate No.	PAM No.	Plate No.	PAM No.	Plate No.	PAM No.	Plate No.	PAM No.	Plate No.	PAM No.
573	42.009	631	42.070	689	42.187	746	42.267	803	42.378
574	42.010	632	42.071	690	42.188	747	42.268	804	42.379
575	42.011	633	42.072			748	42.269	805	42.380
576	42.012	634	42.073	691	42.189	749	42.270	806	42.381
577	42.013	635	42.074	692	42.190	750	42.271	807	42.382
578	42.014	636	42.075	693	42.191			808	42.383
579	42.015	637	42.076	694	42.192	751	42.272	809	42.384
580	42.016	638	42.077	695	42.193	752	42.273	810	42.385
		639	42.078	696	42.194	753	42.274		
581	42.017	640	42.079	697	42.196	754	42.275	811	42.386
582	42.018			698	42.197	755	42.276	812	42.387
583	42.019	641	42.081	699	42.198	756	42.277	813	42.388
584	42.020	642	42.082	700	42.199	757	42.278	814	42.389
585	42.021	643	42.085			758	42.279	815	42.390
586	42.022	644	42.086	701	42.200	759	42.280	816	42.391
587	42.023	645	42.087	702	42.201	760	42.281	817	42.392
588	42.024	646	42.088	703	42.202			818	42.393
589	42.025	647	42.089	704	42.203	761	42.282	819	42.394
590	42.026	648	42.090	705	42.204	762	42.283	820	42.395
		649	42.100	706	42.205	763	42.284		
591	42.027	650	42.132	707	42.206	764	42.285	821	42.396
592	42.028			708	42.207	765	42.286	822	42.397
593	42.029	651	42.136	709	42.208	766	42.287	823	42.398
594	42.030	652	42.137	710	42.209	767	42.288	824	42.399
595	42.031	653	42.143			768	42.289	825	42.400
596	42.032	654	42.144	711	42.210	769	42.324	826	42.401
597	42.033	655	42.145	712	42.211	770	42.325	827	42.402
598	42.034	656	42.146	713	42.212			828	42.403
599	42.035	657	42.147	714	42.213	771	42.326	829	42.404
600	42.036	658	42.151	715	42.214	772	42.327	830	42.405
		659	42.152	716	42.215	773	42.328		
601	42.037	660	42.153	717	42.216	774	42.330	831	42.406
602	42.038			718	42.217	775	42.331	832	42.407
603	42.039	661	42.154	719	42.218	776	42.332	833	42.408
604	42.040	662	42.155	720	42.219	777	42.333	834	42.409
605	42.041	663	42.156			778	42.334	835	42.410
606	42.042	664	42.157	721	42.220	779	42.335	836	42.411
607	42.043	665	42.158	722	42.221	780	42.338A	837	42.412
608	42.044	666	42.159	723	42.222			838	42.413
609	42.045	667	42.160	724	42.223	781	42.356	839	42.414
610	42.046	668	42.161	725	42.224	782	42.357	840	42.415
		669	42.162	726	42.225	783	42.358		
611	42.047	670	42.163	727	42.226	784	42.359	841	42.416
612	42.048			728	42.232	785	42.360	842	42.417
613	42.049	671	42.164	729	42.233	786	42.361	843	42.418
614	42.050	672	42.165	730	42.239	787	42.362	844	42.419
615	42.051	673	42.166			788	42.363	845	42.420
616	42.052	674	42.167	731	42.240	789	42.364	846	42.421
617	42.053	675	42.168	732	42.241	790	42.365	847	42.422
618	42.055	676	42.169	733	42.242			848	42.423
619	42.056	677	42.170	734	42.243	791	42.366	849	42.424
620	42.057	678	42.171	735	42.244	792	42.367	850	42.425
		679	42.172	736	42.245	793	42.368		
621	42.058	680	42.173	737	42.246	794	42.369	851	42.426
622	42.059			738	42.247	795	42.370	852	42.427
623	42.060	681	42.174	739	42.260	796	42.371	853	42.428
624	42.061	682	42.175	740	42.261	797	42.372	854	42.429
625	42.062	683	42.176			798	42.373	855	42.430
626	42.064	684	42.177	741	42.262	799	42.374	856	42.431
627	42.066	685	42.182	742	42.263	800	42.375	857	42.435
628	42.067	686	42.184	743	42.264			858	42.436
629	42.068	687	42.185	744	42.265	801	42.376	859	42.438
630	42.069	688	42.186	745	42.266	802	42.377	860	42.439

Plate No.	PAM No.	Plate No.	PAM No.	Plate No.	PAM No.	Plate No.	PAM No.	Plate No.	PAM No.
861	42.440	919	42.592	976	42.727	1033	42.824	1091	43.007
862	42.443	920	42.597	977	42.729	1034	42.825	1092	43.008
863	42.443A			978	42.730	1035	42.826	1093	43.009
864	42.445	921	42.598	979	42.731	1036	42.827	1094	43.010
865	42.446	922	42.599	980	42.732	1037	42.830	1095	43.011
866	42.447	923	42.600			1038	42.831	1096	43.012
867A–B	42.448	924	42.601	981	42.733	1039	42.832	1097	43.013
868	42.459	925	42.602	982	42.734	1040	42.833	1098	43.014
869	42.470	926	42.603	983	42.735			1099	43.015
870	42.471	927	42.604	984	42.736	1041	42.834	1100	43.016
		928	42.609	985	42.737	1042	42.835		
871	42.472	929	42.611	986	42.738	1043	42.836	1101	43.017
872	42.473	930	42.630	987	42.739	1044	42.837	1102	43.018
873	42.474			988	42.740	1045	42.838	1103	43.019
874	42.475	931	42.631	989	42.741	1046	42.839	1104	43.020
875	42.476	932	42.632	990	42.742	1047	42.858	1105	43.021
876	42.477	933	42.633			1048	42.859	1106	43.022
877	42.478	934	42.634	991	42.743	1049	42.860	1107	43.023
878	42.479	935	42.635	992	42.744	1050	42.862	1108	43.024
879	42.480	936	42.636	993	42.745			1109	43.025
880	42.481	937	42.638	994	42.746	1051	42.908	1110	43.026
		938	42.639	995	42.747	1052	42.909		
881	42.482	939	42.640	996	42.748	1053	42.912	1111	43.027
882	42.484	940	42.641	997	42.749	1054	42.913	1112	43.028
883	42.488			998	42.750	1055	42.914	1113	43.029
884	42.489	941	42.642	999	42.751	1056	42.915	1114	43.030
885	42.490	942	42.643	1000	42.752	1057	42.916	1115	43.031
886	42.495	943	42.644			1058	42.917	1116	43.032
887	42.496	944	42.645	1001	42.753	1059	42.927	1117	43.033
888	42.498	945	42.646	1002	42.754	1060	42.928	1118	43.034
889	42.499	946	42.647	1003	42.755			1119	43.035
890	42.500	947	42.648	1004	42.756	1061	42.929	1120	43.036
		948	42.649	1005	42.757	1062	42.930		
891	42.501	949	42.650	1006	42.758	1063	42.931	1121	43.037
892	42.504	950	42.701	1007	42.759	1064	42.932	1122	43.038
893	42.505			1008	42.760	1065	42.933	1123	43.039
894	42.506	951	42.702	1009	42.761	1066	42.934	1124	43.040
895	42.507	952	42.703	1010	42.762	1067	42.935	1125	43.041
896	42.508	953	42.704			1068	42.936	1126	43.042
897	42.509	954	42.705	1011	42.763	1069	42.937	1127	43.043
898	42.510	955	42.706	1012	42.793	1070	42.938	1128	43.044
899	42.511	956	42.707	1013	42.802			1129	43.045
900	42.513	957	42.708	1014	42.803	1071	42.940	1130	43.046
		958	42.709	1015	42.806	1072	42.941		
901	42.514	959	42.710	1016	42.807	1073	42.951	1131	43.047
902	42.515	960	42.711	1017	42.808	1074	42.966	1132	43.048
903	42.554			1018	42.809	1075	42.967	1133	43.049
904	42.555	961	42.712	1019	42.810	1076	42.968	1134	43.050
905	42.556	962	42.713	1020	42.811	1077	42.969	1135	43.051
906	42.557	963	42.714			1078	42.970	1136	43.052
907	42.558	964	42.715	1021	42.812	1079	42.971	1137	43.053
908	42.561	965	42.716	1022	42.813	1080	42.972	1138	43.054
909	42.578	966	42.717	1023	42.814			1139	43.055
910	42.579	967	42.718	1024	42.815	1081	42.973	1140	43.056
		968	42.719	1025	42.816	1082	42.974		
911	42.580	969	42.720	1026	42.817	1083	42.975	1141	43.057
912	42.581	970	42.721	1027	42.818	1084	42.976	1142	43.058
913	42.582			1028	42.819	1085	43.001	1143	43.059
914	42.583	971	42.722	1029	42.820	1086	43.002	1144	43.060
915	42.584	972	42.723	1030	42.821	1087	43.003	1145	43.061
916	42.586	973	42.724			1088	43.004	1146	43.062
917	42.586A	974	42.725	1031	42.822	1089	43.005	1147	43.063
918	42.586B	975	42.726	1032	42.823	1090	43.006	1148	43.064

Plate No.	PAM No.	Plate No.	PAM No.	Plate No.	PAM No.	Plate No.	PAM No.	Plate No.	PAM No.
1149	43.065	1206	43.123	1263	43.226	1321	43.285	1379	43.385
1150	43.066	1207	43.124	1264	43.227	1322	43.286	1380	43.386
		1208	43.125	1265	43.228	1323	43.287		
1151	43.067	1209	43.154	1266	43.229	1324	43.288	1381	43.387
1152	43.068	1210	43.155	1267	43.230	1325	43.289	1382	43.388
1153	43.069			1268	43.231	1326	43.290	1383	43.389
1154	43.070	1211	43.156	1269	43.232	1327	43.291	1384	43.390
1155	43.071	1212	43.157	1270	43.233	1328	43.293	1385	43.391
1156	43.072	1213	43.158			1329	43.294	1386	43.392
1157	43.073	1214	43.159	1271	43.234	1330	43.295	1387	43.393
1158	43.074	1215	43.160	1272	43.236			1388	43.394
1159	43.075	1216	43.161	1273	43.237	1331	43.296	1389	43.395
1160	43.076	1217	43.162	1274	43.238	1332	43.297	1390	43.396
		1218	43.163	1275	43.239	1333	43.298		
1161	43.077	1219	43.164	1276	43.240	1334	43.299	1391	43.397
1162	43.078	1220	43.165	1277	43.241	1335	43.300	1392	43.398
1163	43.079			1278	43.242	1336	43.301	1393	43.399
1164	43.080	1221	43.166	1279	43.243	1337	43.302	1394	43.400
1165	43.081	1222	43.167	1280	43.244	1338	43.303	1395	43.401
1166	43.082	1223	43.168			1339	43.304	1396	43.402
1167	43.083	1224	43.169	1281	43.245	1340	43.305	1397	43.403
1168	43.084	1225	43.170	1282	43.246			1398	43.404
1169	43.085	1226	43.171	1283	43.247	1341	43.306	1399	43.405
1170	43.086	1227	43.172	1284	43.248	1342	43.307	1400	43.406
		1228	43.173	1285	43.249	1343	43.308		
1171	43.087	1229	43.174	1286	43.250	1344	43.309	1401	43.407
1172	43.088	1230	43.175	1287	43.251	1345	43.310	1402	43.408
1173	43.089			1288	43.252	1346	43.311	1403	43.409
1174	43.090	1231	43.176	1289	43.253	1347	43.312	1404	43.410
1175	43.091	1232	43.177	1290	43.254	1348	43.313	1405	43.411
1176	43.092	1233	43.178			1349	43.314	1406	43.412
1177	43.093	1234	43.179	1291	43.255	1350	43.315	1407	43.413
1178	43.094	1235	43.180	1292	43.256			1408	43.414
1179	43.095	1236	43.181	1293	43.257	1351	43.316	1409	43.430
1180	43.096	1237	43.182	1294	43.258	1352	43.325	1410	43.437
		1238	43.183	1295	43.259	1353	43.326		
1181	43.097	1239	43.184	1296	43.260	1354	43.327	1411	43.448
1182	43.098	1240	43.185	1297	43.261	1355	43.328	1412	43.462
1183	43.099			1298	43.262	1356	43.329	1413	43.463
1184	43.100	1241	43.186	1299	43.263	1357	43.330	1414	43.464
1185	43.101	1242	43.187	1300	43.264	1358	43.331	1415	43.465
1186	43.102	1243	43.188			1359	43.332	1416	43.466
1187	43.103	1244	43.189	1301	43.265	1360	43.333	1417	43.467
1188	43.104	1245	43.190	1302	43.266			1418	43.468
1189	43.105	1246	43.191	1303	43.267	1361	43.334	1419	43.469
1190	43.106	1247	43.192	1304	43.268	1362	43.335	1420	43.470
		1248	43.193	1305	43.269	1363	43.336		
1191	43.107	1249	43.194	1306	43.270	1364	43.337	1421	43.471
1192	43.108	1250	43.195	1307	43.271	1365	43.338	1422	43.472
1193	43.109			1308	43.272	1366	43.339	1423	43.473
1194	43.110	1251	43.196	1309	43.273	1367	43.340	1424	43.474
1195	43.112	1252	43.215	1310	43.274	1368	43.374	1425	43.475
1196	43.113	1253	43.216			1369	43.375	1426	43.476
1197	43.114	1254	43.217	1311	43.275	1370	43.376	1427	43.477
1198	43.115	1255	43.218	1312	43.276			1428	43.478
1199	43.116	1256	43.219	1313	43.277	1371	43.377	1429	43.479
1200	43.117	1257	43.220	1314	43.278	1372	43.378	1430	43.480
		1258	43.221	1315	43.279	1373	43.379		
1201	43.118	1259	43.222	1316	43.280	1374	43.380	1431	43.481
1202	43.119	1260	43.223	1317	43.281	1375	43.381	1432	43.482
1203	43.120			1318	43.282	1376	43.382	1433	43.483
1204	43.121	1261	43.224	1319	43.283	1377	43.383	1434	43.484
1205	43.122	1262	43.225	1320	43.284	1378	43.384	1435	43.485

Plate No.	PAM No.	Plate No.	PAM No.	Plate No.	PAM No.	Plate No.	PAM No.	Plate No.	PAM No.
1436	43.486	1493	43.544	1551	43.604	1609	43.685	1666	43.954
1437	43.487	1494	43.545	1552	43.605	1610	43.686	1667	43.955
1438	43.488	1495	43.546	1553	43.606			1668	43.956
1439	43.489	1496	43.547	1554	43.607	1611	43.687	1669	43.957
1440	43.490	1497	43.548	1555	43.610	1612	43.688	1670	43.958
		1498	43.549	1556	43.611	1613	43.689		
1441	43.491	1499	43.550	1557	43.612	1614	43.690	1671	43.959
1442	43.492	1500	43.552	1558	43.613	1615	43.691	1672	43.960
1443	43.493			1559	43.617	1616	43.692	1673	43.961
1444	43.494	1501	43.553	1560	43.618	1617	43.693	1674	43.962
1445	43.495	1502	43.554			1618	43.694	1675	43.963
1446	43.496	1503	43.555	1561	43.635	1619	43.695	1676	43.964
1447	43.497	1504	43.556	1562	43.636	1620	43.696	1677	43.965
1448	43.498	1505	43.557	1563	43.639			1678	43.966
1449	43.499	1506	43.558	1564	43.640	1621	43.697	1679	43.967
1450	43.500	1507	43.559	1565	43.641	1622	43.698	1680	43.968
		1508	43.560	1566	43.642	1623	43.699		
1451	43.501	1509	43.561	1567	43.643	1624	43.700	1681	43.969
1452	43.502	1510	43.562	1568	43.644	1625	43.701	1682	43.970
1453	43.503			1569	43.645	1626	43.727	1683	43.971
1454	43.504	1511	43.563	1570	43.646	1627	43.732	1684	43.972
1455	43.505	1512	43.564			1628	43.745	1685	43.973
1456	43.506	1513	43.565	1571	43.647	1629	43.747	1686	43.974
1457	43.507	1514	43.566	1572	43.648	1630	43.750	1687	43.977
1458	43.508	1515	43.567	1573	43.649			1688	43.979
1459	43.509	1516	43.568	1574	43.650	1631	43.750A	1689	43.980
1460	43.510	1517	43.569	1575	43.651	1632	43.772	1690	43.981
		1518	43.570	1576	43.652	1633	43.773		
1461	43.511	1519	43.571	1577	43.653	1634	43.774	1691	43.982
1462	43.512	1520	43.572	1578	43.654	1635	43.775	1692	43.983
1463	43.513			1579	43.655	1636	43.794	1693	43.984
1464	43.514	1521	43.573	1580	43.656	1637	43.855	1694	43.985
1465	43.515	1522	43.574			1638	43.856	1695	43.986
1466	43.516	1523	43.575	1581	43.657	1639	43.857	1696	43.987
1467	43.517	1524	43.576	1582	43.658	1640	43.858	1697	43.988
1468	43.518	1525	43.577	1583	43.659			1698	43.989
1469	43.519	1526	43.578	1584	43.660	1641	43.859	1699	43.990
1470	43.520	1527	43.580	1585	43.661	1642	43.860	1700	43.991
		1528	43.581	1586	43.662	1643	43.861		
1471	43.521	1529	43.582	1587	43.663	1644	43.862	1701	43.992
1472	43.522	1530	43.583	1588	43.664	1645	43.863	1702	43.993
1473	43.523			1589	43.665	1646	43.864	1703	43.994
1474	43.524	1531	43.584	1590	43.666	1647	43.865	1704	43.995
1475	43.525	1532	43.585			1648	43.866	1705	43.996
1476	43.526	1533	43.586	1591	43.667	1649	43.867	1706	43.997
1477	43.527	1534	43.587	1592	43.668	1650	43.868	1707	43.998
1478	43.528	1535	43.588	1593	43.669			1708	43.999
1479	43.529	1536	43.589	1594	43.670	1651	43.869	1709	44.000
1480	43.530	1537	43.590	1595	43.671	1652	43.870	1710	44.001
		1538	43.591	1596	43.672	1653	43.871		
1481	43.531	1539	43.592	1597	43.673	1654	43.873	1711	44.002
1482	43.533	1540	43.593	1598	43.674	1655	43.874	1712	44.003
1483	43.534			1599	43.675	1656	43.944	1713	44.004
1484	43.535	1541	43.594	1600	43.676	1657	43.945	1714	44.005
1485	43.536	1542	43.595			1658	43.946	1715	44.006
1486	43.537	1543	43.596	1601	43.677	1659	43.947	1716	44.007
1487	43.538	1544	43.597	1602	43.678	1660	43.948	1717	44.008
1488	43.539	1545	43.598	1603	43.679			1718	44.009
1489	43.540	1546	43.599	1604	43.680	1661	43.949	1719	44.011
1490	43.541	1547	43.600	1605	43.681	1662	43.950	1720	44.012
		1548	43.601	1606	43.682	1663	43.951		
1491	43.542	1549	43.602	1607	43.683	1664	43.952	1721	44.016
1492	43.543	1550	43.603	1608	43.684	1665	43.953	1722	44.017

Plate No.	PAM No.	Plate No.	PAM No.	Plate No.	PAM No.	Plate No.	PAM No.	Plate No.	PAM No.
1723	44.043	1736	44.056	1749	44.069	1761	44.081	1774	44.181
1724	44.044	1737	44.057	1750	44.070	1762	44.082	1775	44.182
1725	44.045	1738	44.058			1763	44.083	1776	44.183
1726	44.046	1739	44.059	1751	44.071	1764	44.100	1777	44.184
1727	44.047	1740	44.060	1752	44.072	1765	44.101	1778	44.185
1728	44.048			1753	44.073	1766	44.102	1779	44.187
1729	44.049	1741	44.061	1754	44.074	1767	44.103	1780	44.188
1730	44.050	1742	44.062	1755	44.075	1768	44.104		
		1743	44.063	1756	44.076	1769	44.113	1781	44.189
1731	44.051	1744	44.064	1757	44.077	1770	44.114	1782	44.190
1732	44.052	1745	44.065	1758	44.078			1783	44.194
1733	44.053	1746	44.066	1759	44.079	1771	44.115	1784	44.195
1734	44.054	1747	44.067	1760	44.080	1772	44.117	1785	44.196
1735	44.055	1748	44.068			1773	44.178		

Plates
1–907

PLATE 1

PLATE 2A

PLATE 2B

PLATE 3

PLATE 5

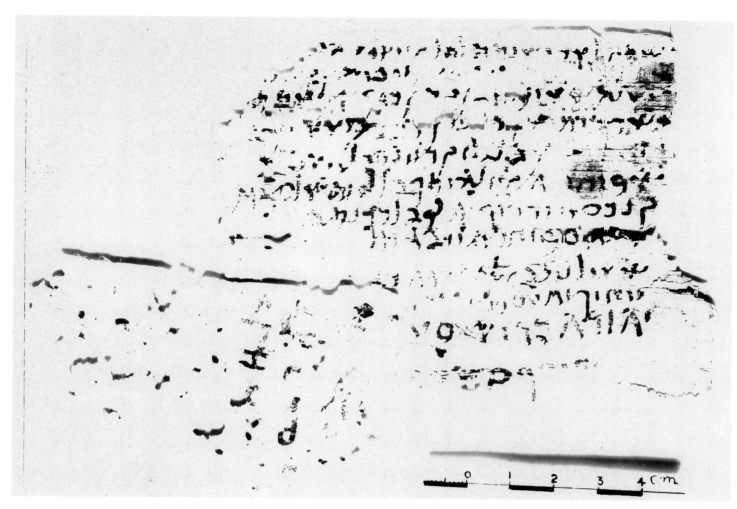

PLATE 6

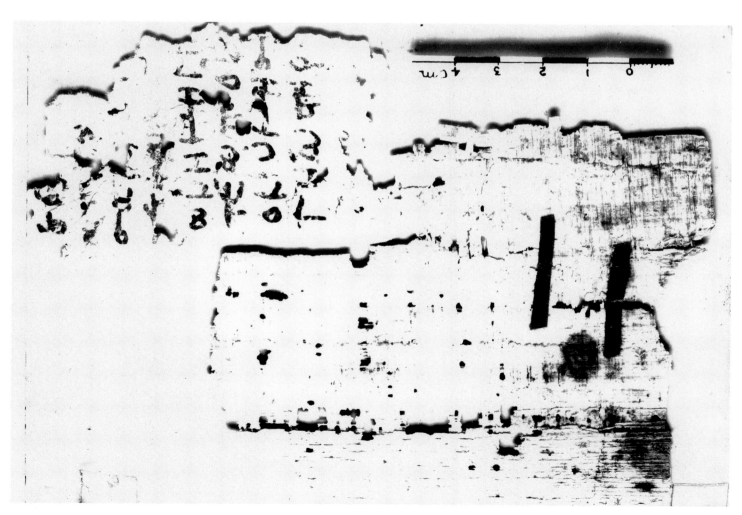

PLATE 7

PLATE 9

PLATE 8

PLATE 10

PLATE 11
PLATE 12

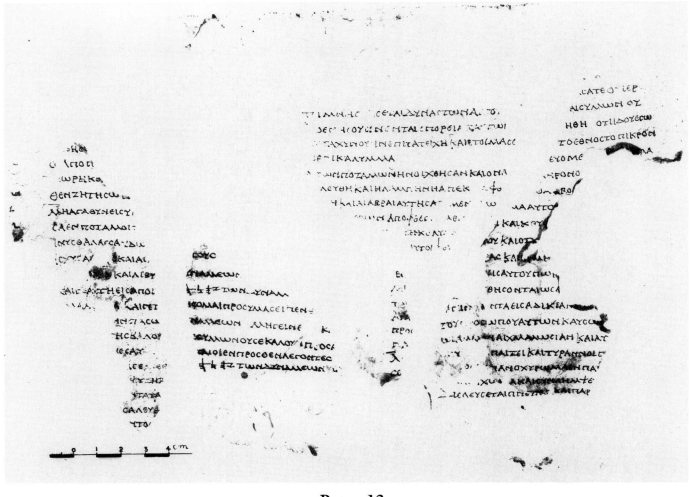

PLATE 13

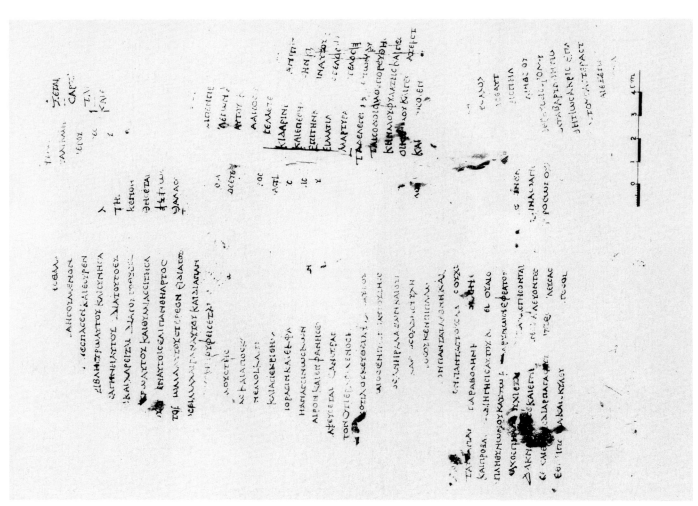

PLATE 14

M.A.B
MiRD
Q2b

PLATE 16

M.A.D
MiRD
Q2b

PLATE 15

PLATE 18

PLATE 17

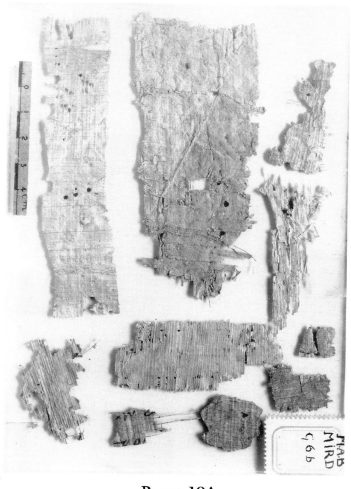

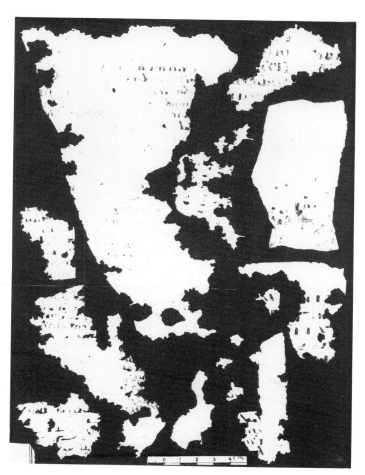

PLATE 19A

PLATE 19B

PLATE 20

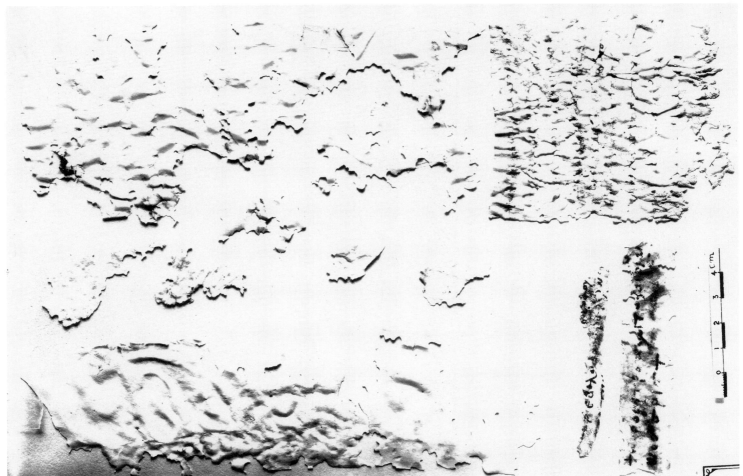

PLATE 22

PLATE 21

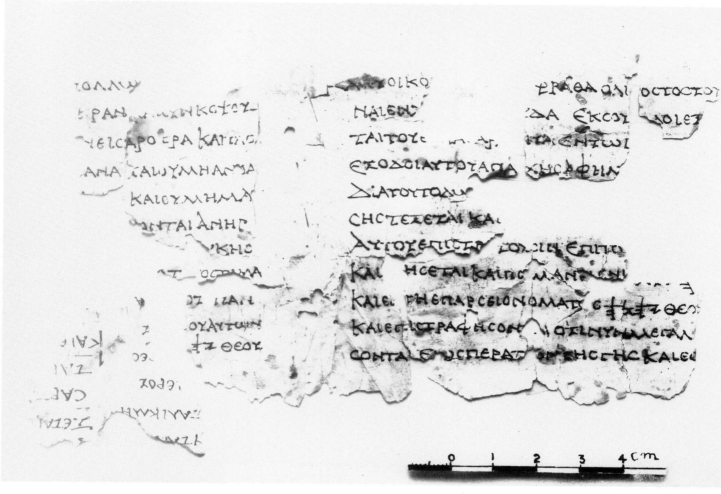

PLATE 23

PLATE 24

PLATE 26

PLATE 25

PLATE 27

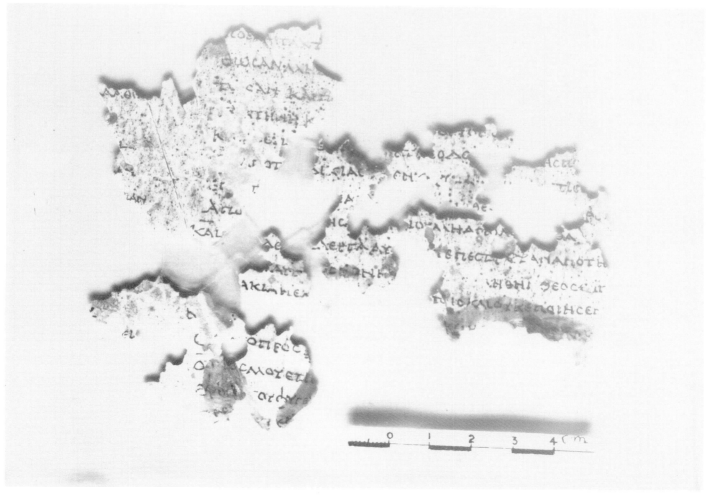

PLATE 28

PLATE 29

PLATE 30

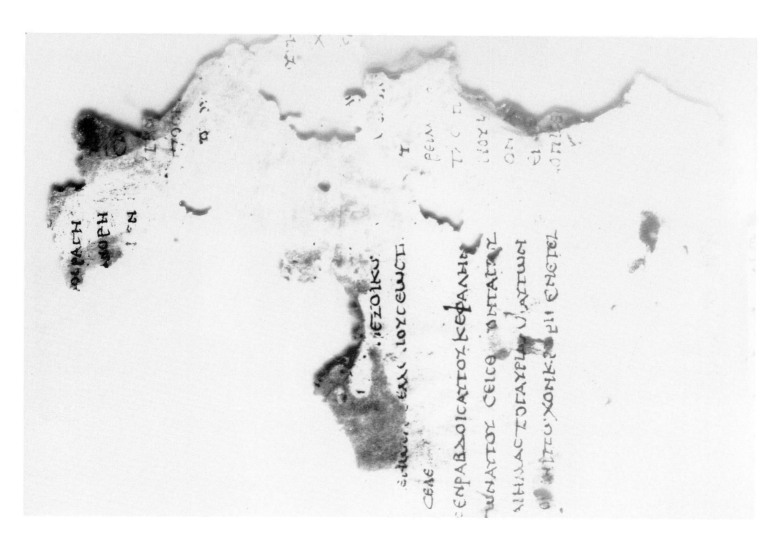

PLATE 33

PLATE 34

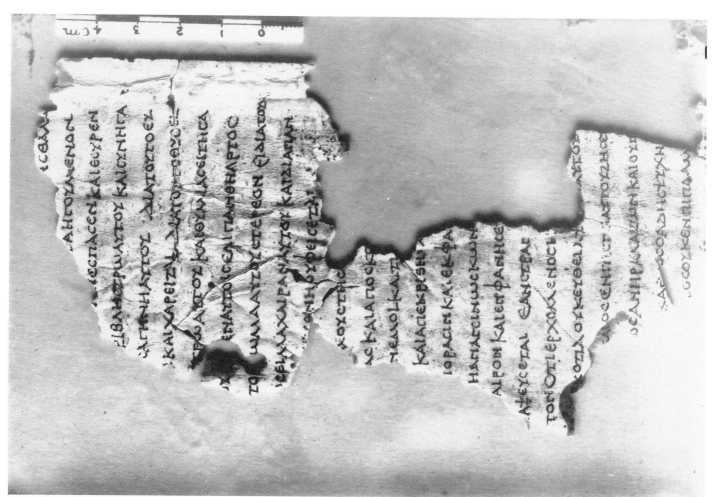

PLATE 35

PLATE 36

PLATE 37

PLATE 38

PLATE 40

PLATE 39

PLATE 42

PLATE 41

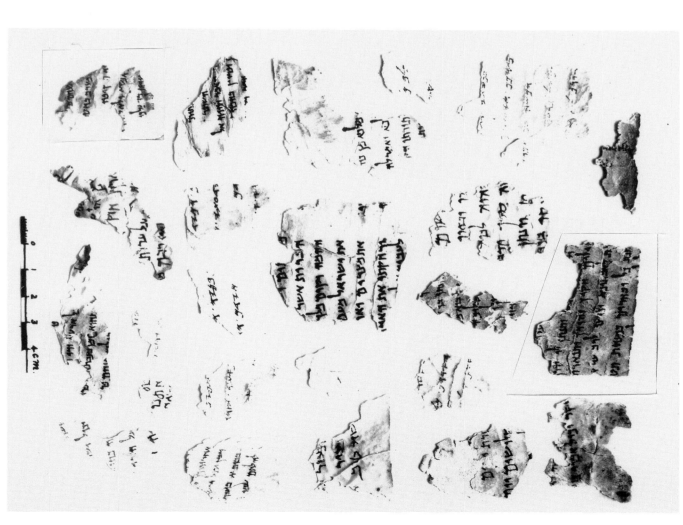

PLATE 44

PLATE 43

PLATE 46

PLATE 45

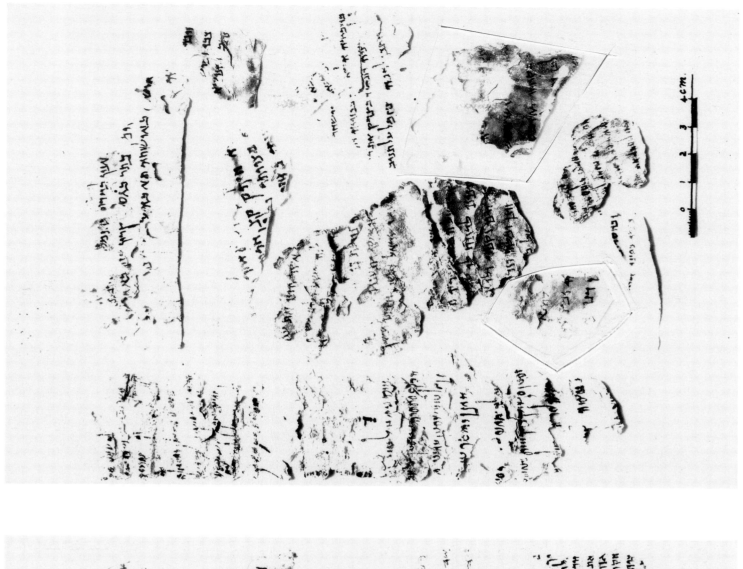

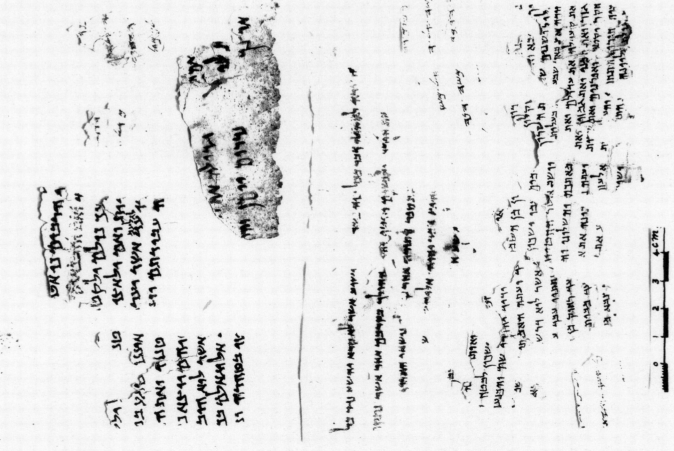

PLATE 48

PLATE 47

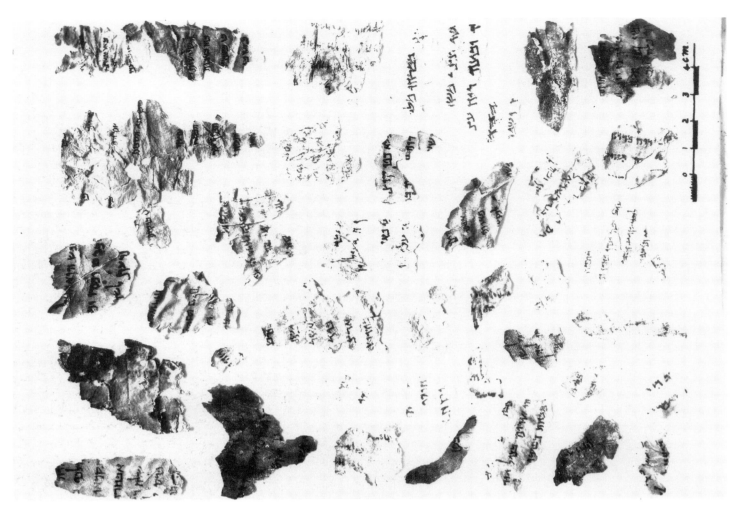

PLATE 50

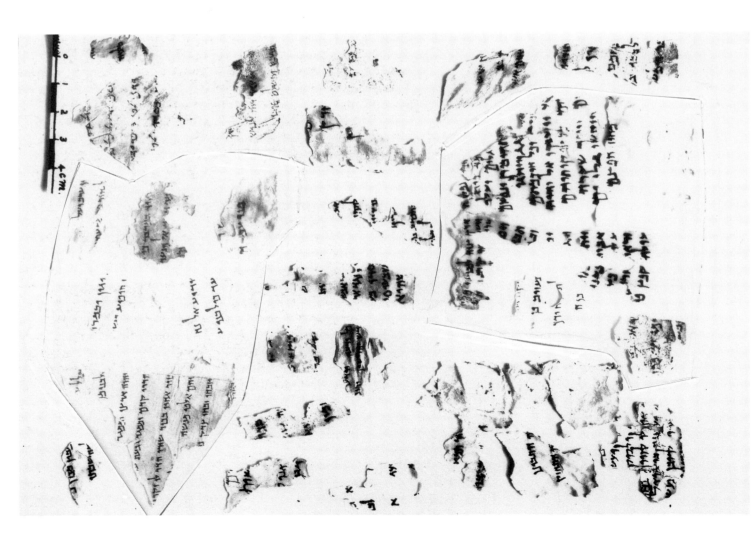

PLATE 49

PLATE 52

PLATE 51

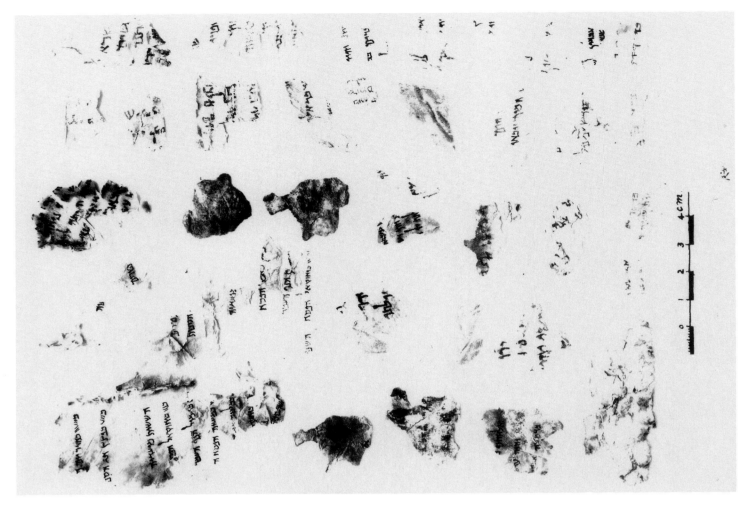

PLATE 54

PLATE 53

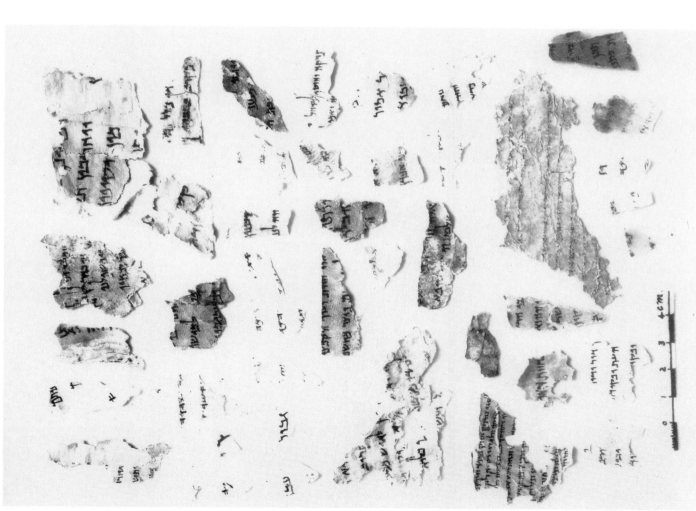

PLATE 56

PLATE 55

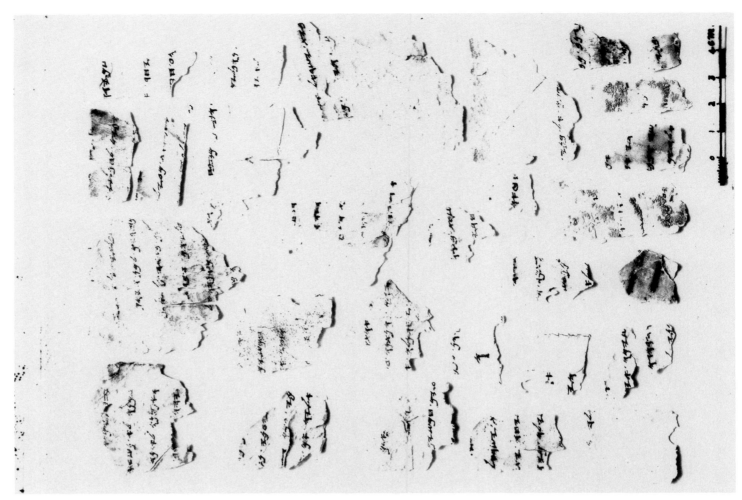

PLATE 58

PLATE 57

Plate 59

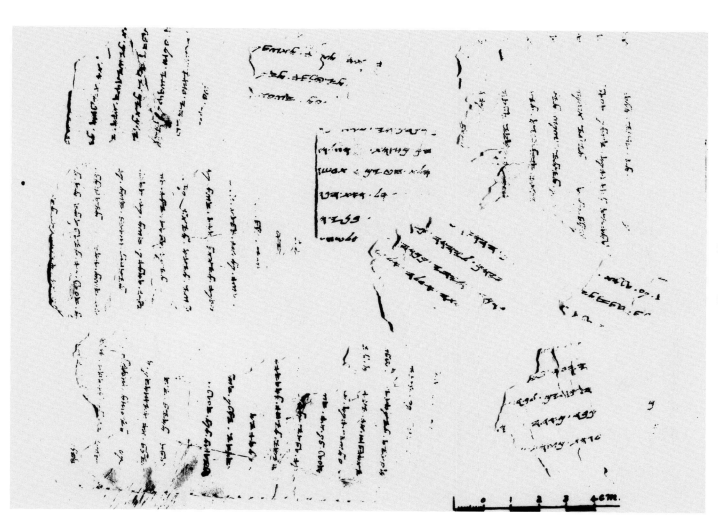

Plate 60

PLATE 61

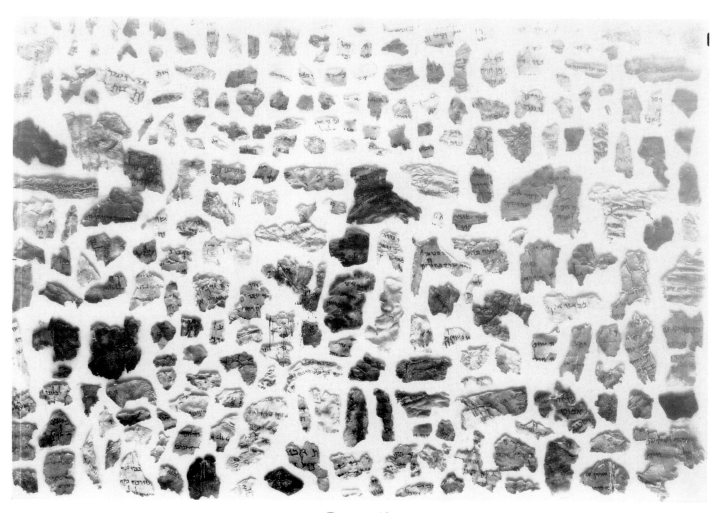

PLATE 62

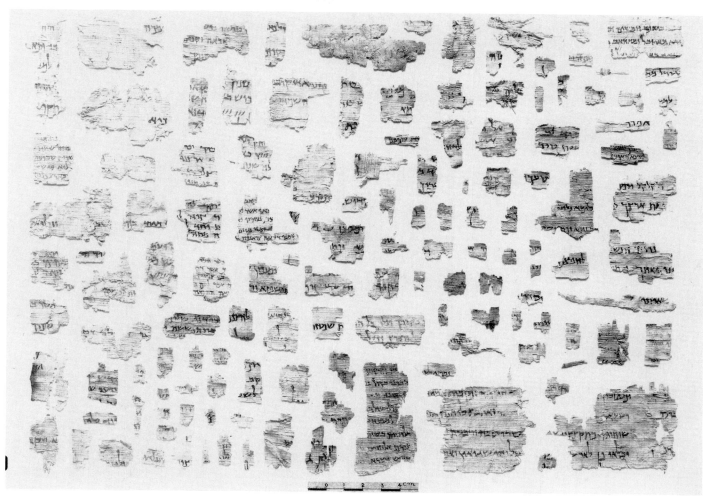

PLATE 63

PLATE 64

PLATE 65

PLATE 66

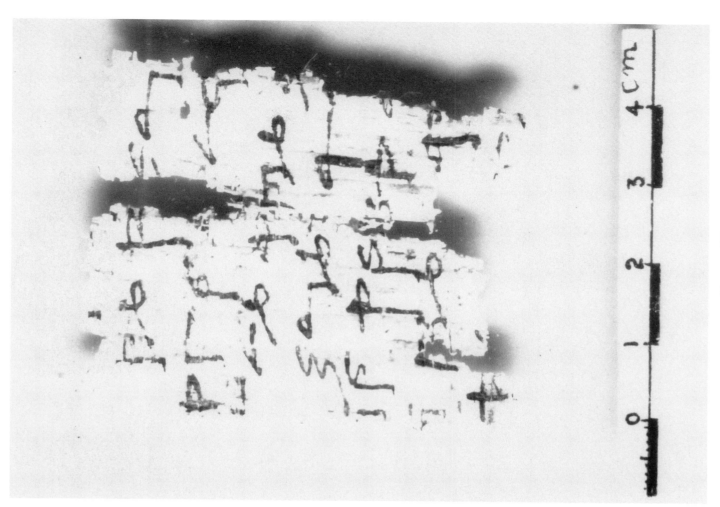

PLATE 67

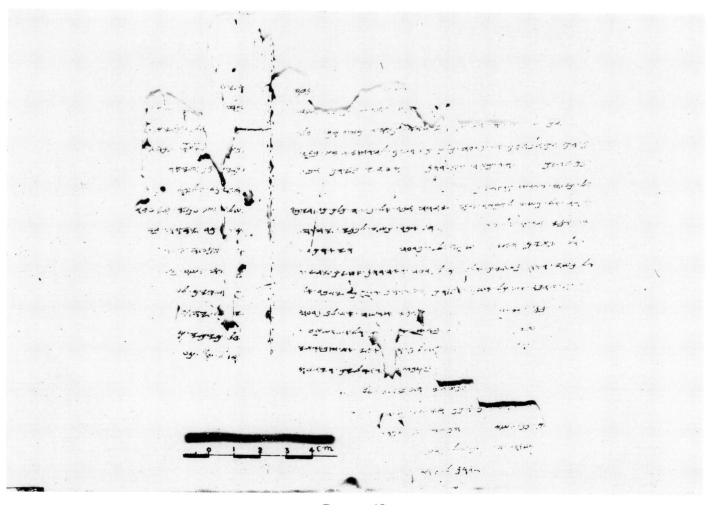

PLATE 68

PLATE 69

PLATE 70

PLATE 71

PLATE 72

PLATE 73

PLATE 74

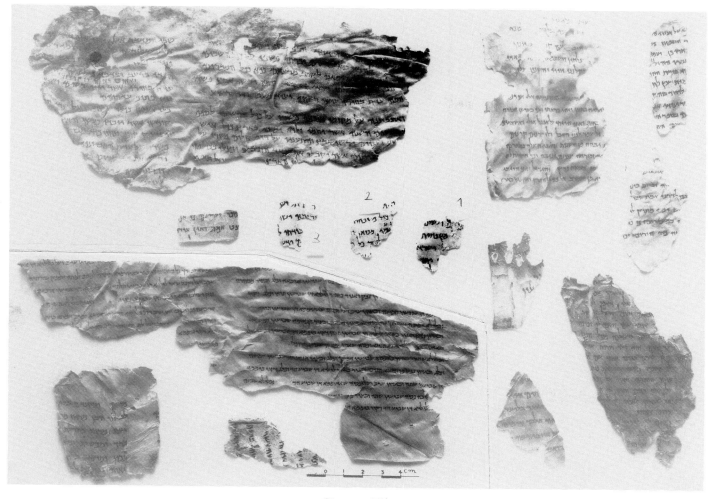

PLATE 75

PLATE 76

PLATE 77

PLATE 78

PLATE 79

PLATE 80

PLATE 81

PLATE 82

PLATE 83

PLATE 84

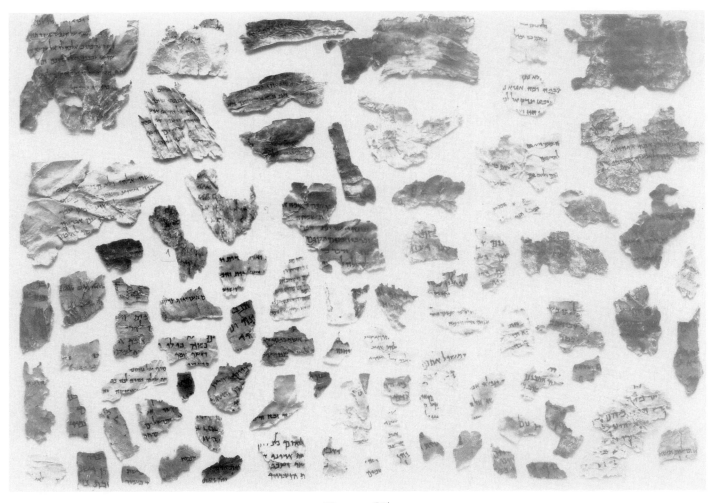

PLATE 85

PLATE 86

PLATE 87

PLATE 88

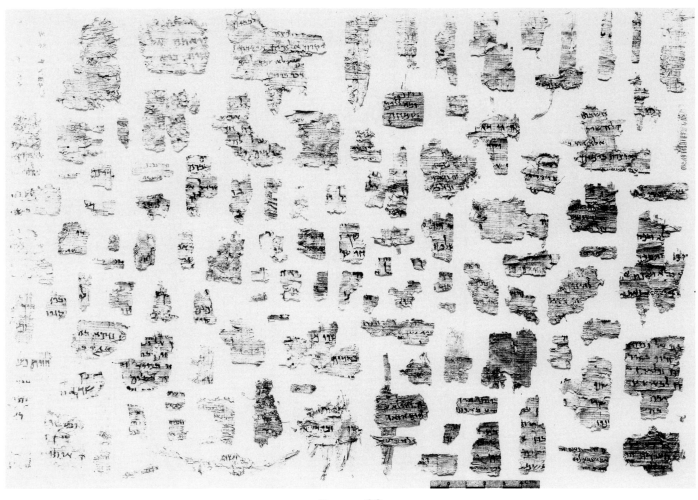

PLATE 89

PLATE 90

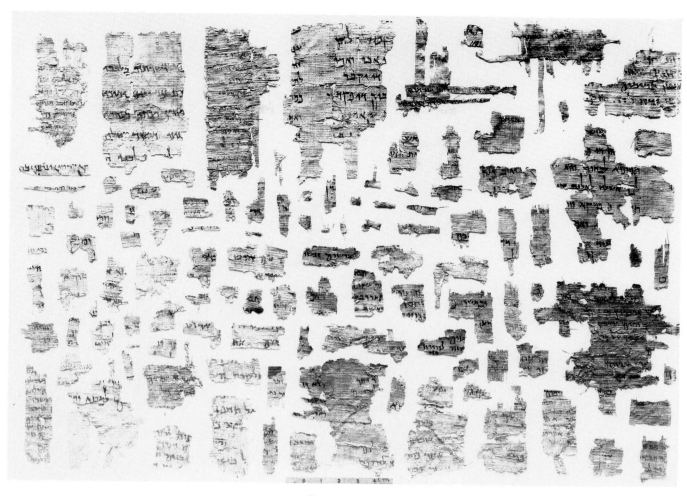

PLATE 91

PLATE 92

PLATE 93

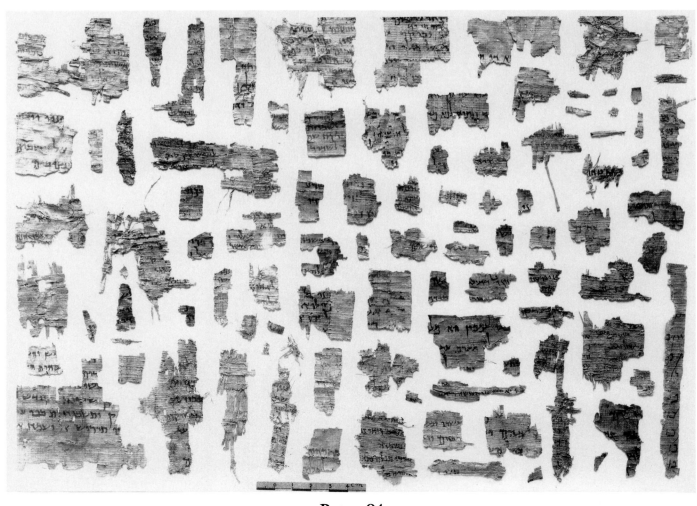

PLATE 94

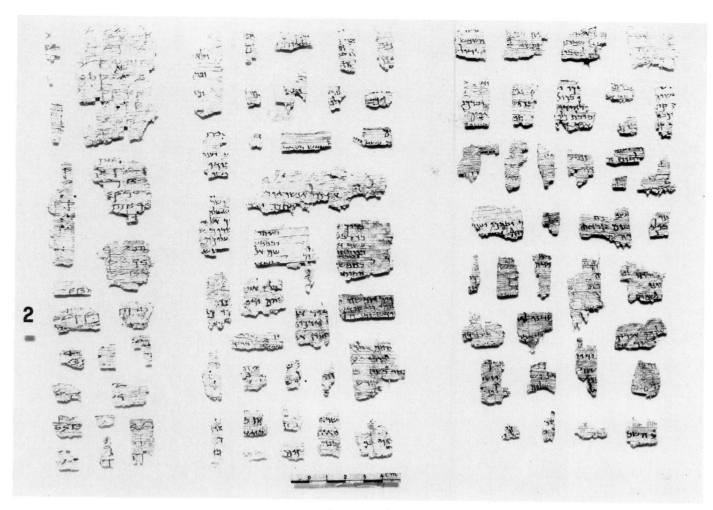

2

PLATE 95

B.

PLATE 96

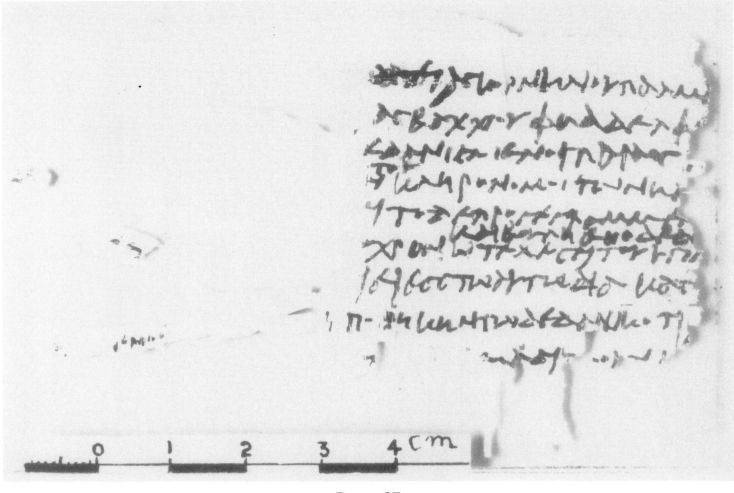

PLATE 97

PLATE 98

PLATE 100

PLATE 99

PLATE 101

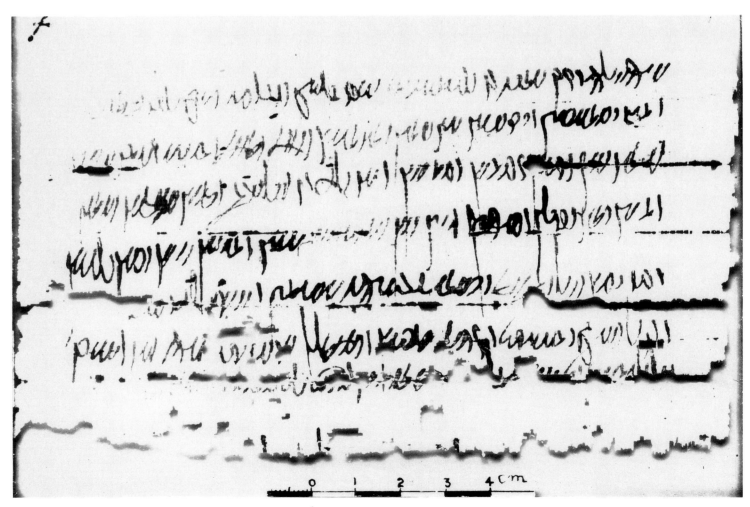

PLATE 102

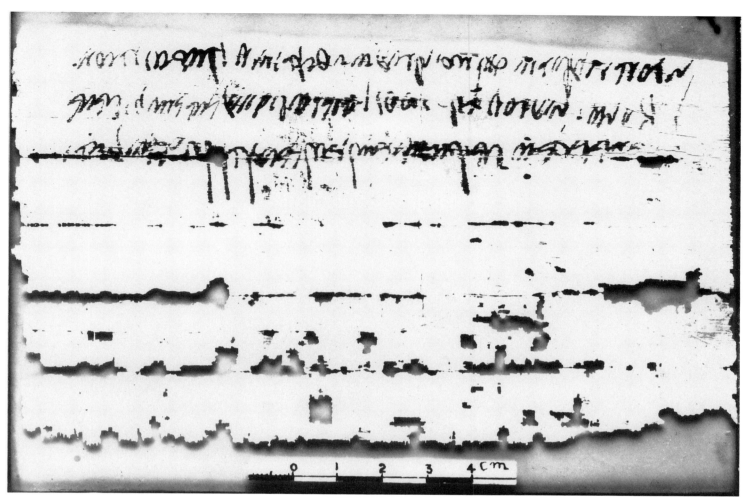

PLATE 103

PLATE 104

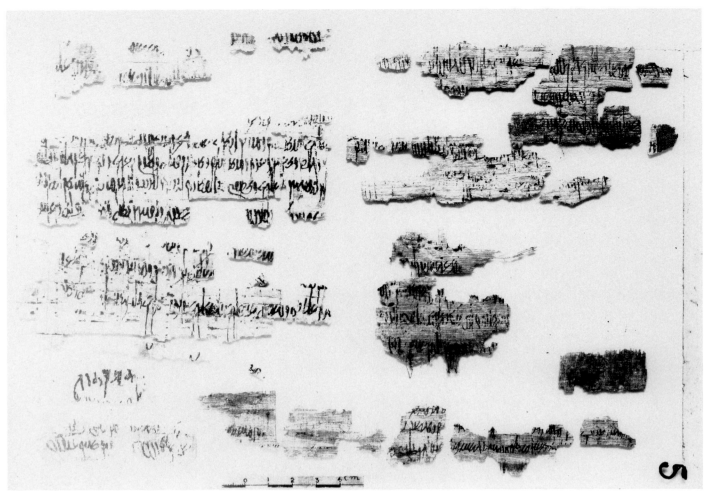

PLATE 105

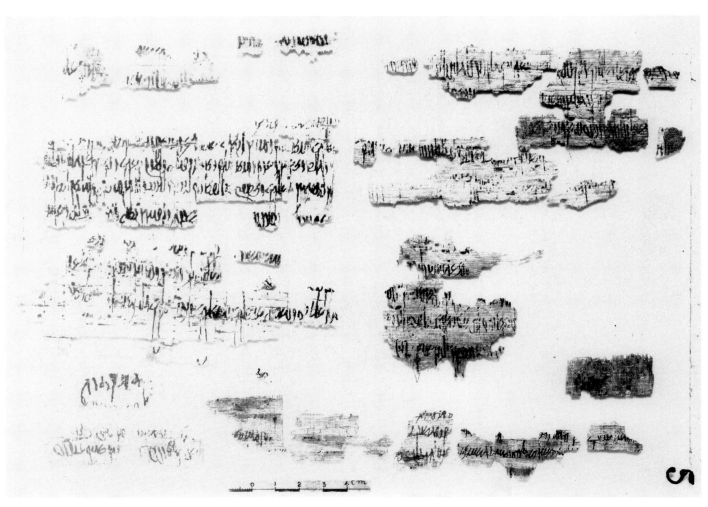

PLATE 106

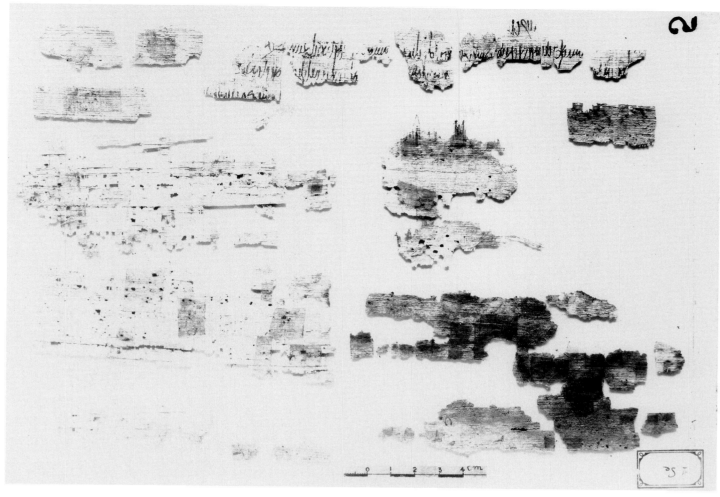

PLATE 107

PLATE 108

PLATE 109

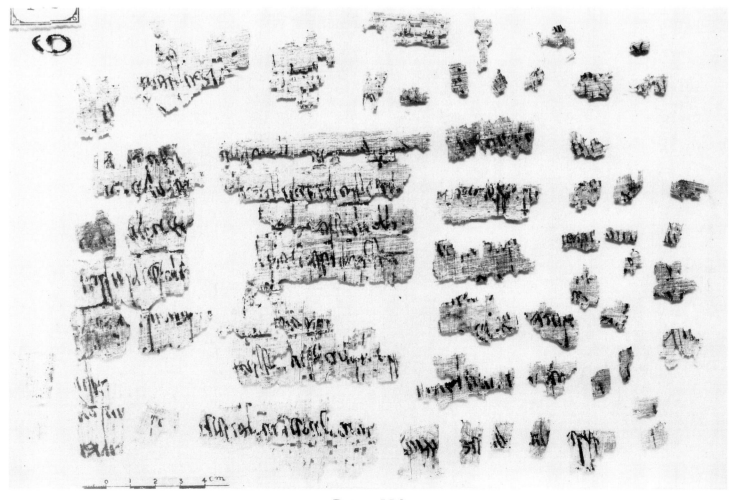

PLATE 110

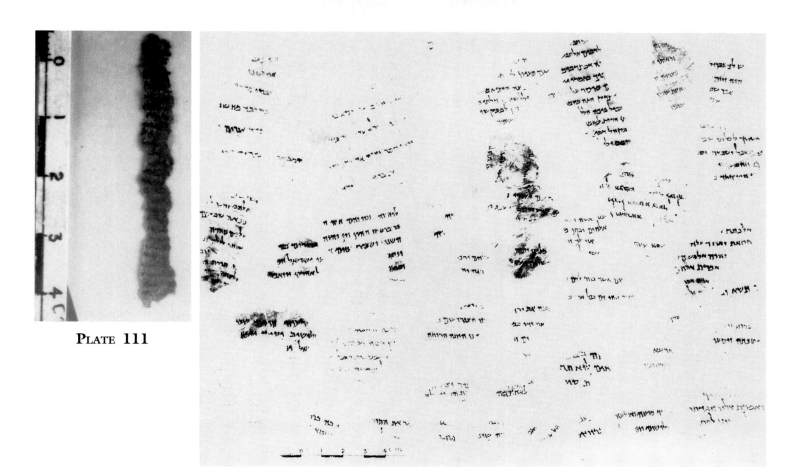

PLATE 111

PLATE 113

PLATE 112

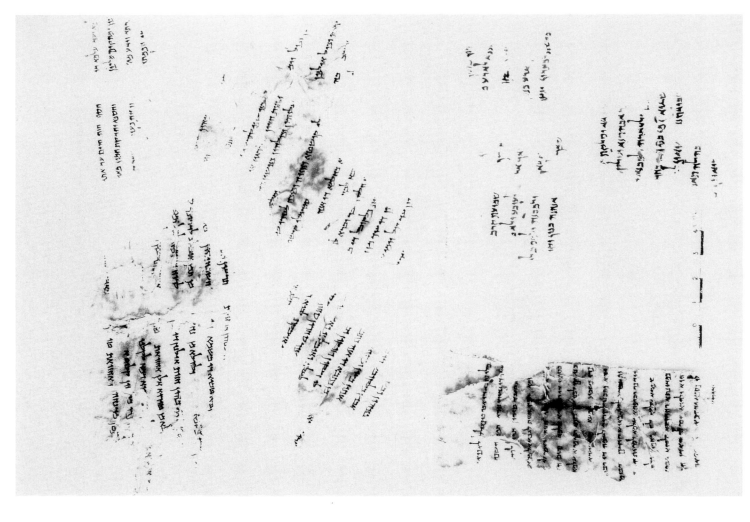

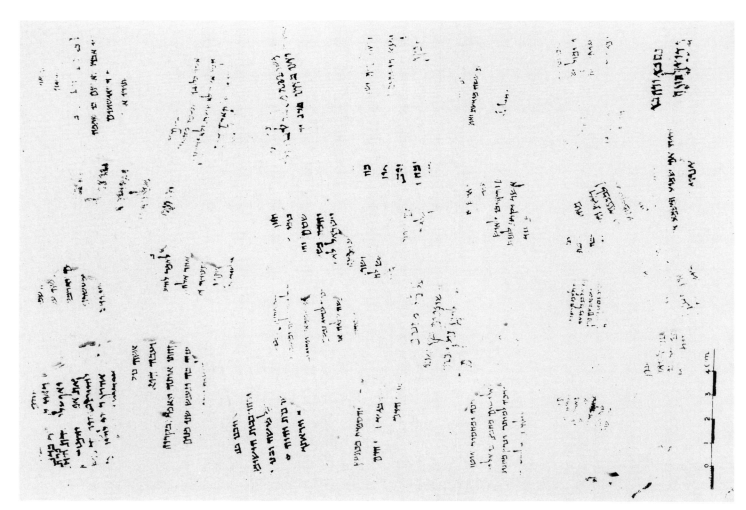

PLATE 115

PLATE 114

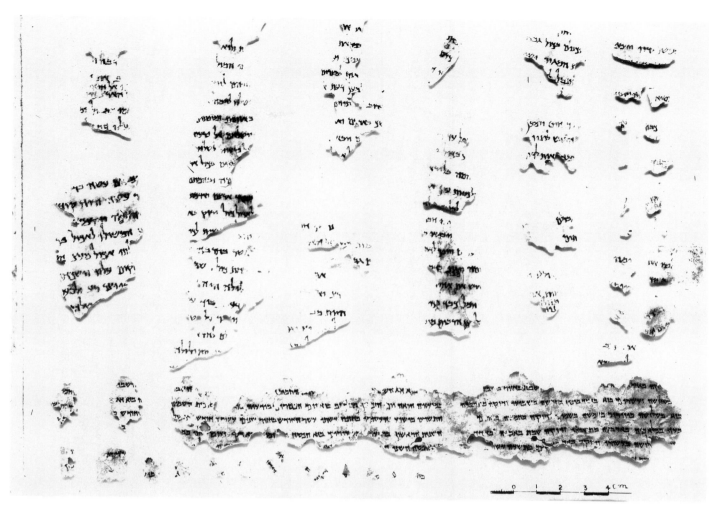

PLATE 116

PLATE 117

Plate 123

Plate 122

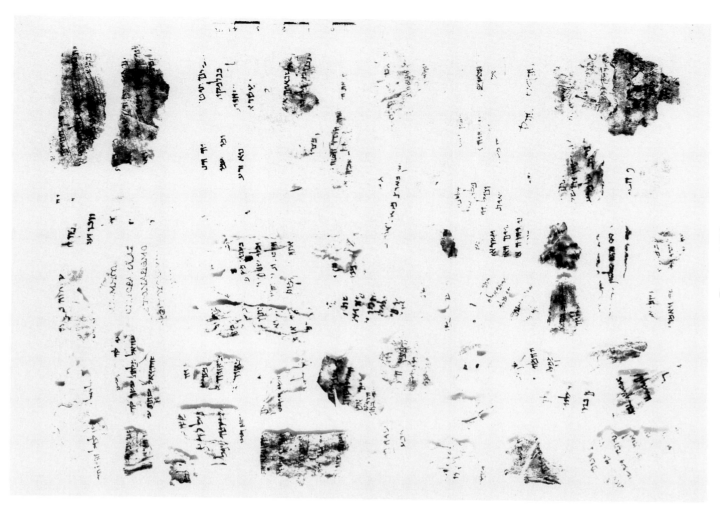

PLATE 125

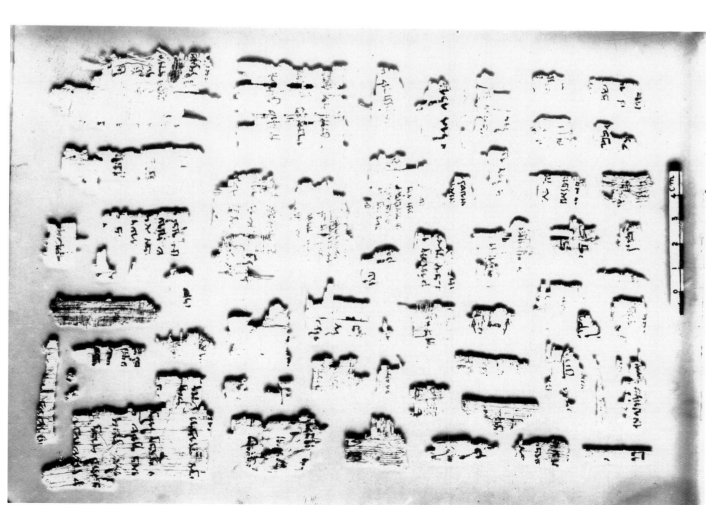

PLATE 124

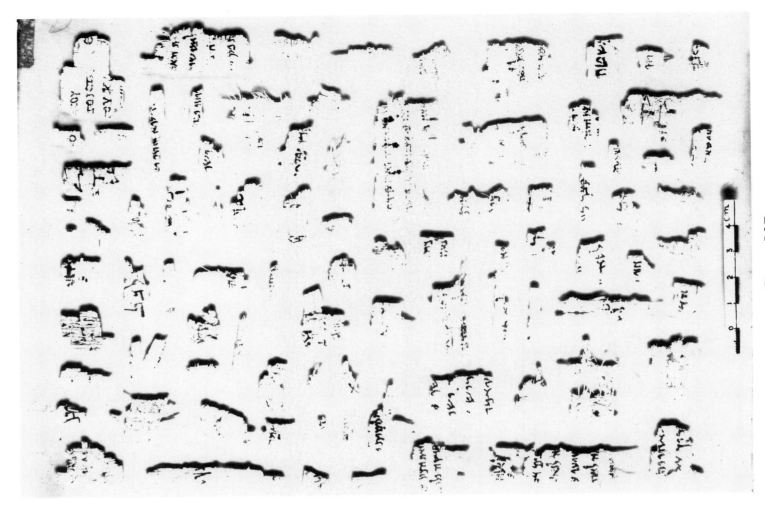

PLATE 127

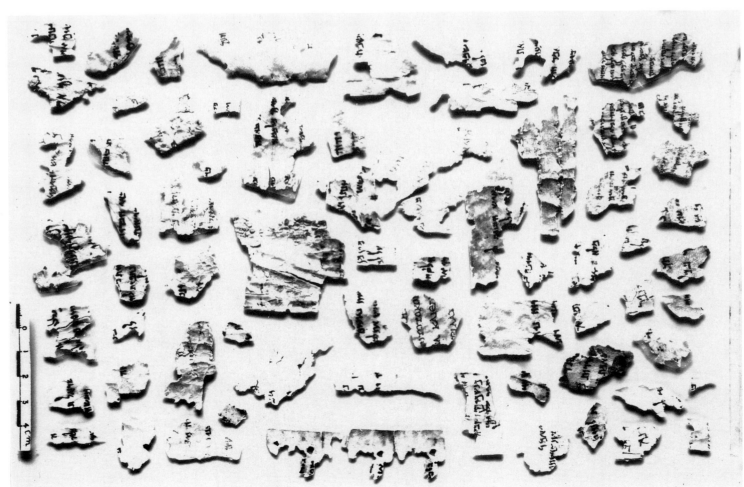

PLATE 126

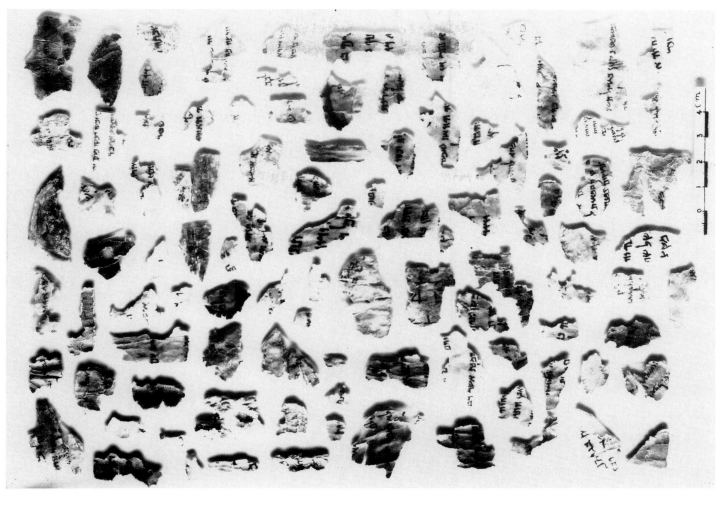

PLATE 129

PLATE 128

PLATE 130

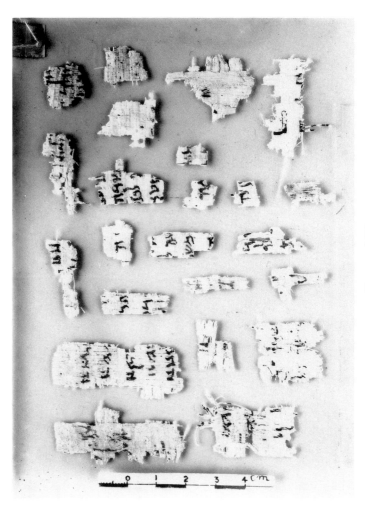

PLATE 131

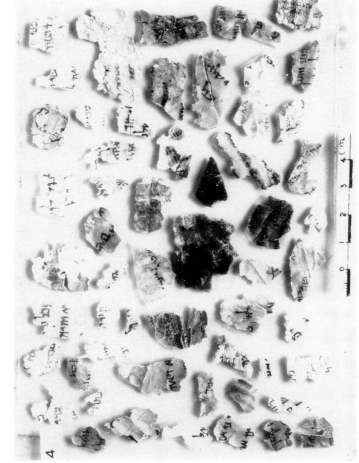

PLATE 132

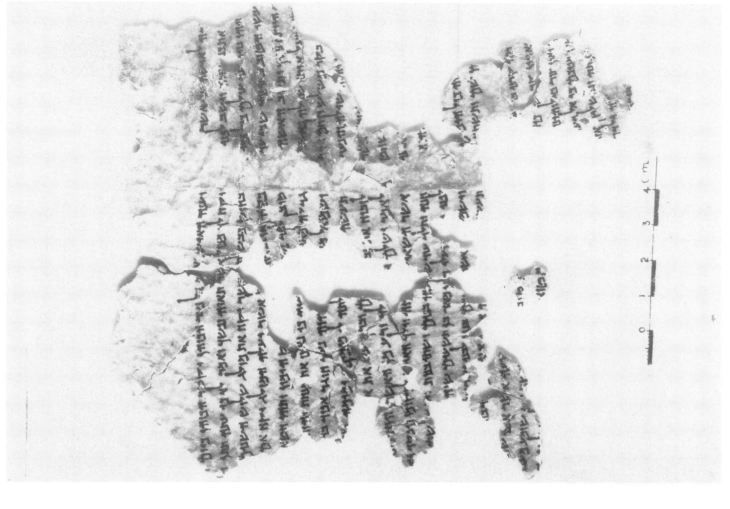

PLATE 134

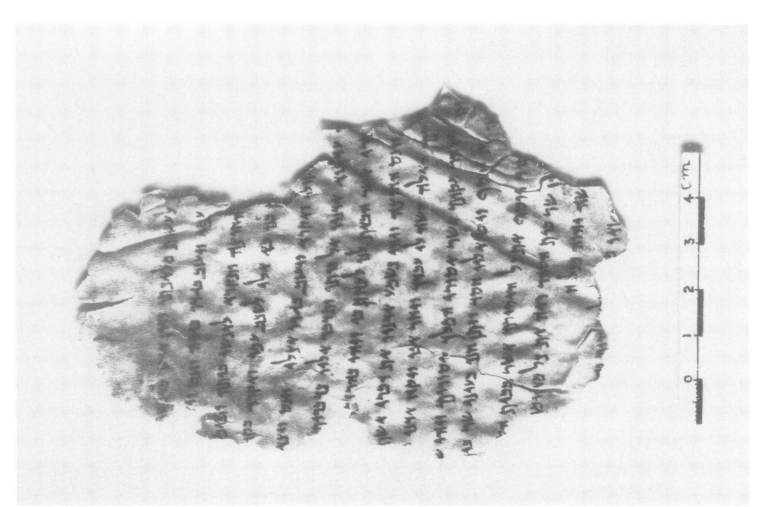

PLATE 133

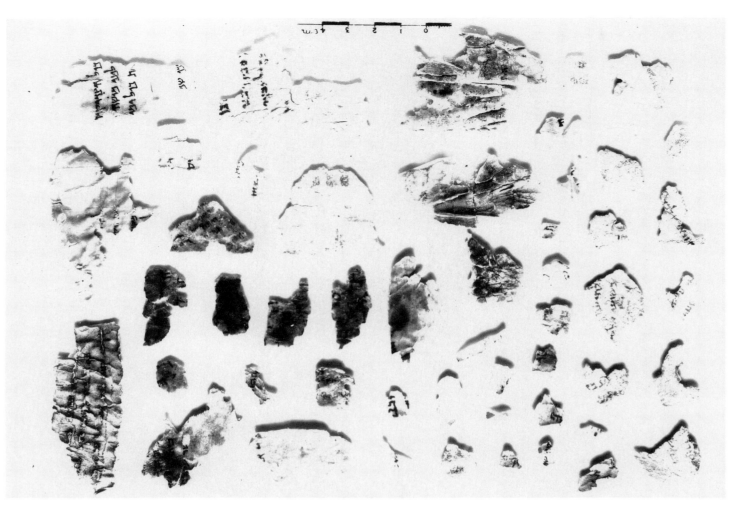

PLATE 135

PLATE 136

PLATE 137

PLATE 138

PLATE 140

PLATE 139

PLATE 141

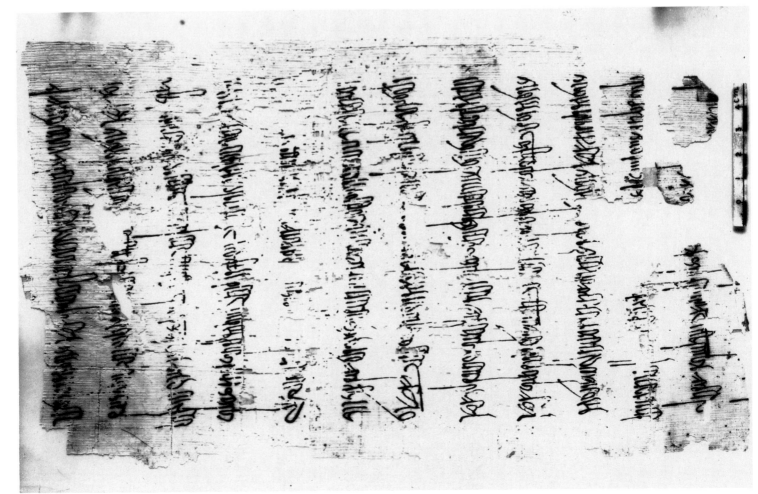

PLATE 143

PLATE 142

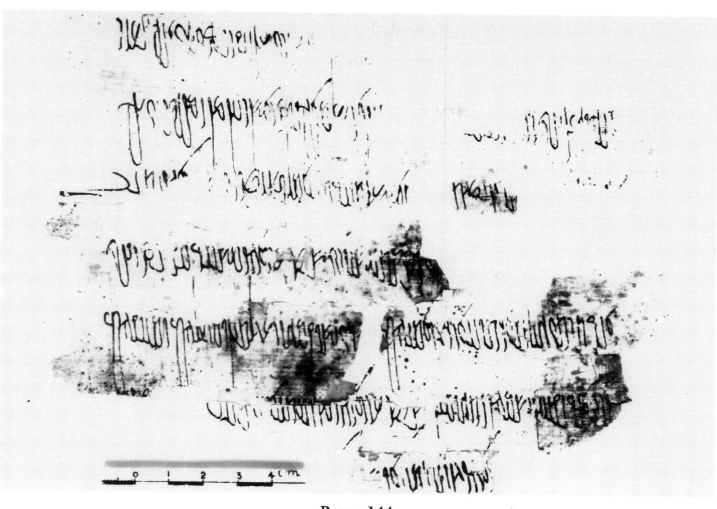

PLATE 144

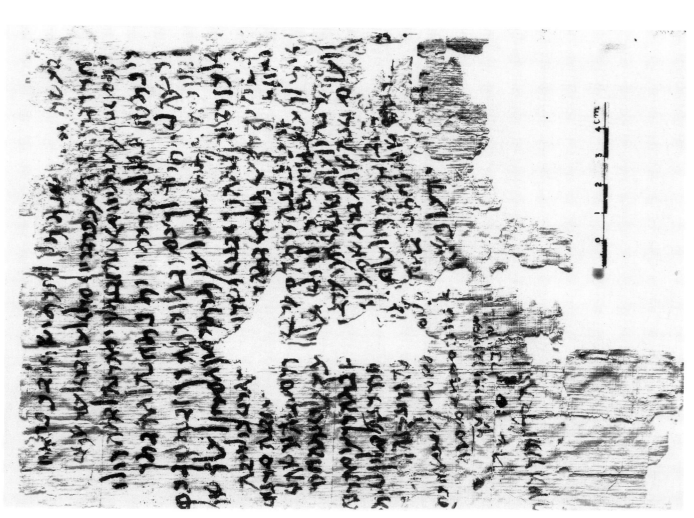

PLATE 145

PLATE 146

PLATE 147

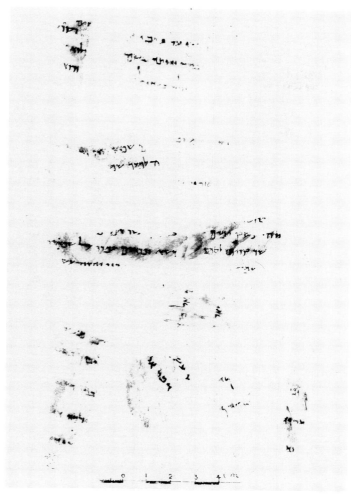

PLATE 148

PLATE 149

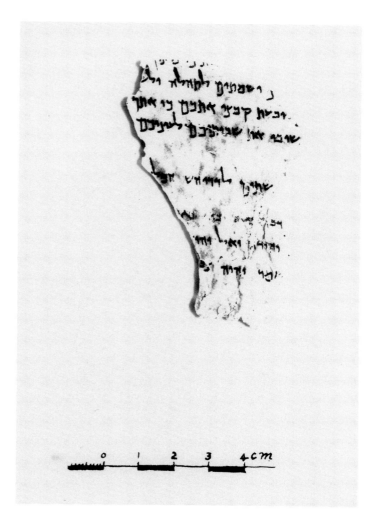

PLATE 150

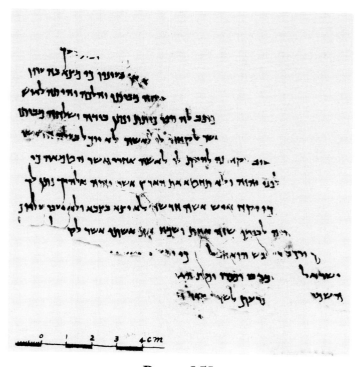

PLATE 151

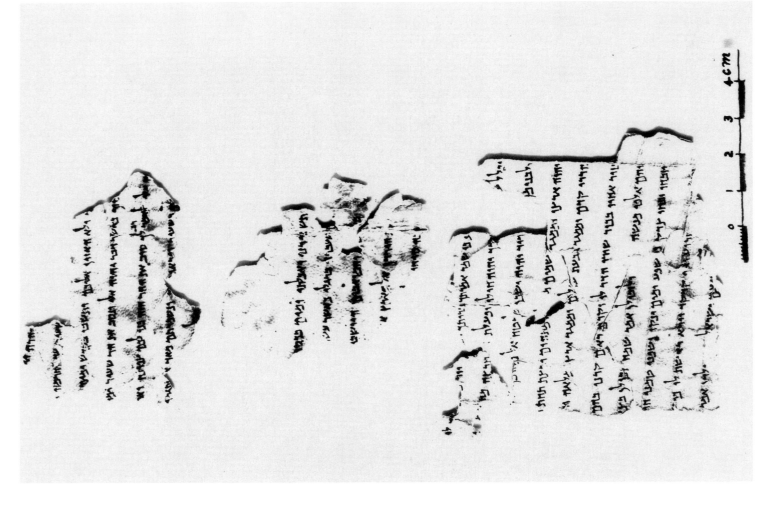

PLATE 153

PLATE 152

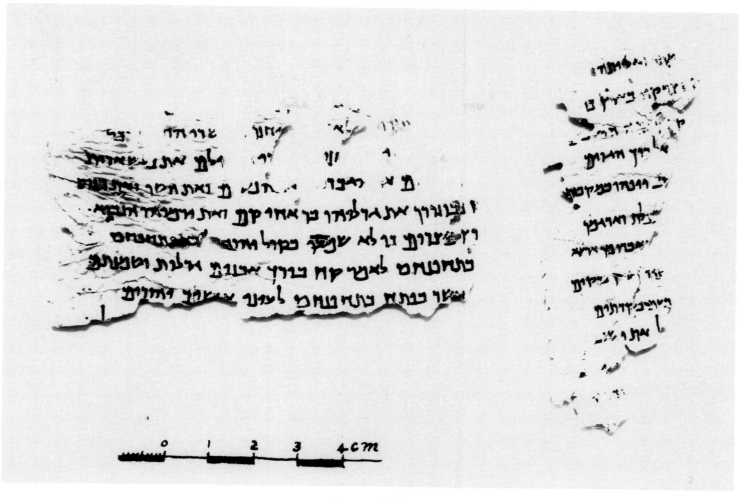

PLATE 154

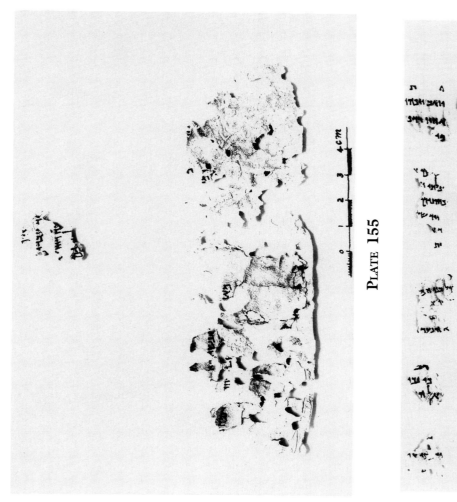

PLATE 155

PLATE 156

PLATE 158

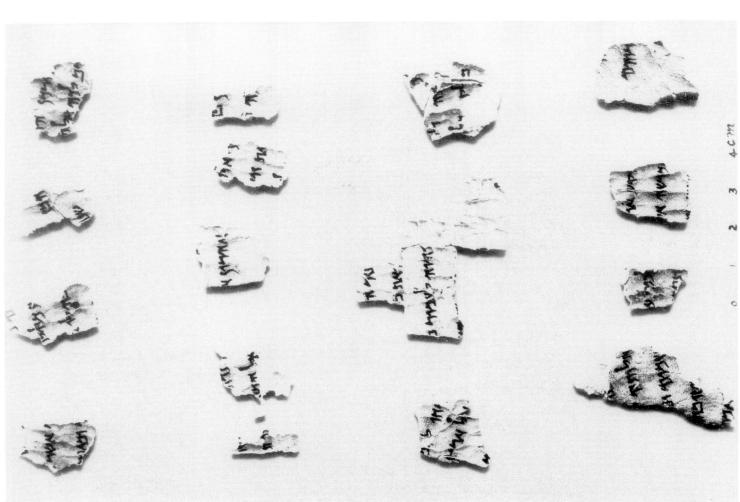

PLATE 157

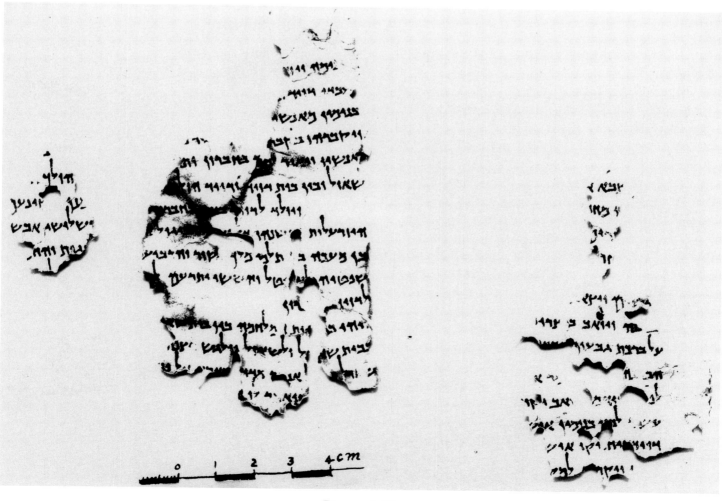

PLATE 159

PLATE 160

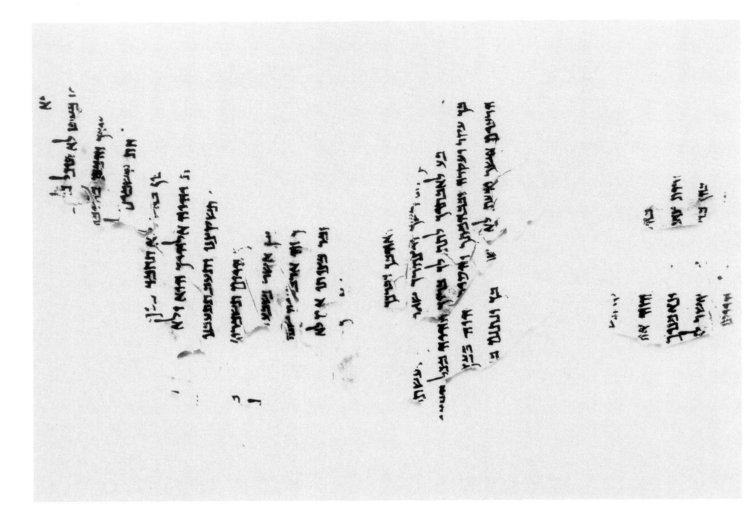

PLATE 162

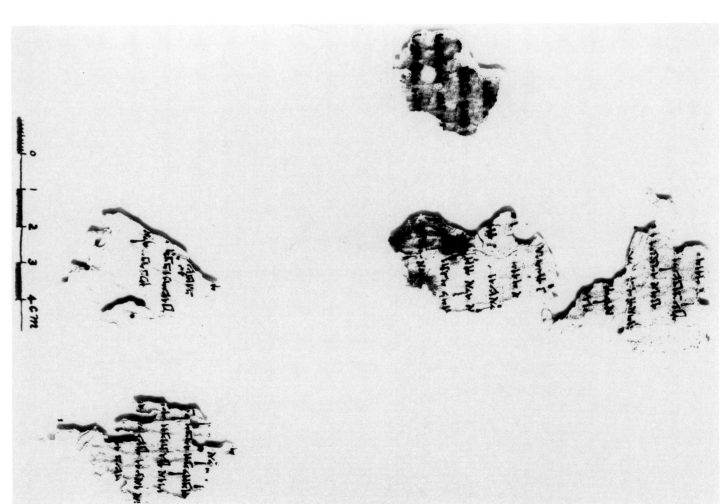

PLATE 161

PLATE 164

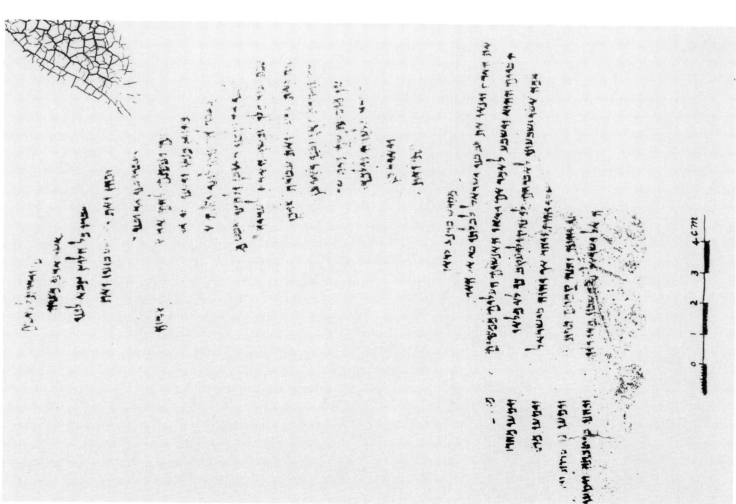

PLATE 163

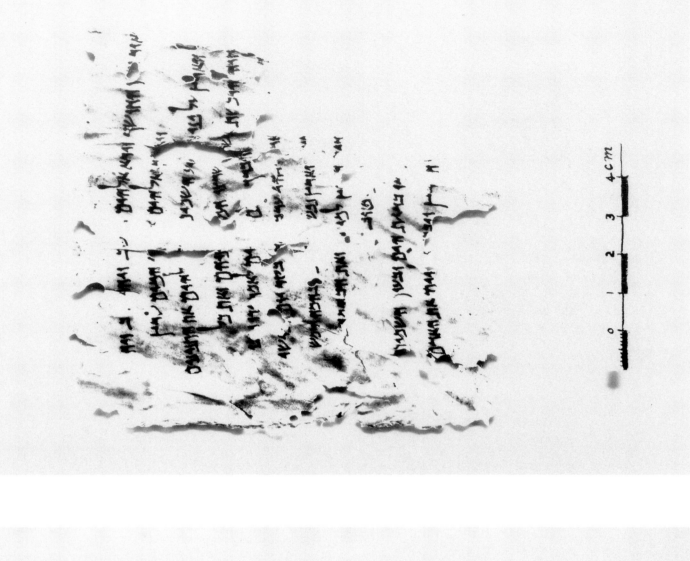

PLATE 166

PLATE 165

PLATE 167

PLATE 168

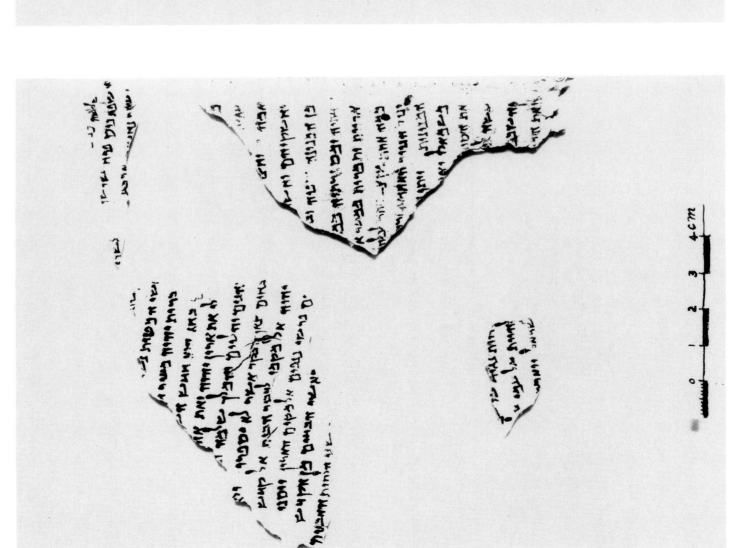

PLATE 170

PLATE 169

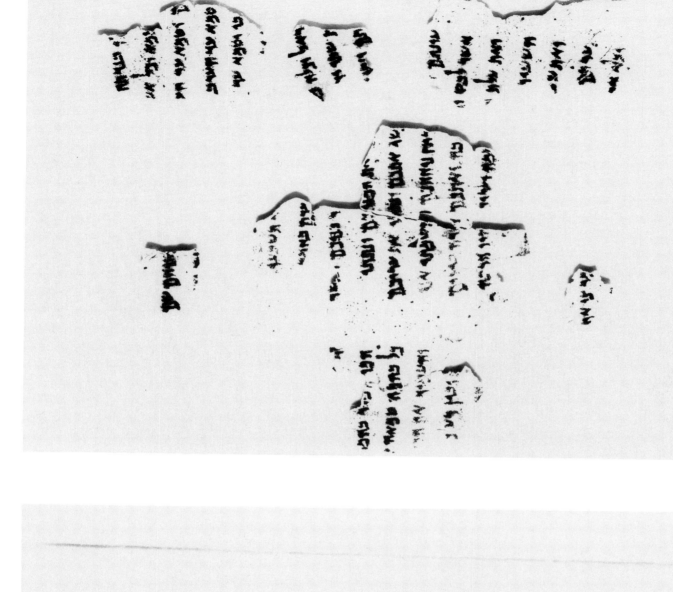

PLATE 172

PLATE 171

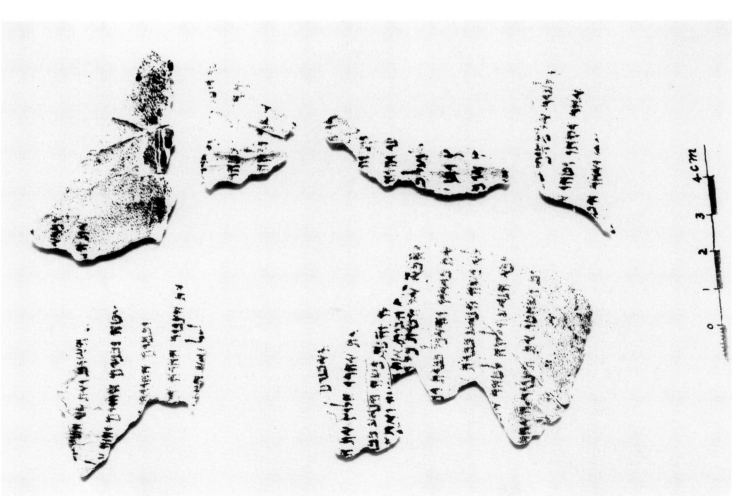

PLATE 173

PLATE 174

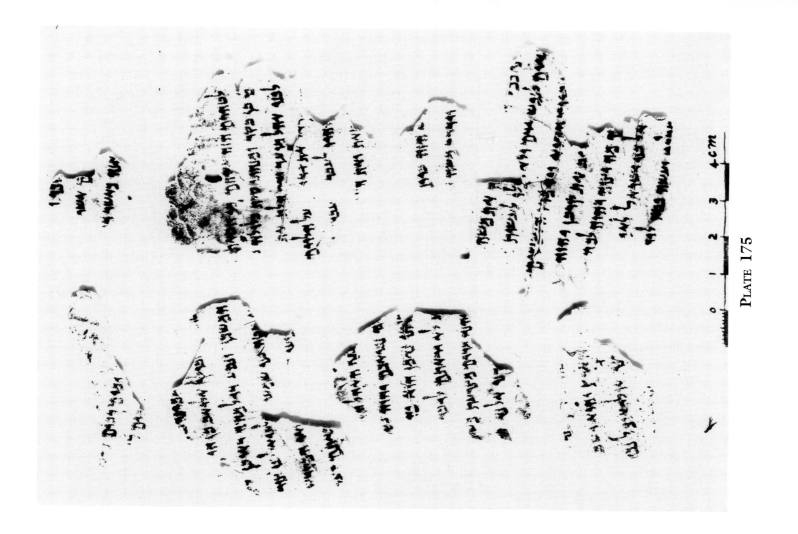

PLATE 175

PLATE 176

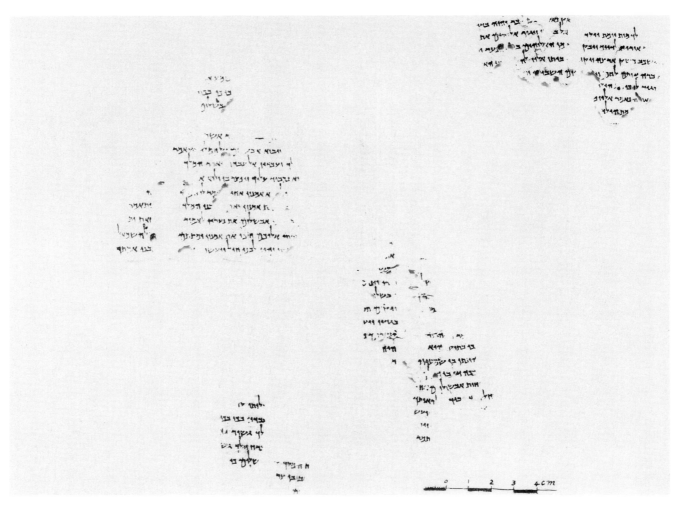

PLATE 177

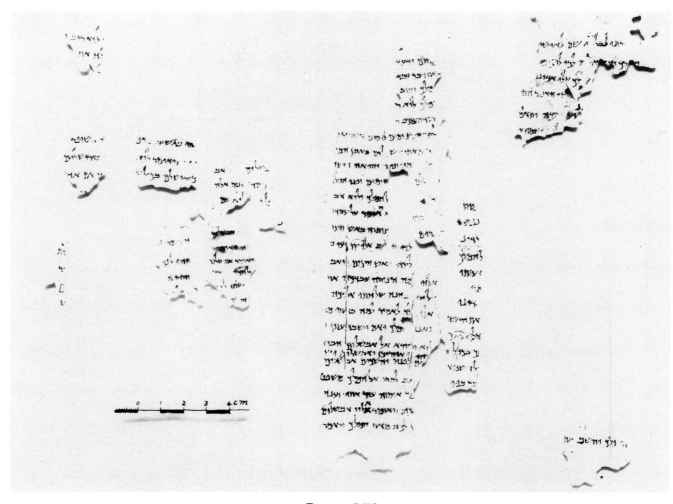

PLATE 178

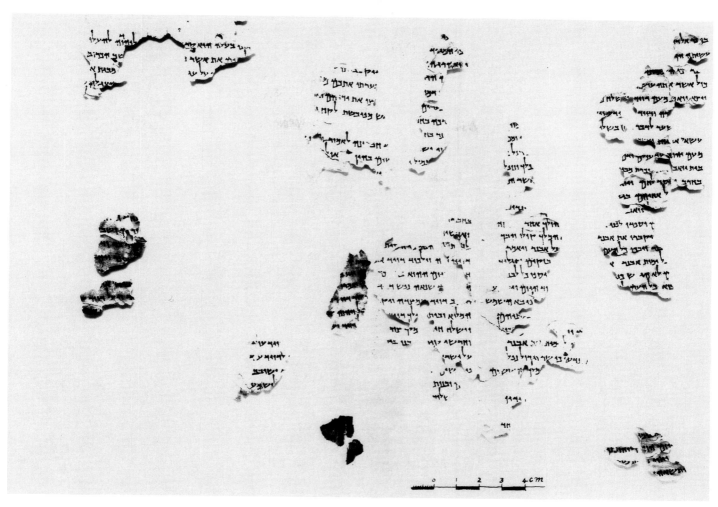

PLATE 179

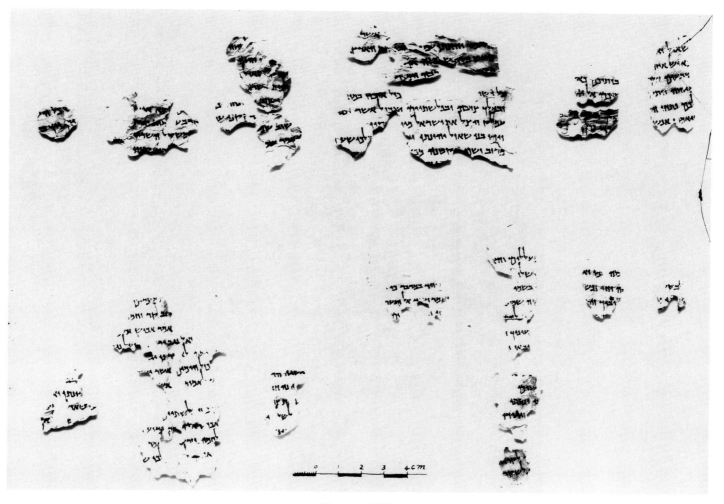

PLATE 180

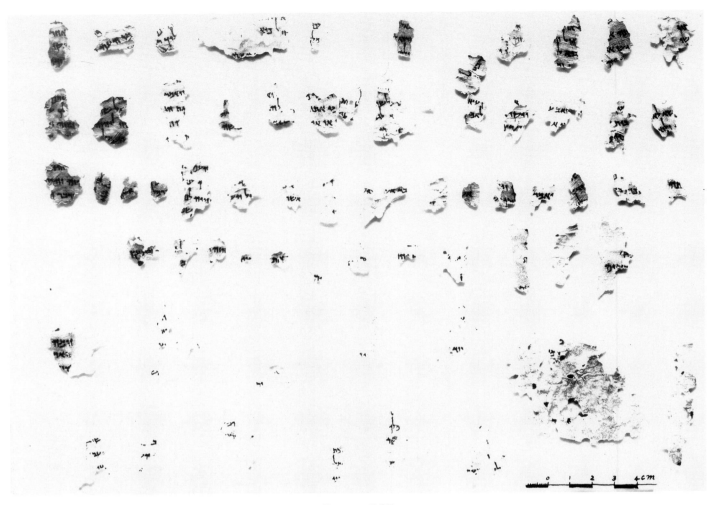

PLATE 181

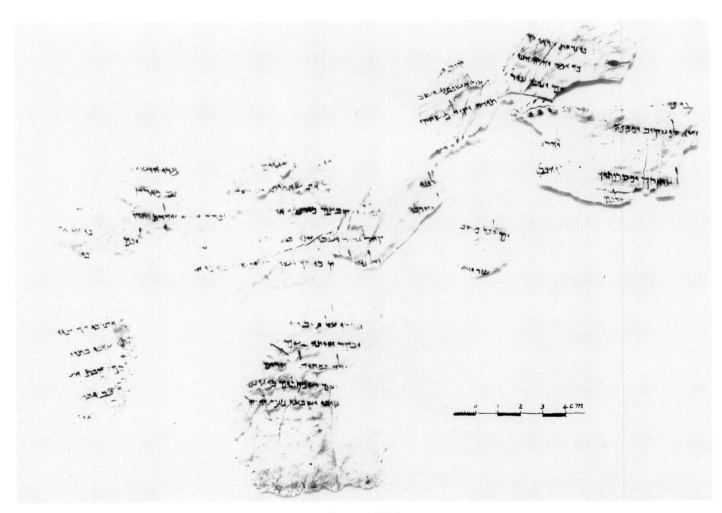

PLATE 182

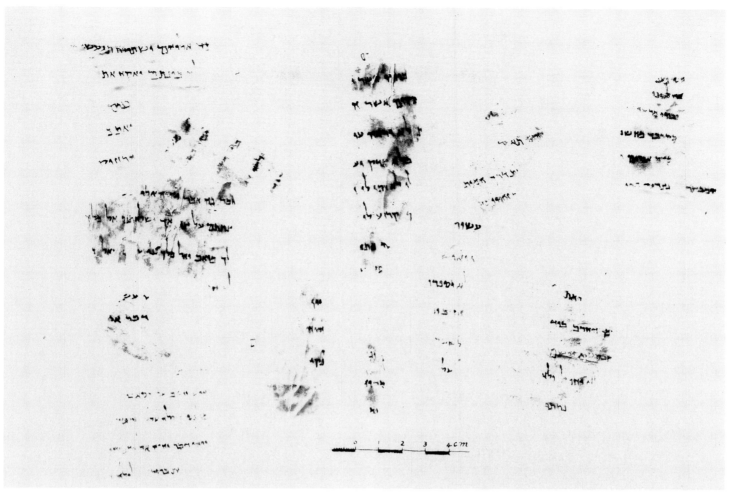

PLATE 183

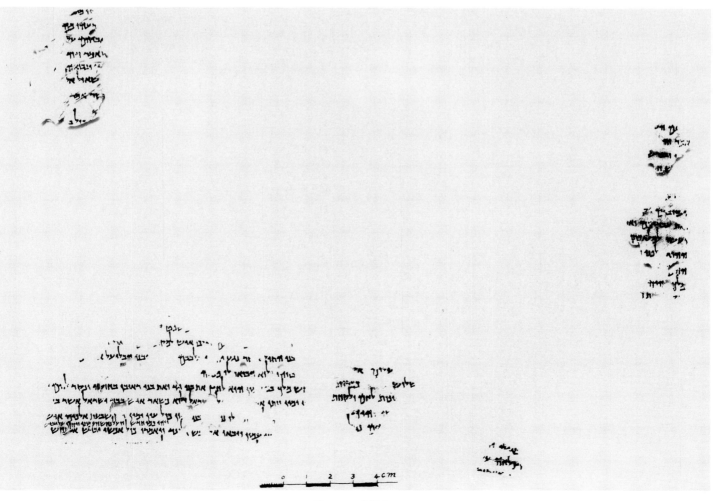

PLATE 184

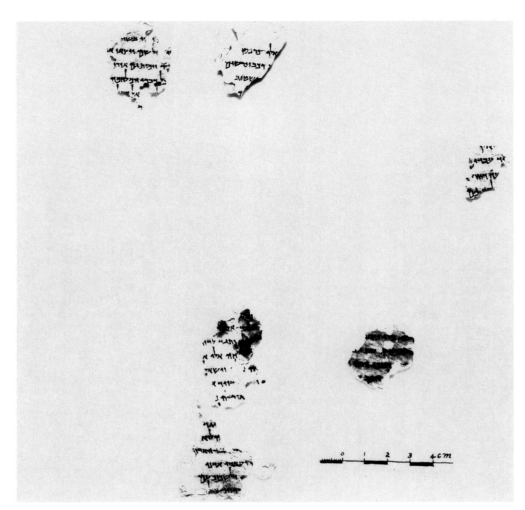

PLATE 185

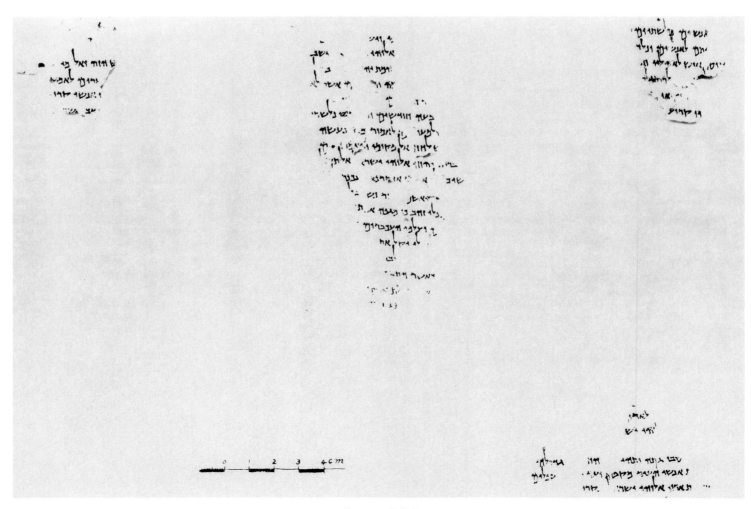

PLATE 186

PLATE 187

PLATE 188

PLATE 189

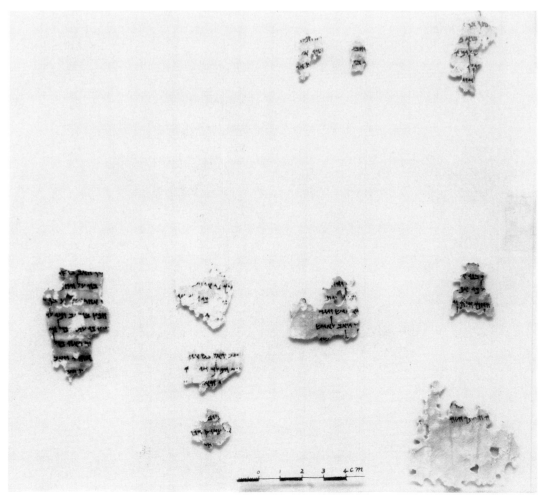

PLATE 190

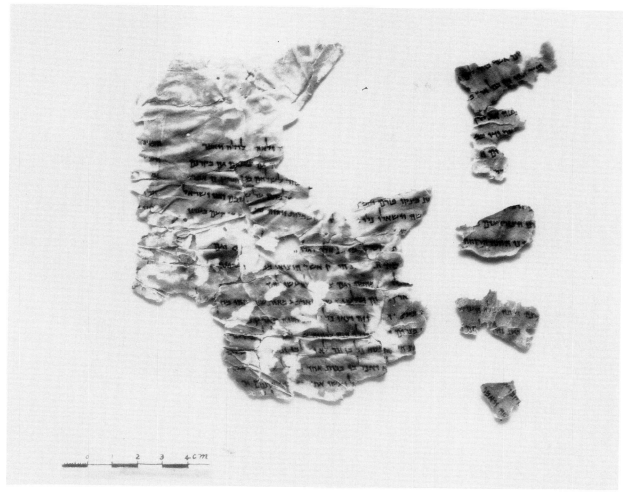

PLATE 191

PLATE 192

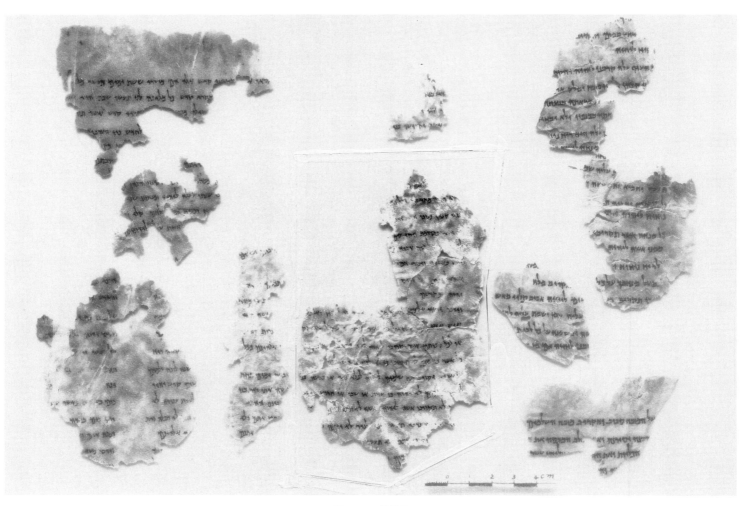

PLATE 193

PLATE 194

PLATE 195

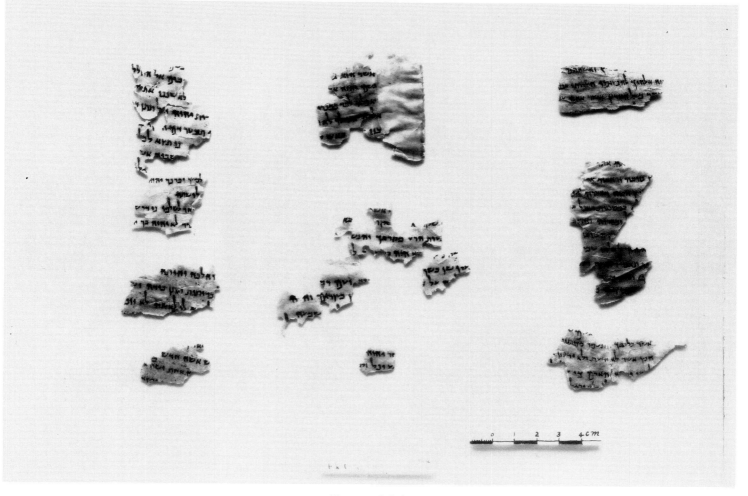

PLATE 196

PLATE 197

PLATE 198

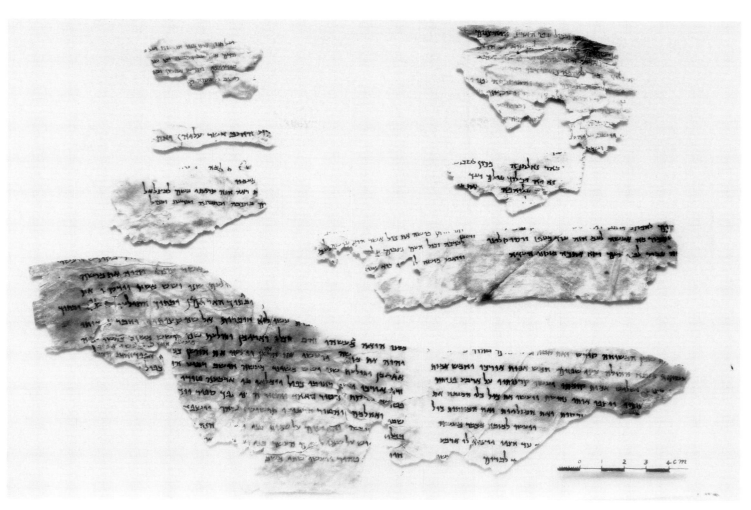

PLATE 199

PLATE 200

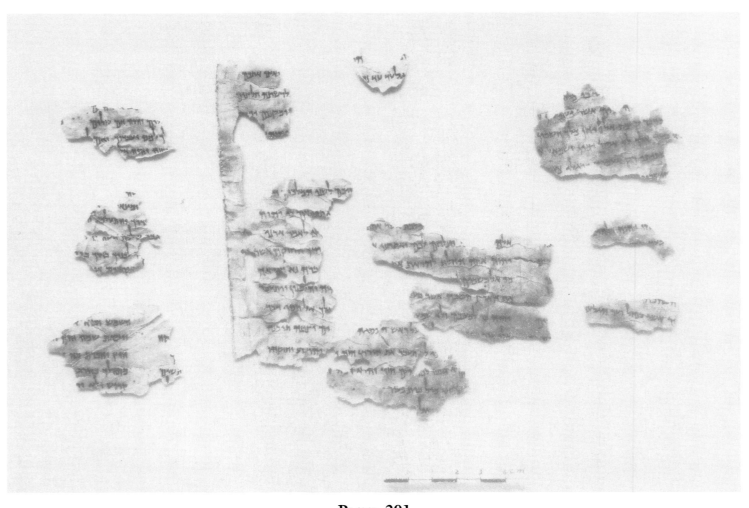

PLATE 201

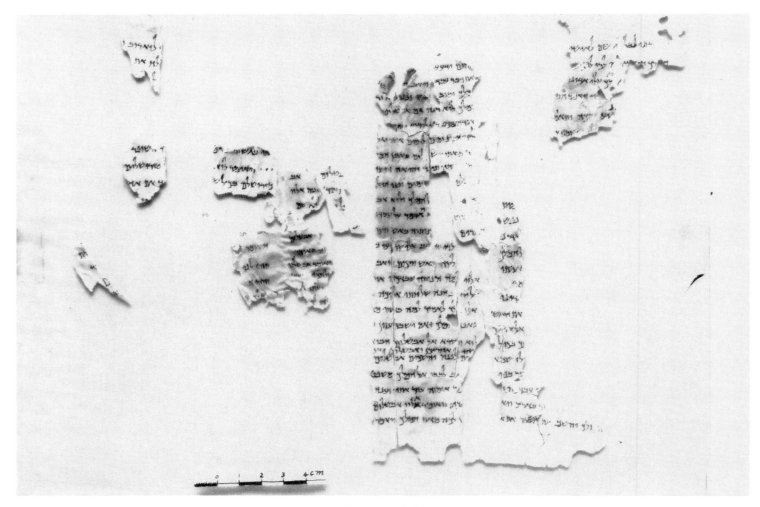

PLATE 202

PLATE 203

PLATE 204

PLATE 205

PLATE 206

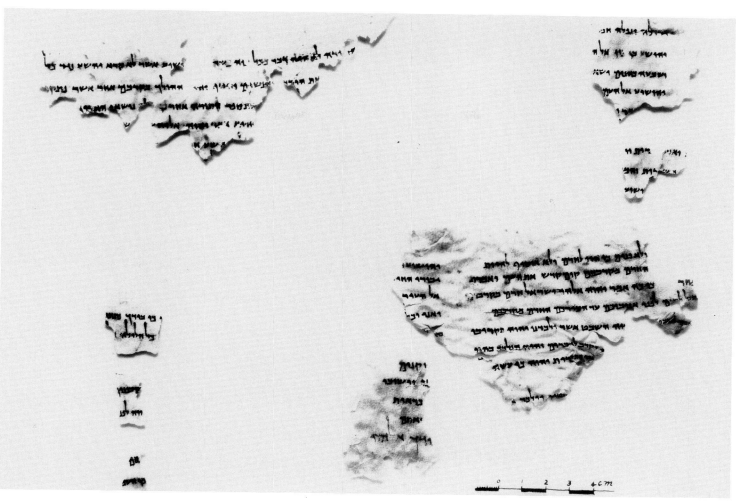

PLATE 207

PLATE 208

PLATE 209

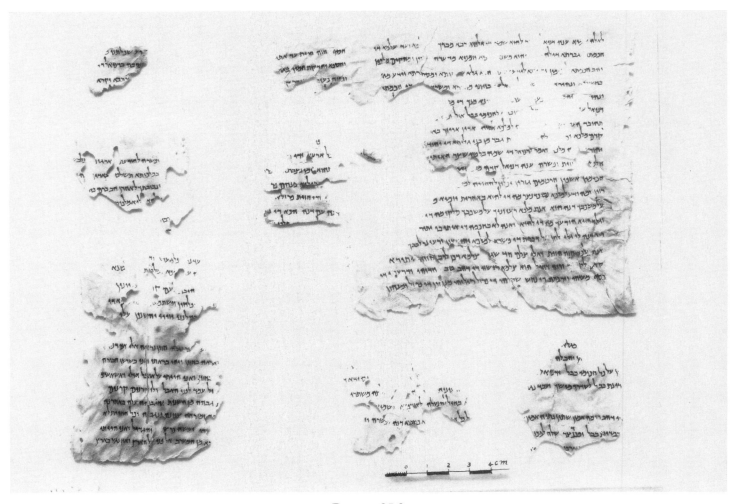

PLATE 210

PLATE 211

PLATE 212

PLATE 213

PLATE 214

PLATE 215

PLATE 216

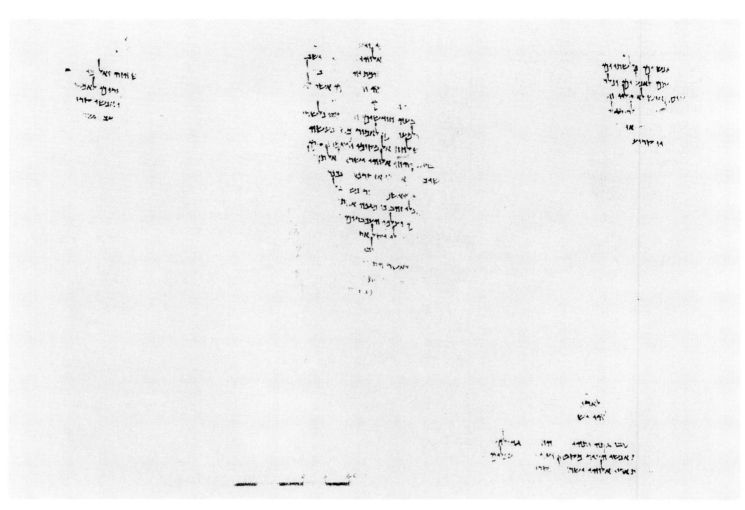

PLATE 221

PLATE 222

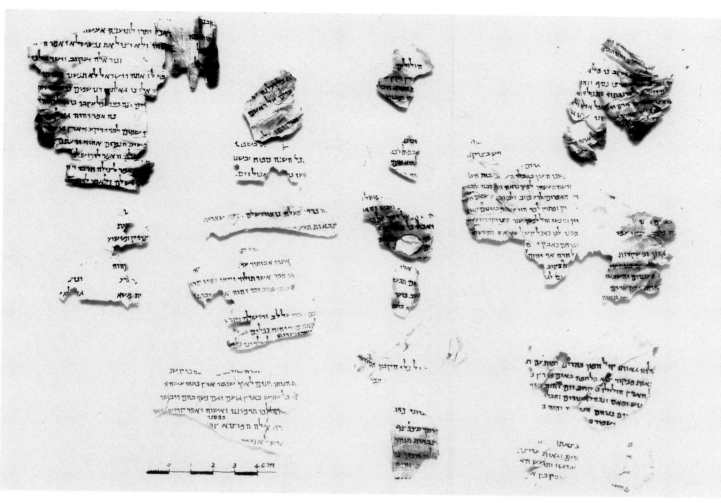

PLATE 223

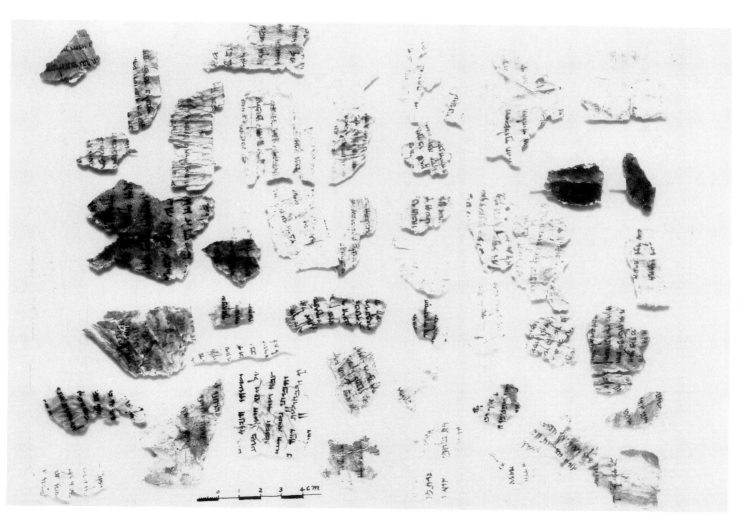

PLATE 224

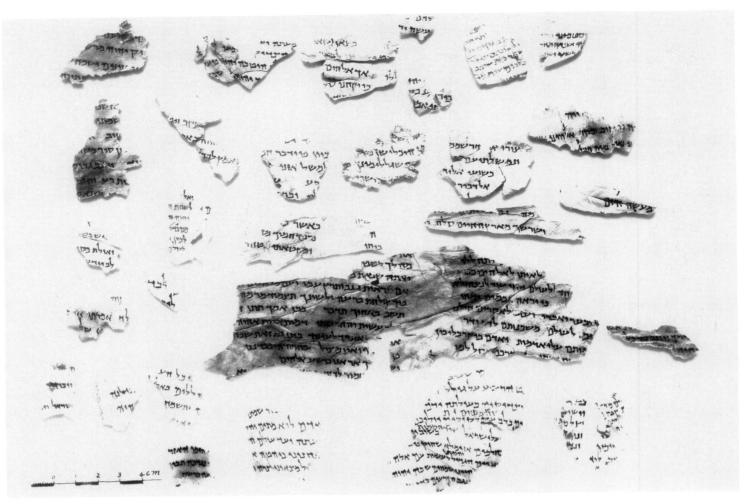

PLATE 225

PLATE 226

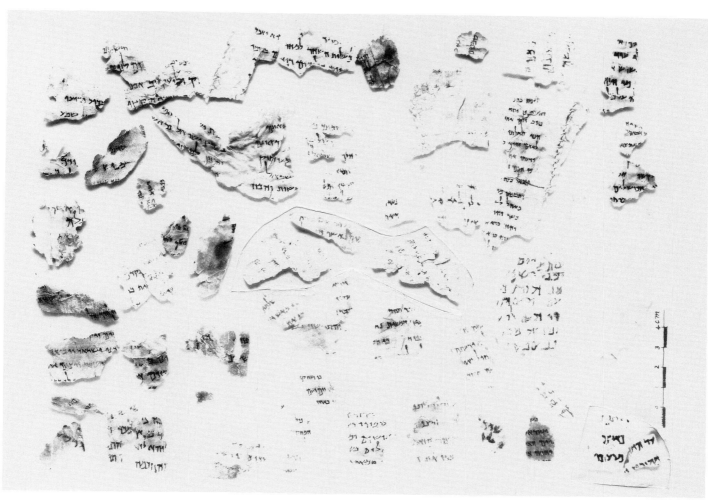

PLATE 227

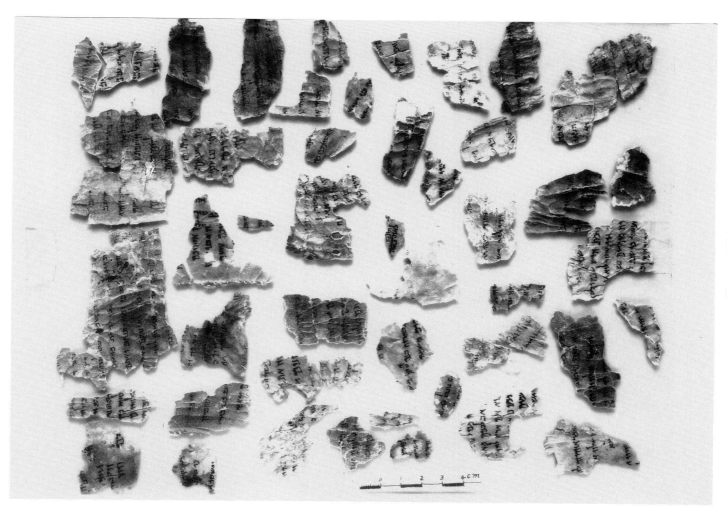

PLATE 228

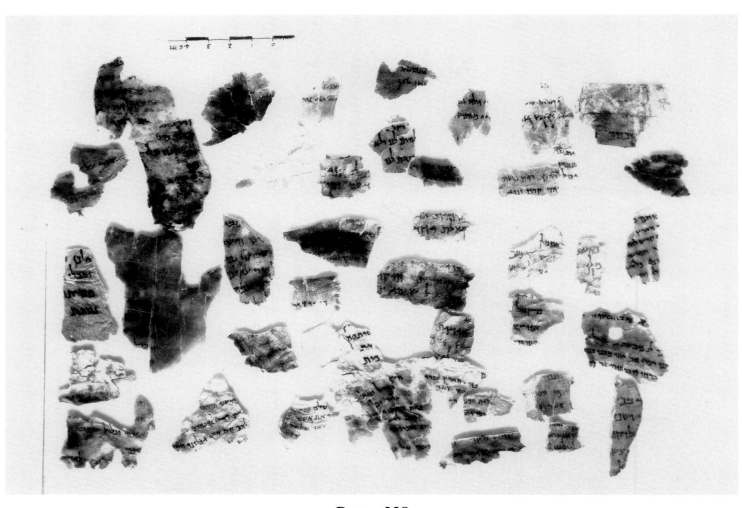

PLATE 229

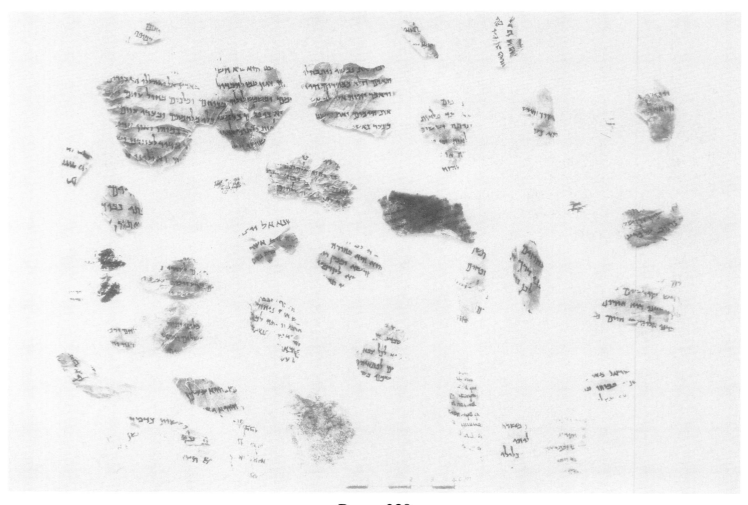

PLATE 230

PLATE 231

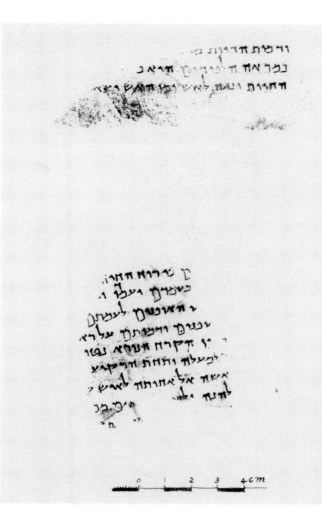

PLATE 232

PLATE 233

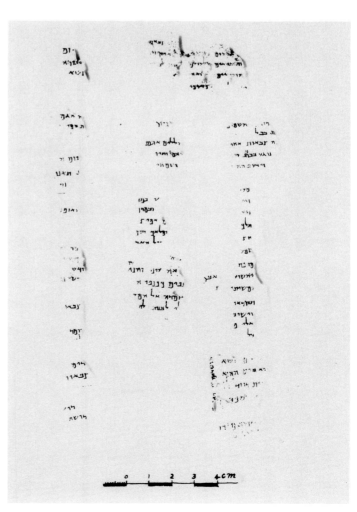

PLATE 234

PLATE 243

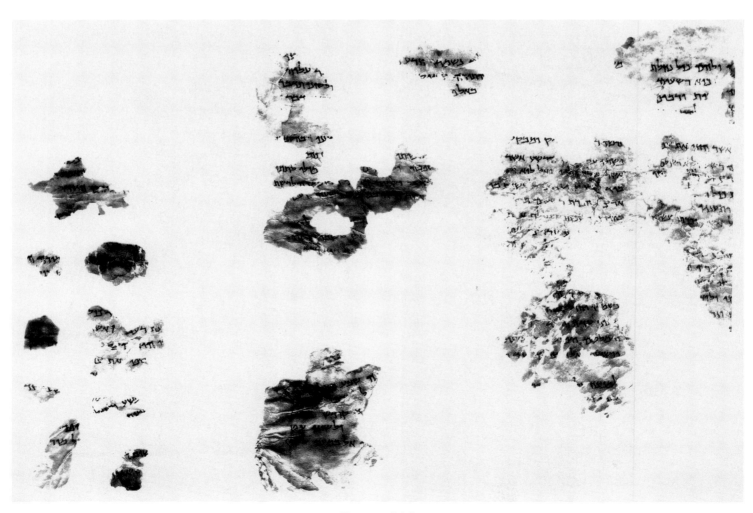

PLATE 244

PLATE 246

PLATE 245

PLATE 247

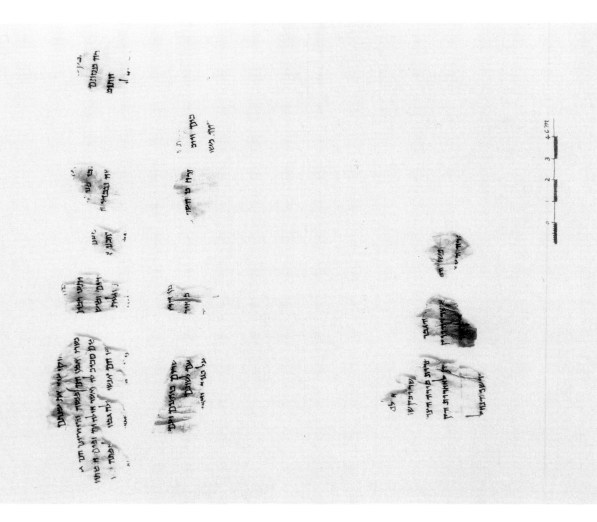

PLATE 248

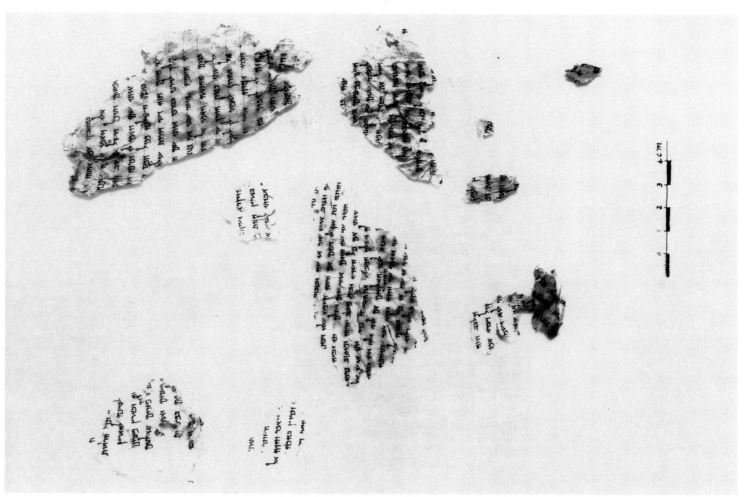

PLATE 249

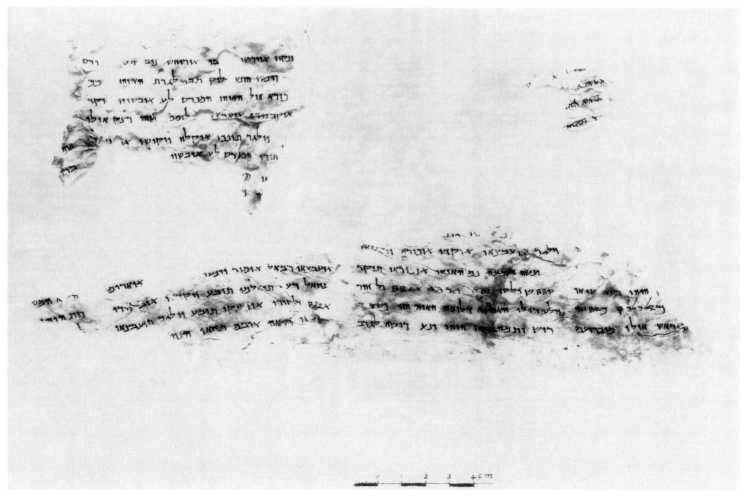

PLATE 250

PLATE 251

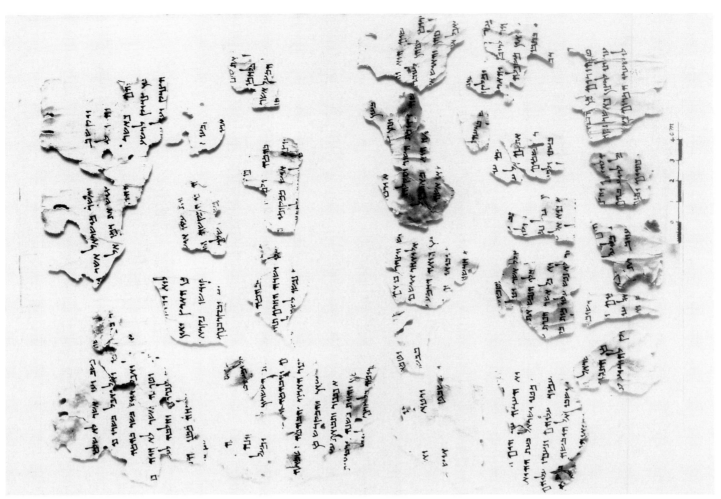

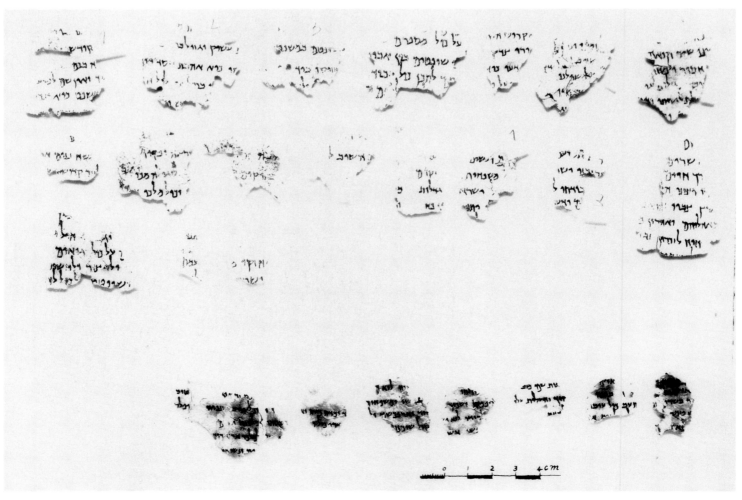

PLATE 252

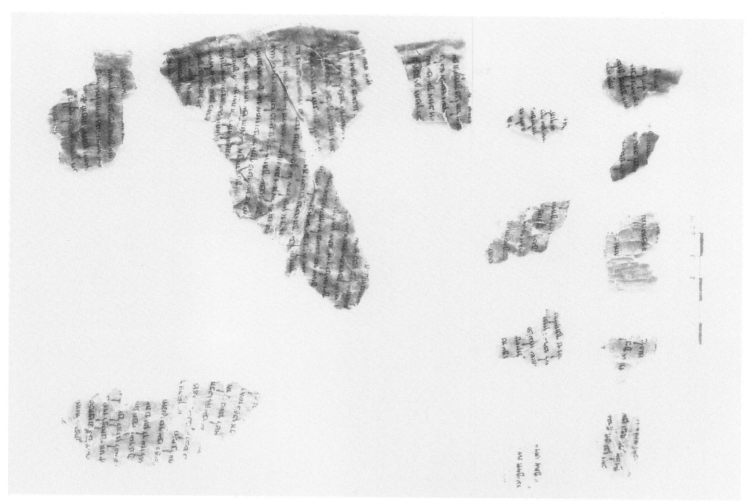

PLATE 253

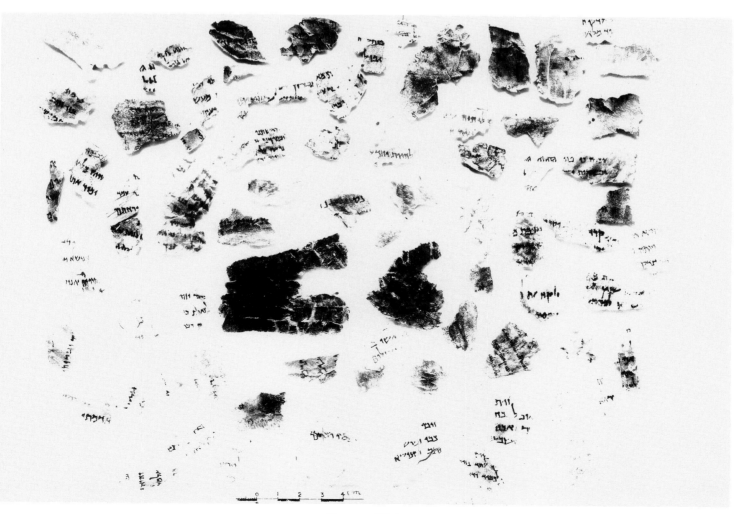

PLATE 254

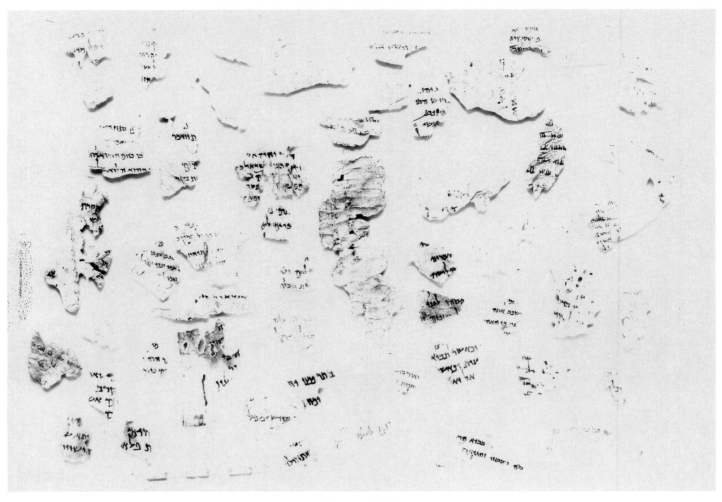

PLATE 255

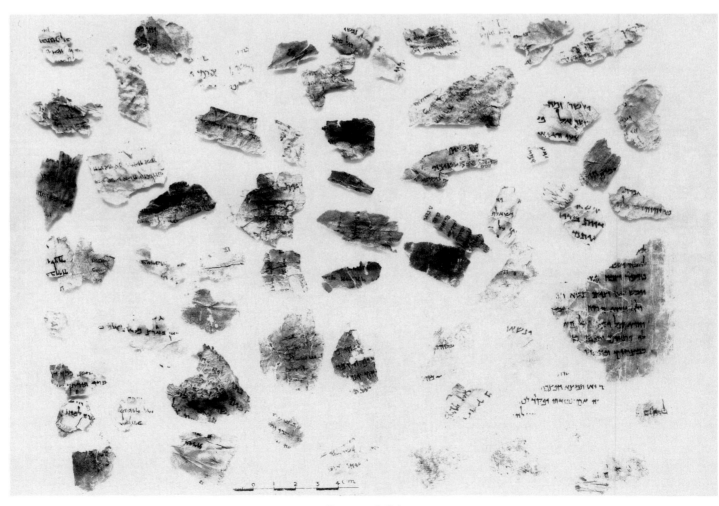

PLATE 256

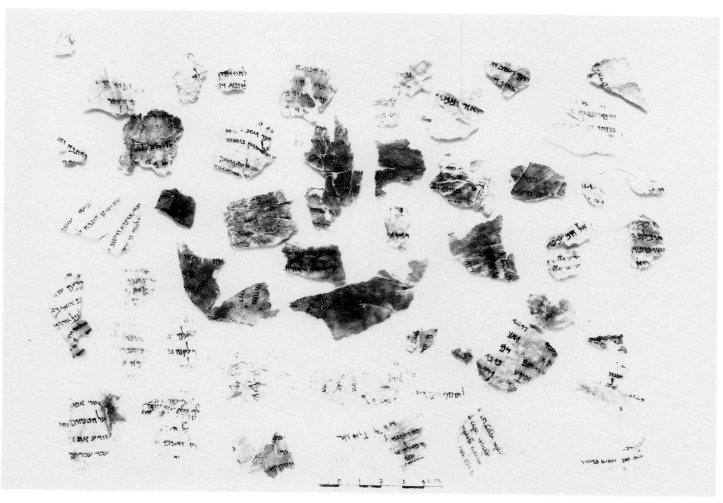

PLATE 257

PLATE 258

PLATE 259

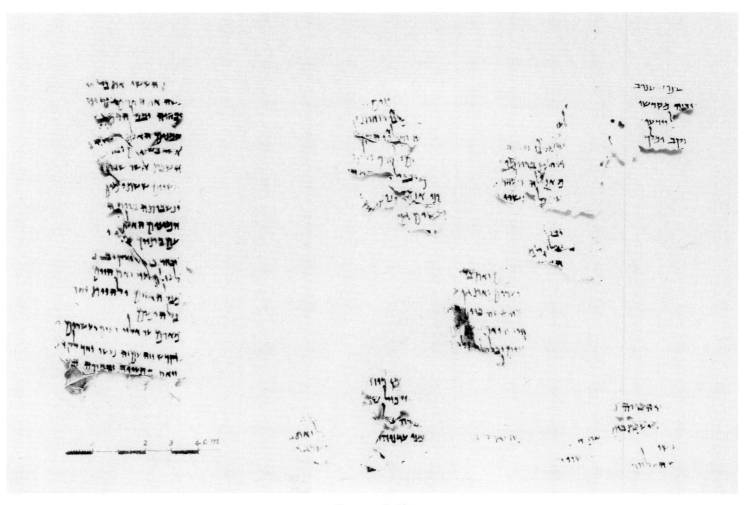

PLATE 260

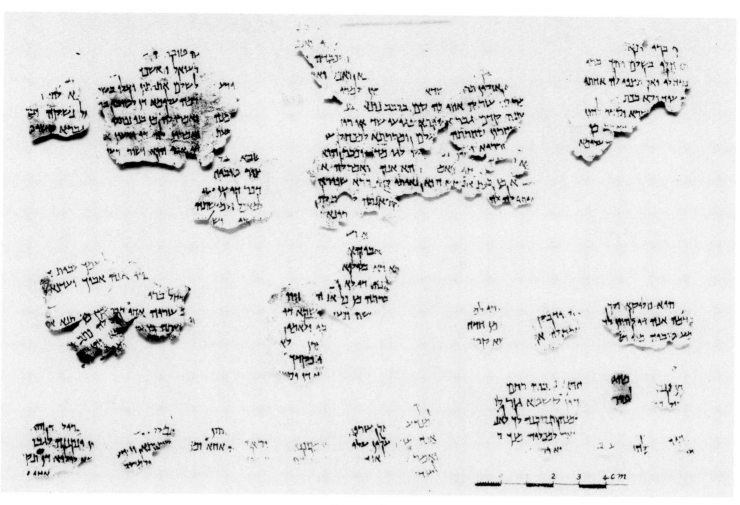

PLATE 261

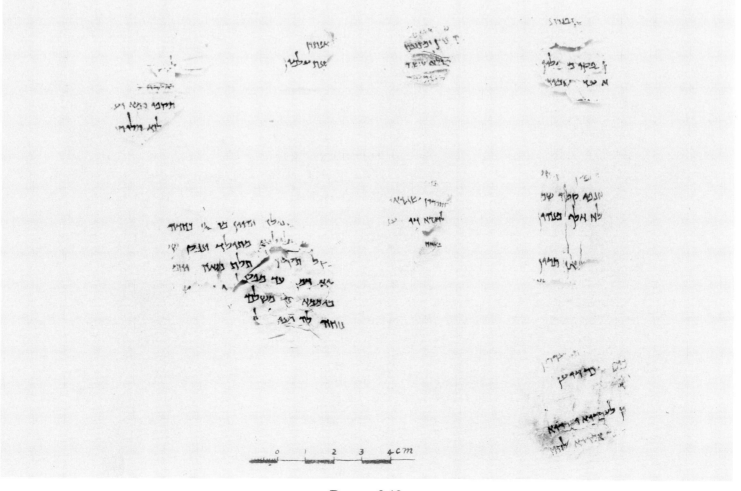

PLATE 262

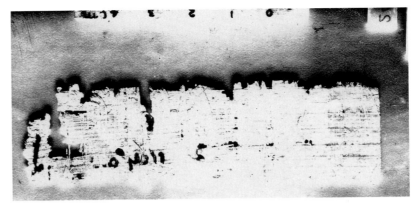

PLATE 263

PLATE 264

PLATE 265

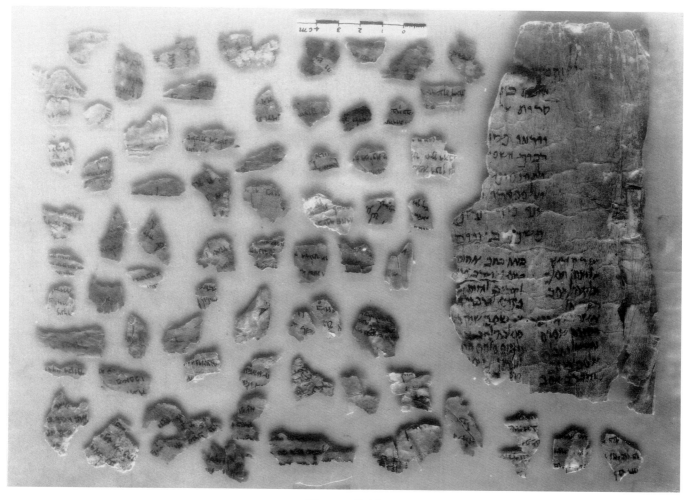

PLATE 266

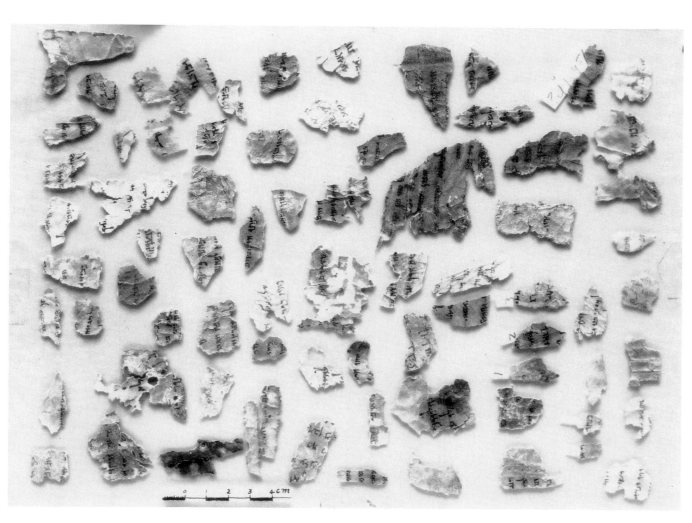

PLATE 267

PLATE 268

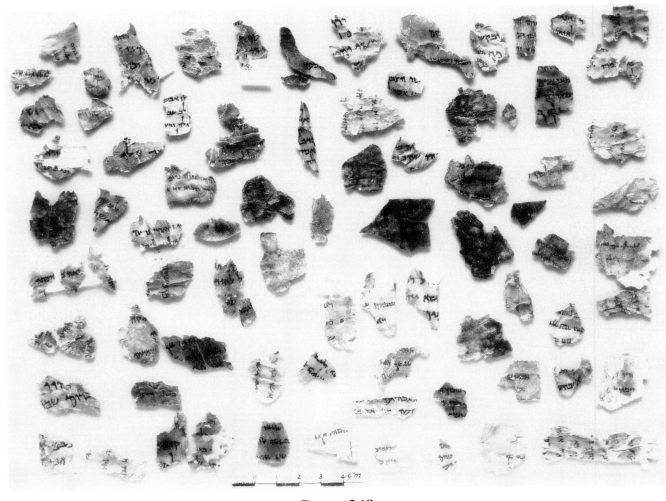

PLATE 269

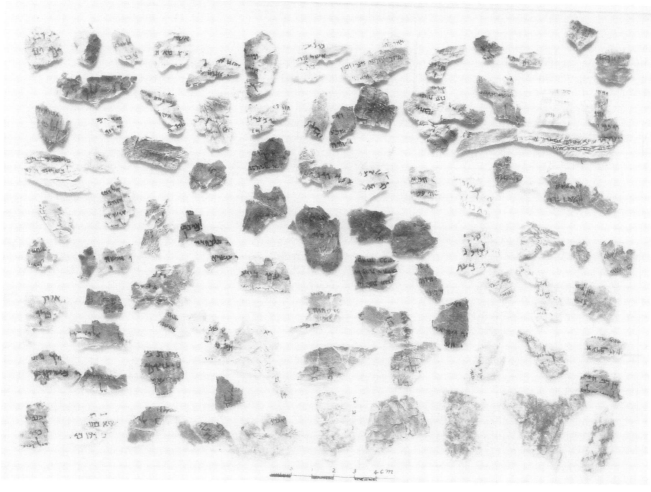

PLATE 270

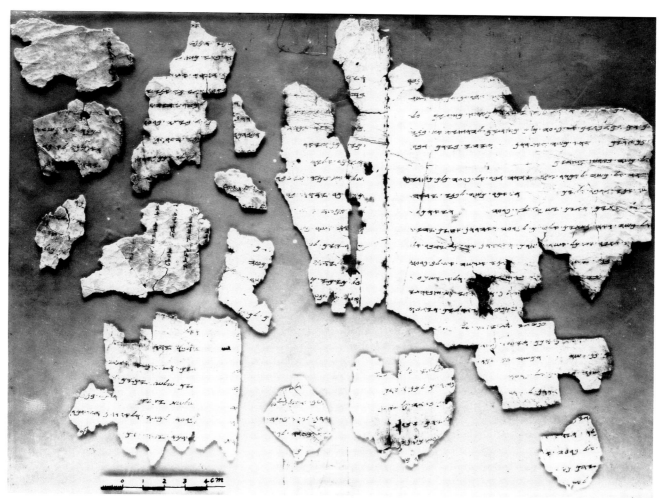

PLATE 271

PLATE 272

PLATE 273

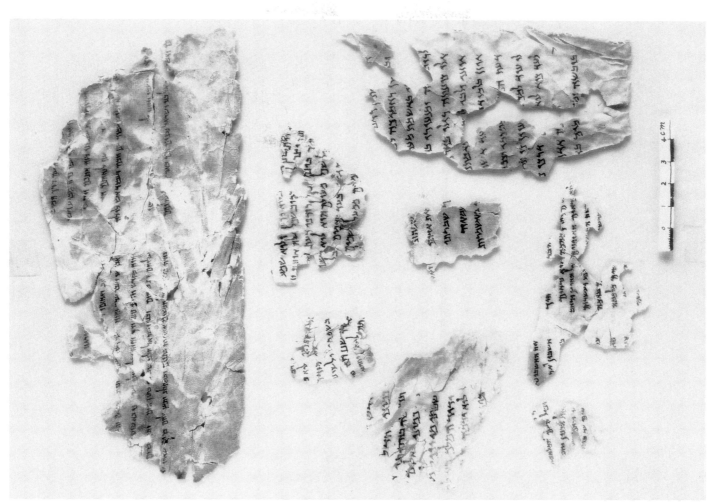

PLATE 274

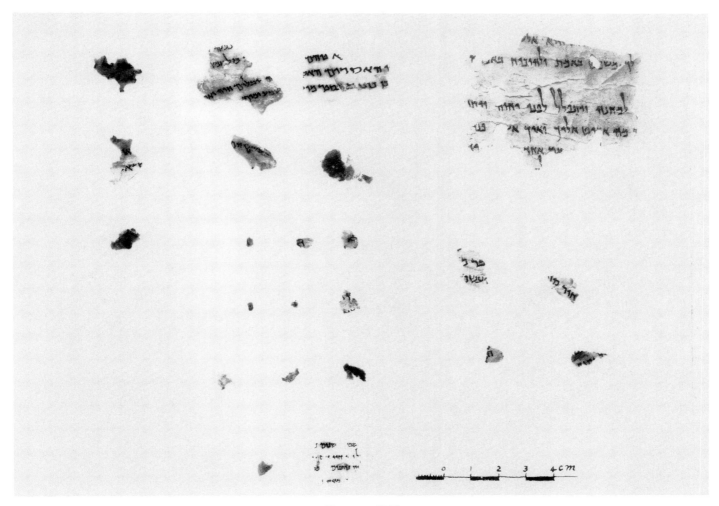

PLATE 275

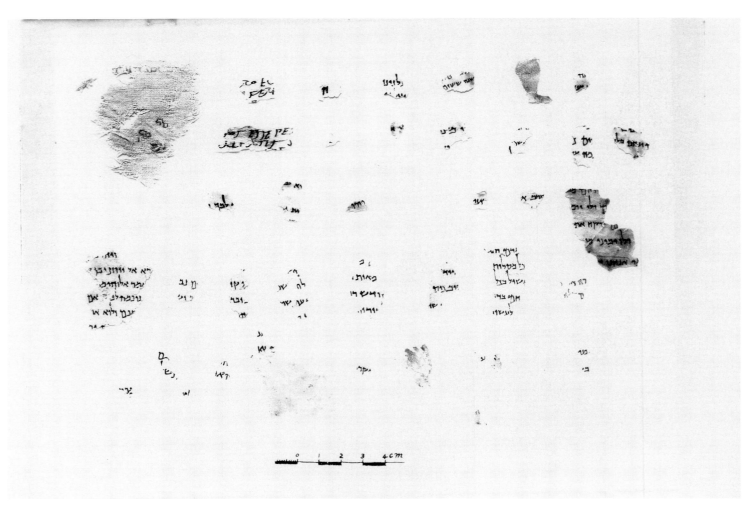

PLATE 276

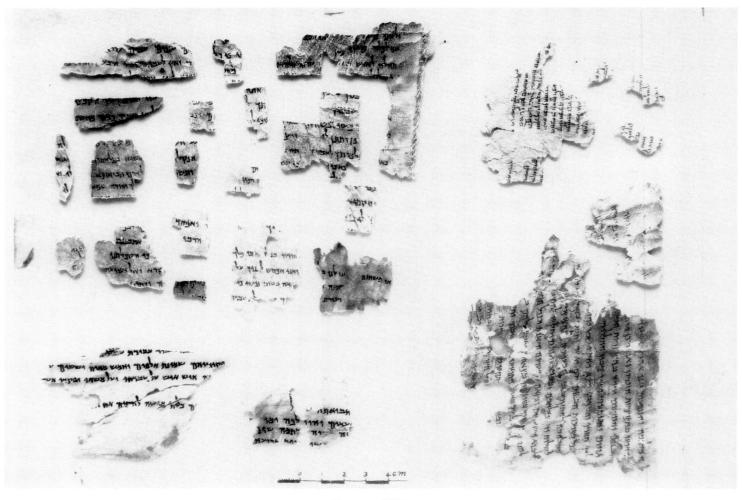

PLATE 277

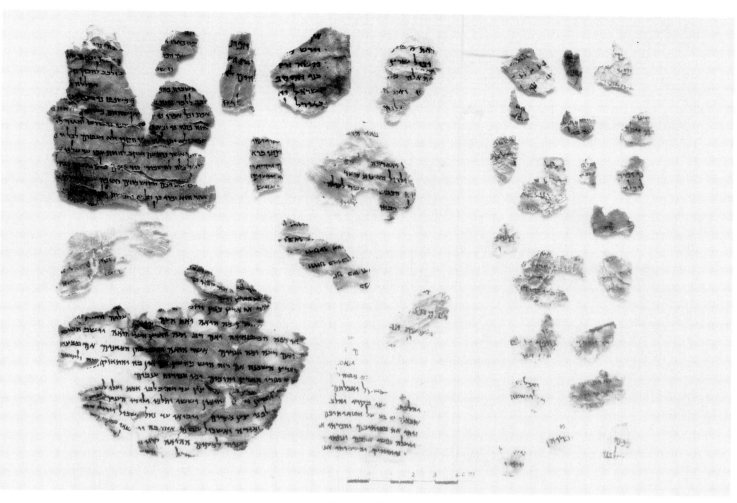

PLATE 278

PLATE 279

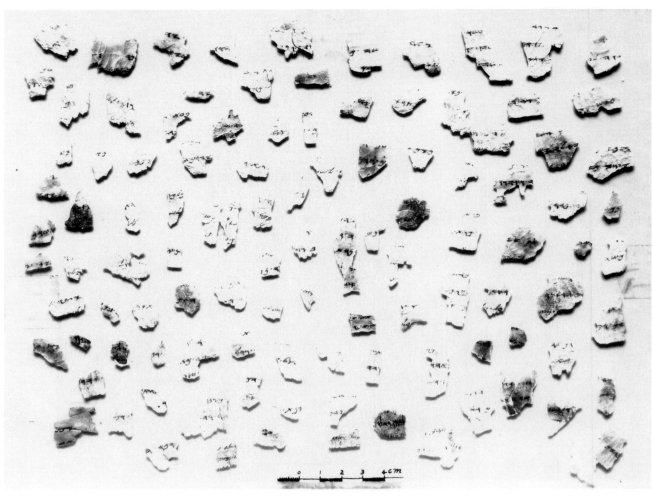

PLATE 280

PLATE 281

PLATE 282

PLATE 283

PLATE 284

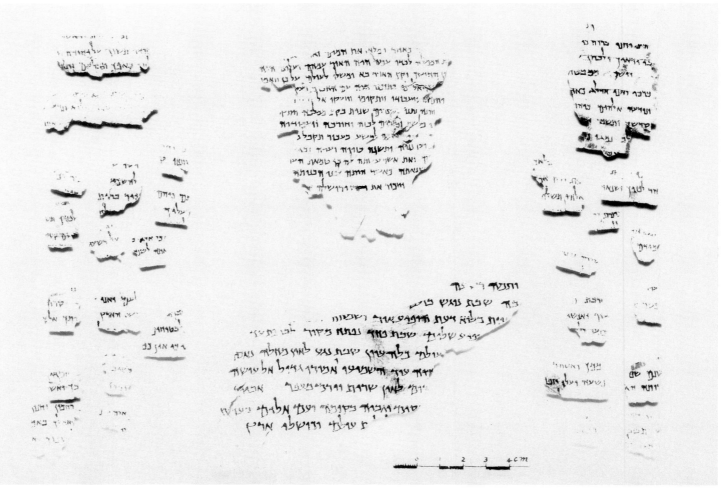

PLATE 285

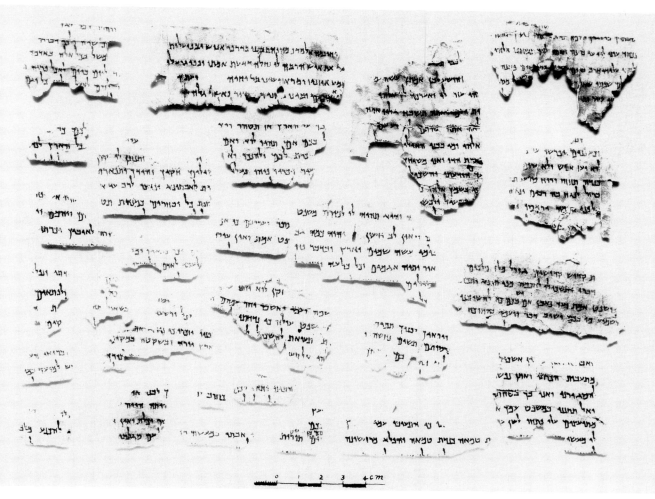

PLATE 286

PLATE 287

PLATE 288

PLATE 289

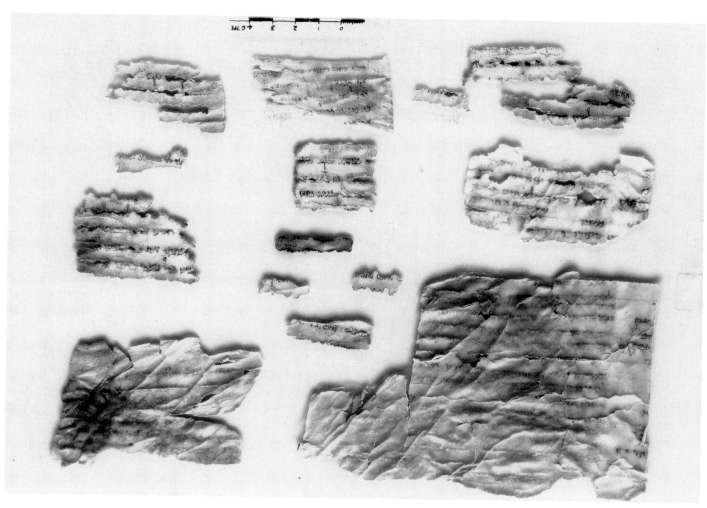

PLATE 290

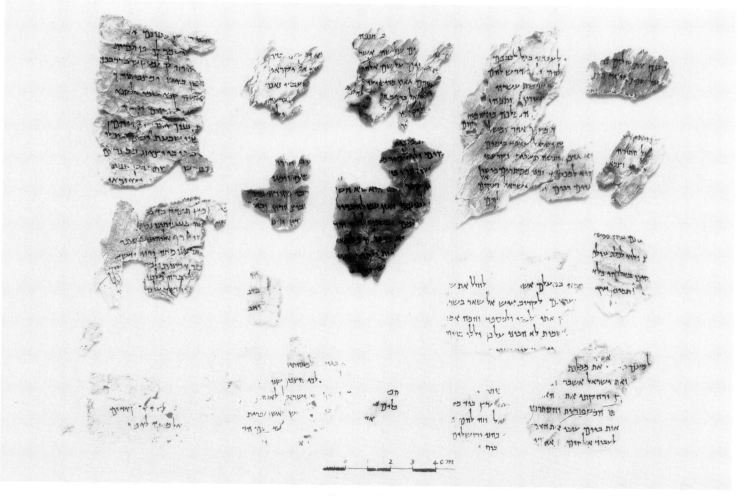

PLATE 291

PLATE 292

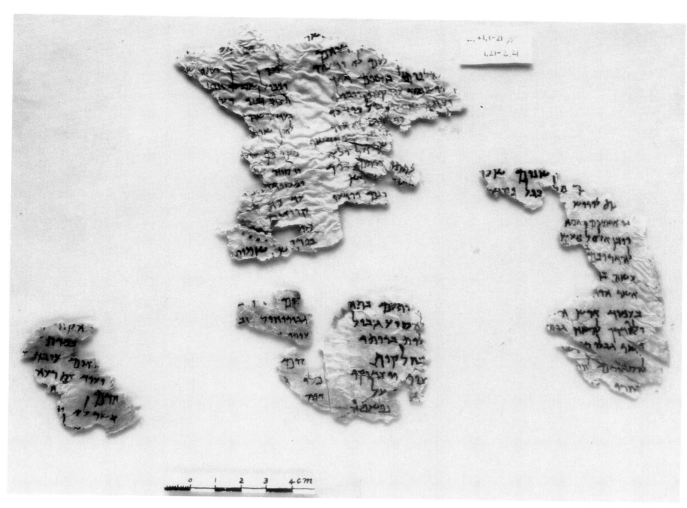

PLATE 297

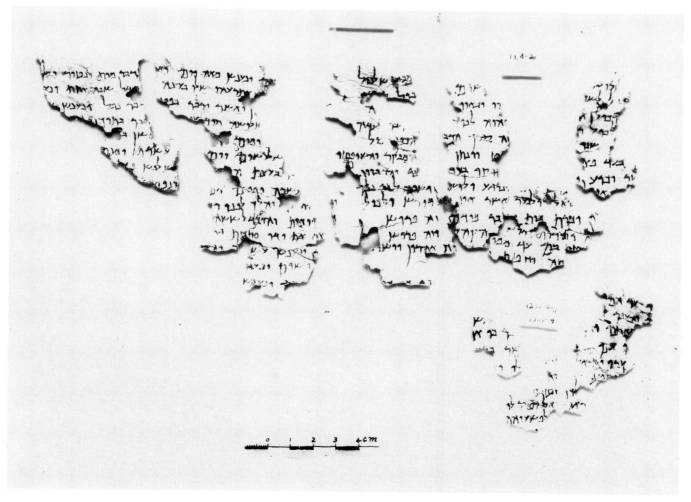

PLATE 298

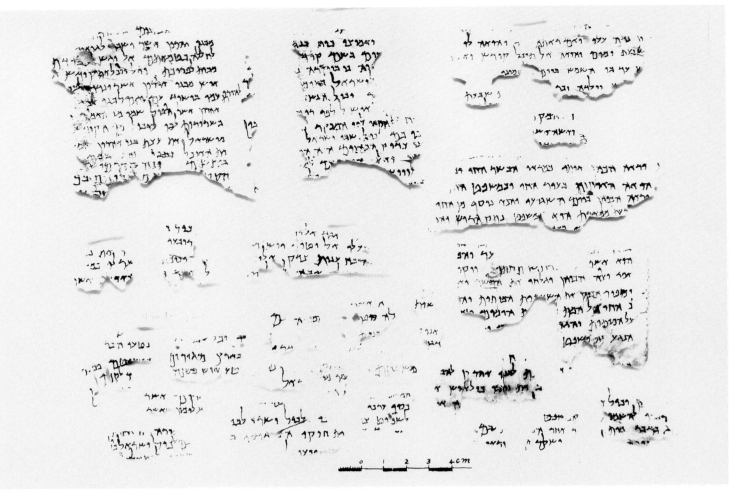

PLATE 299

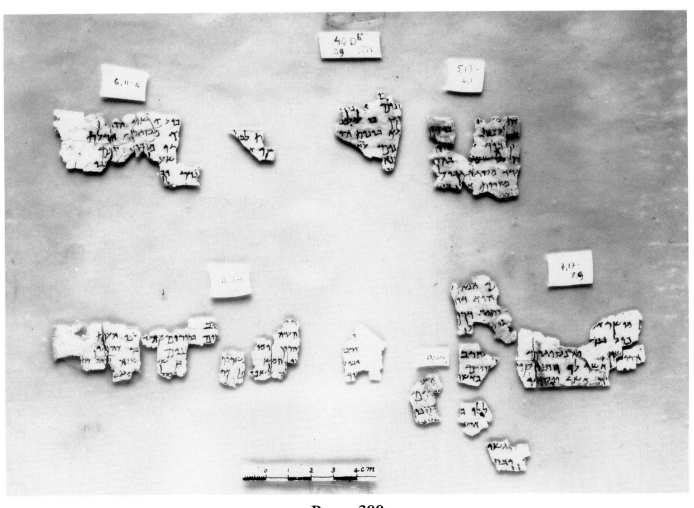

PLATE 300

PLATE 301

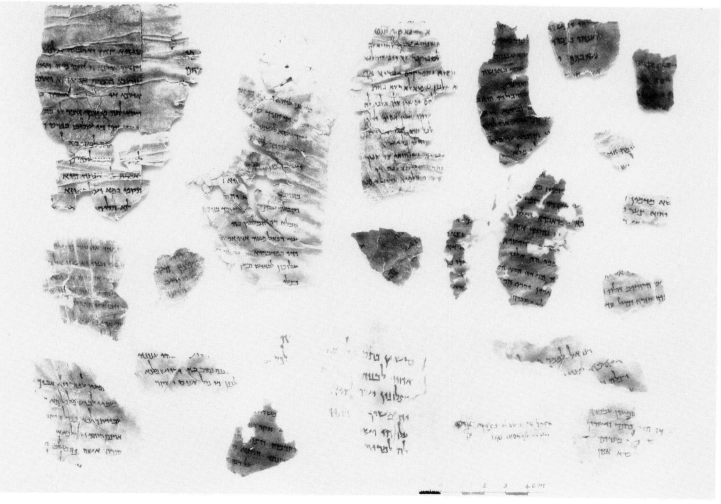

PLATE 302

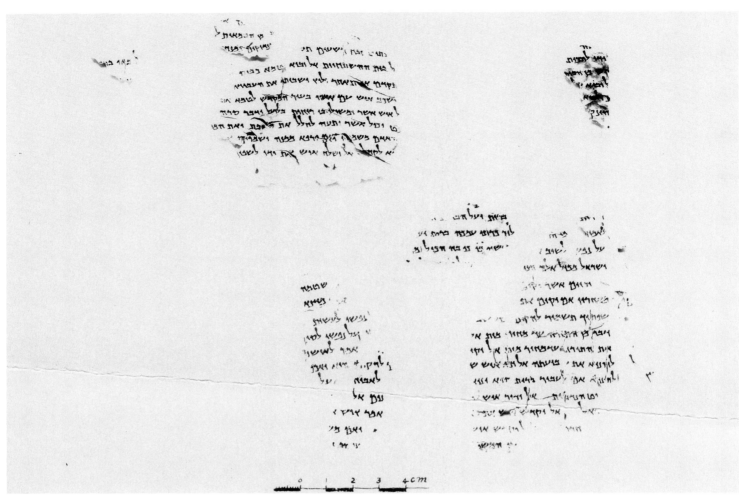

PLATE 303

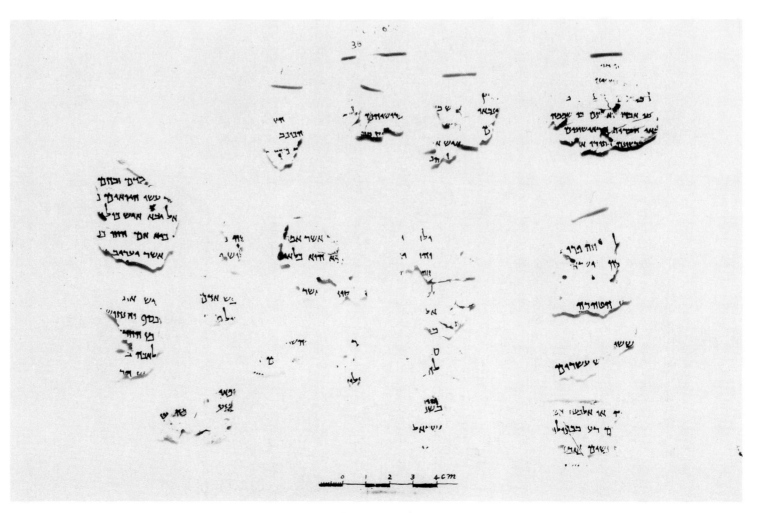

PLATE 304

PLATE 305

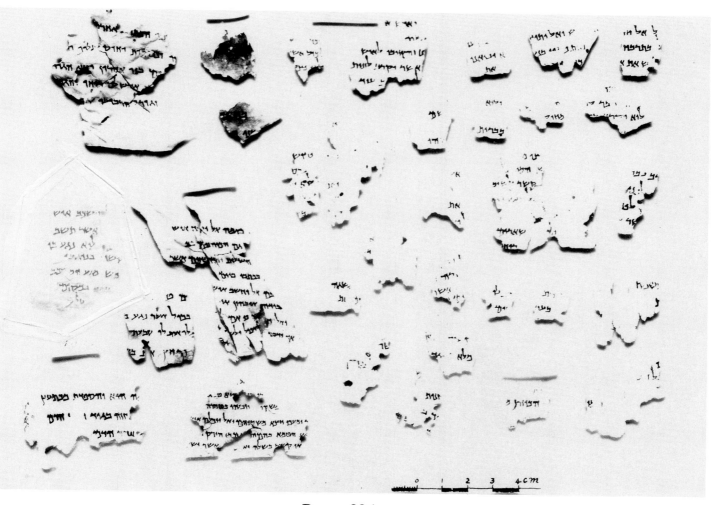

PLATE 306

PLATE 307

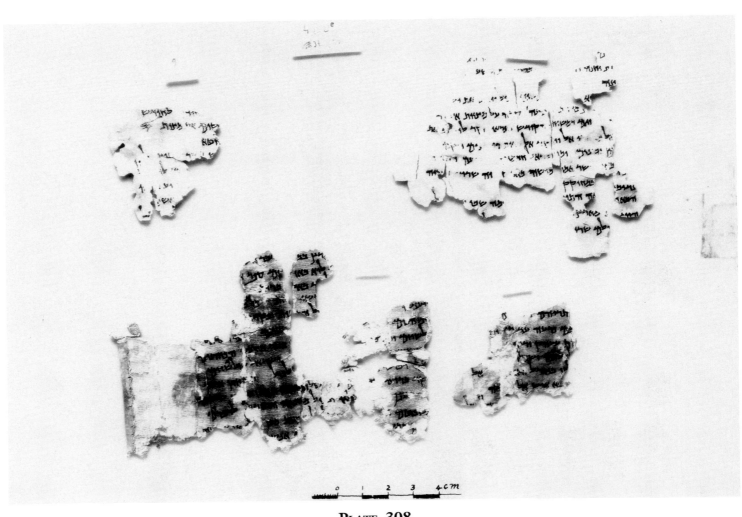

PLATE 308

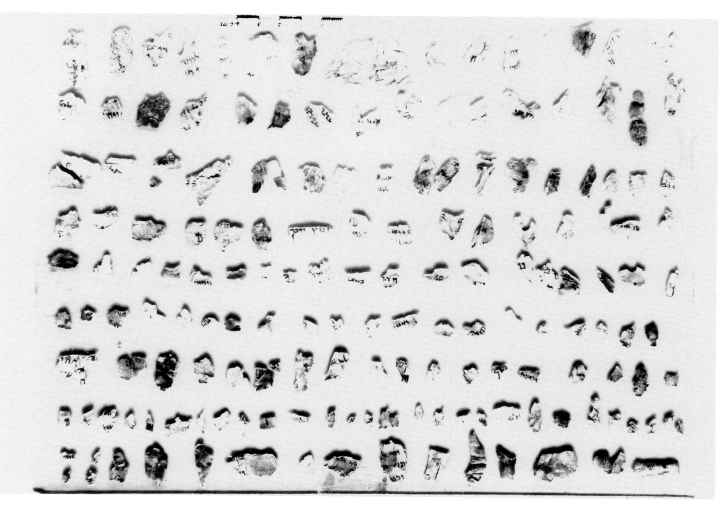

PLATE 309

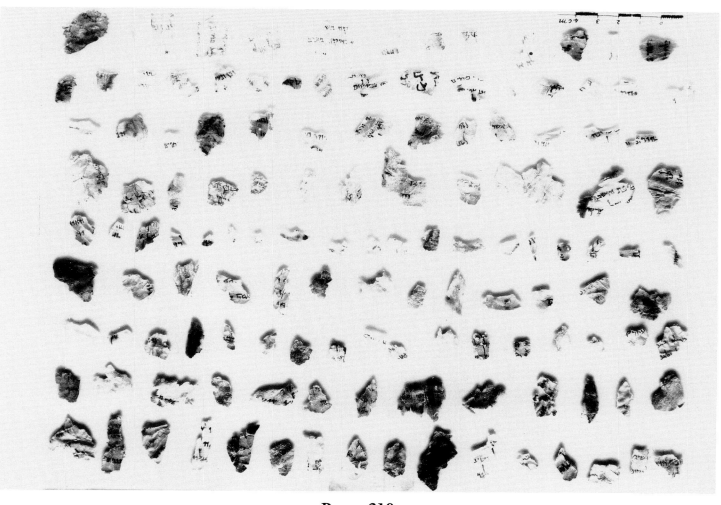

PLATE 310

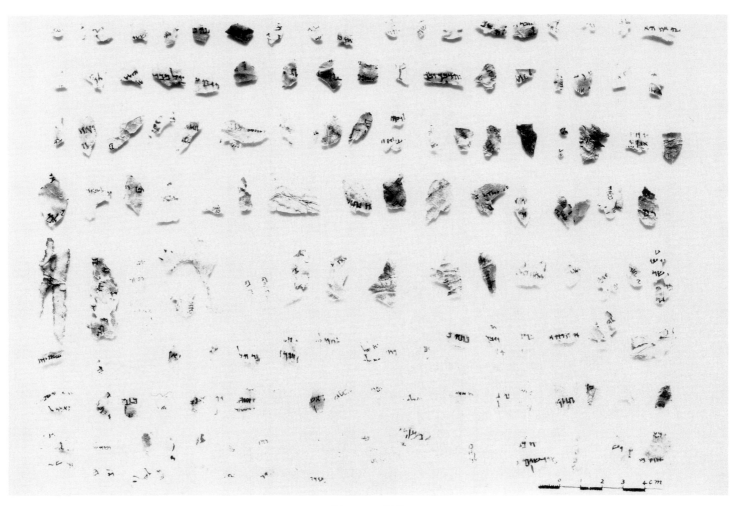

PLATE 311

PLATE 312

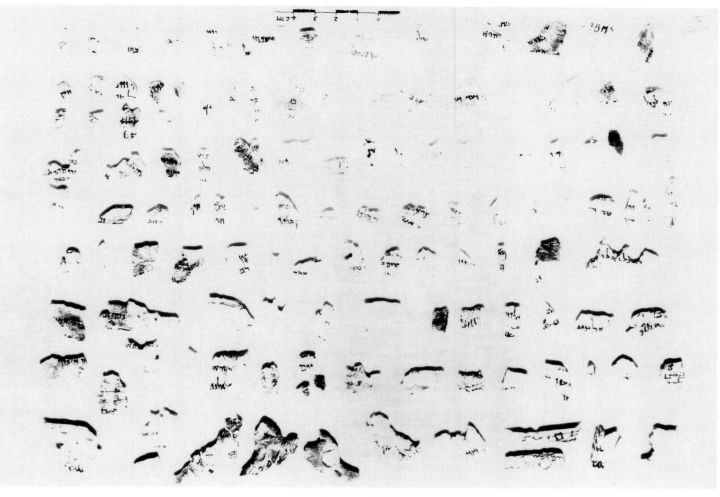

PLATE 313

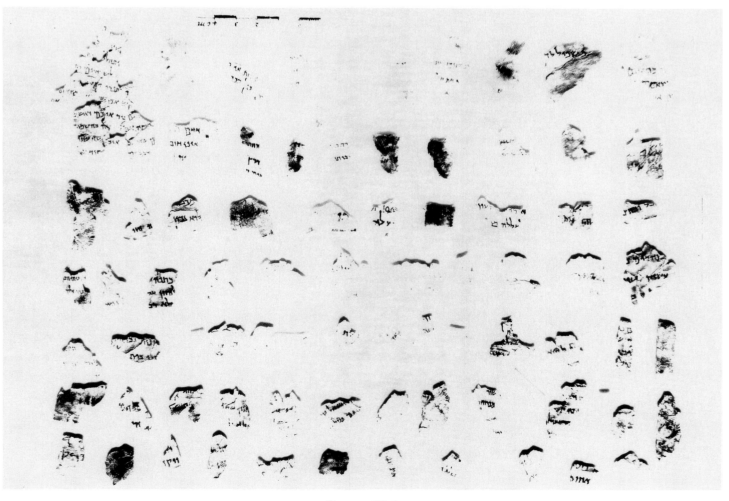

PLATE 314

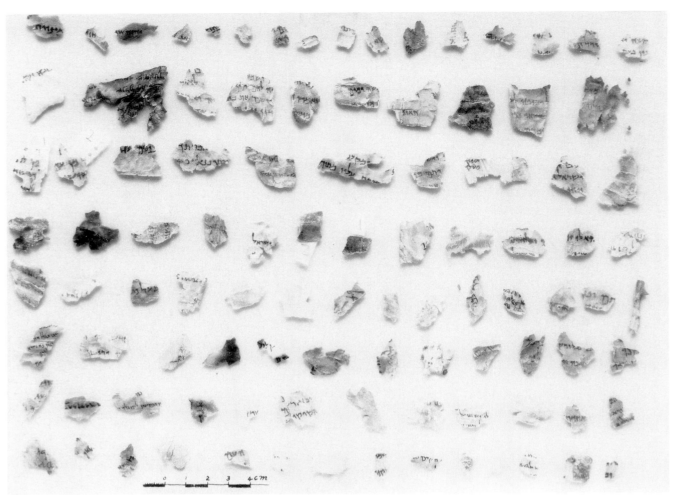

PLATE 315

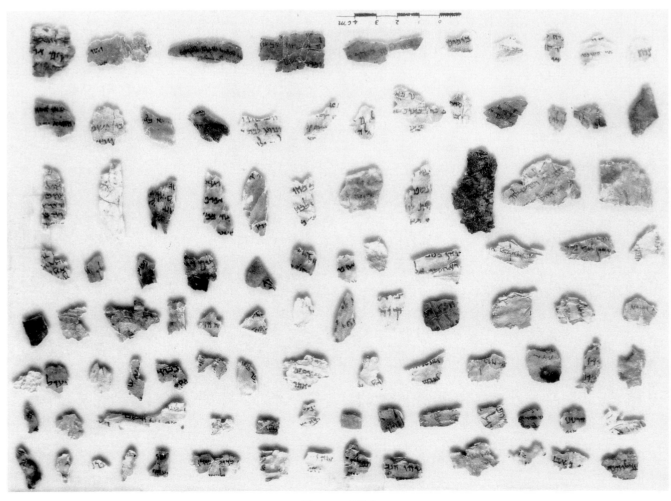

PLATE 316

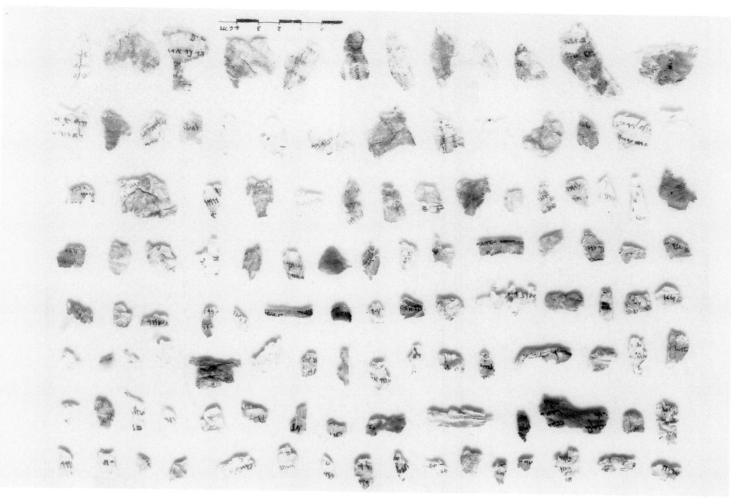

PLATE 317

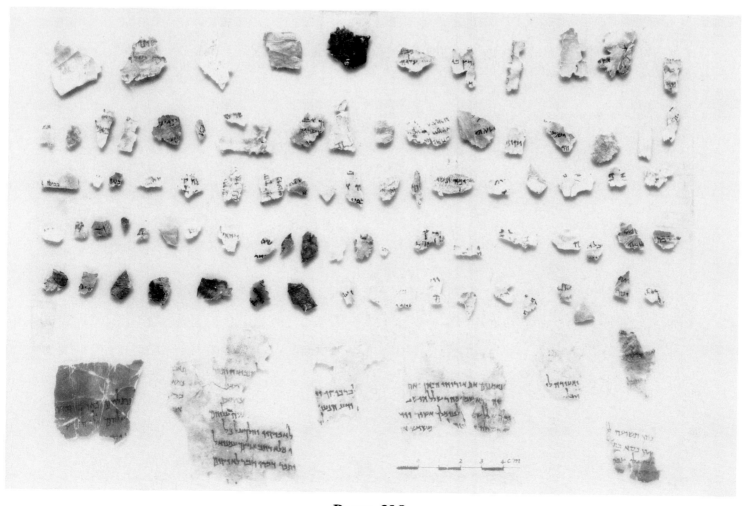

PLATE 318

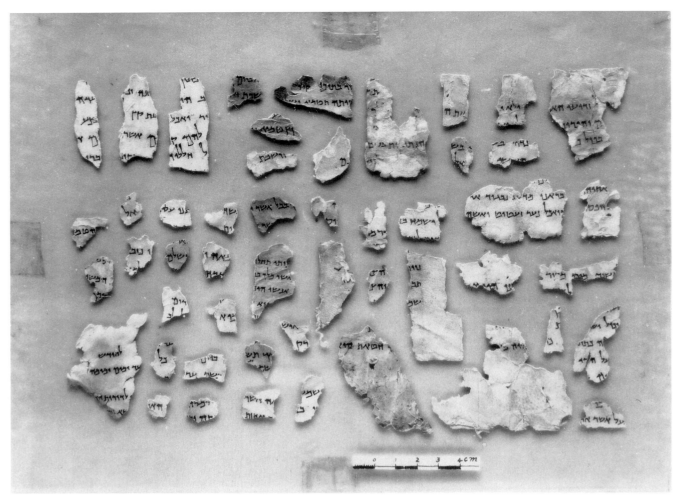

PLATE 319

PLATE 320

PLATE 321

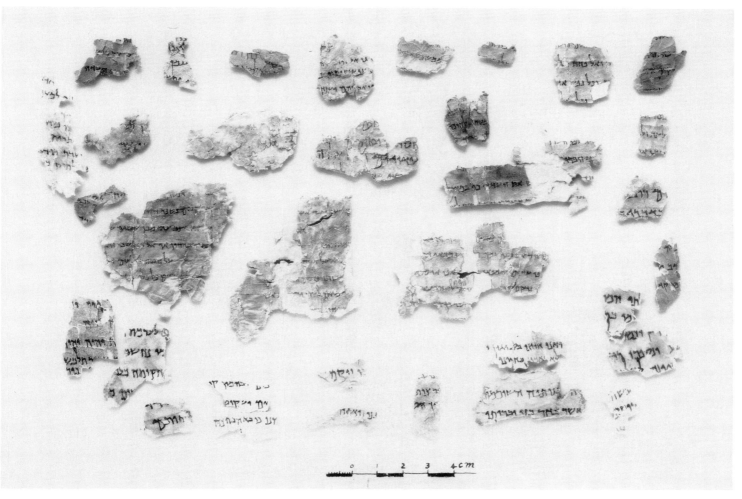

PLATE 322

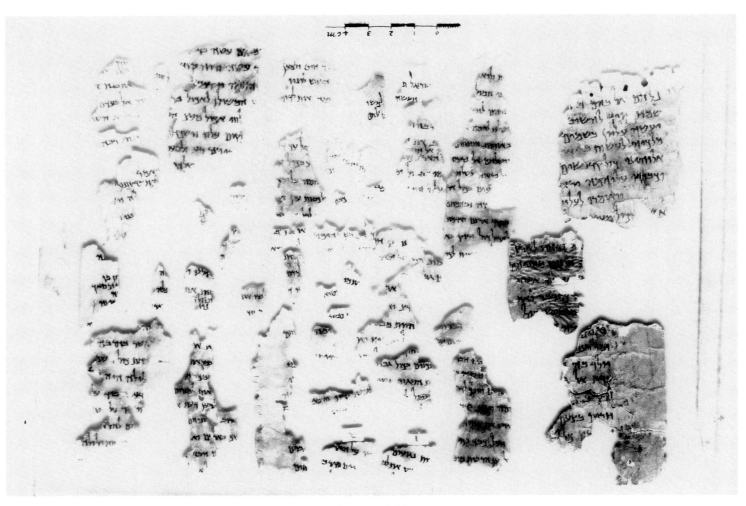

PLATE 323

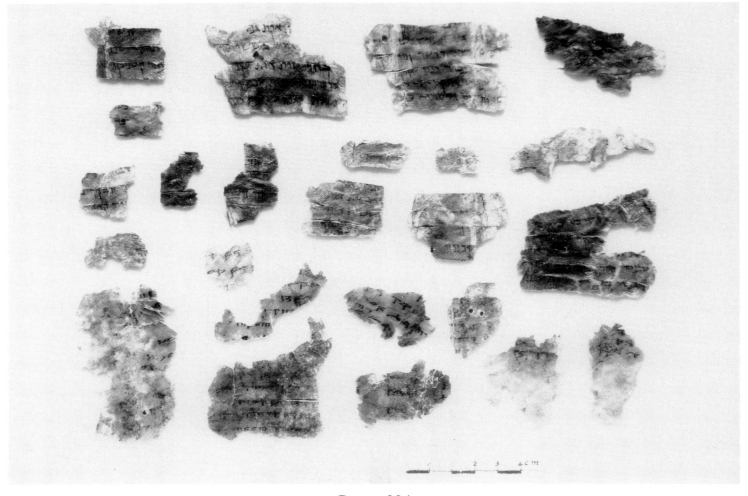

PLATE 324

PLATE 325

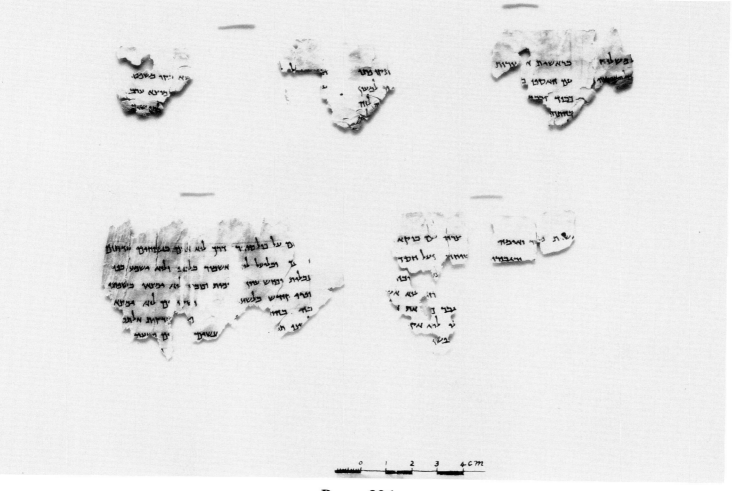

PLATE 326

PLATE 327

PLATE 328

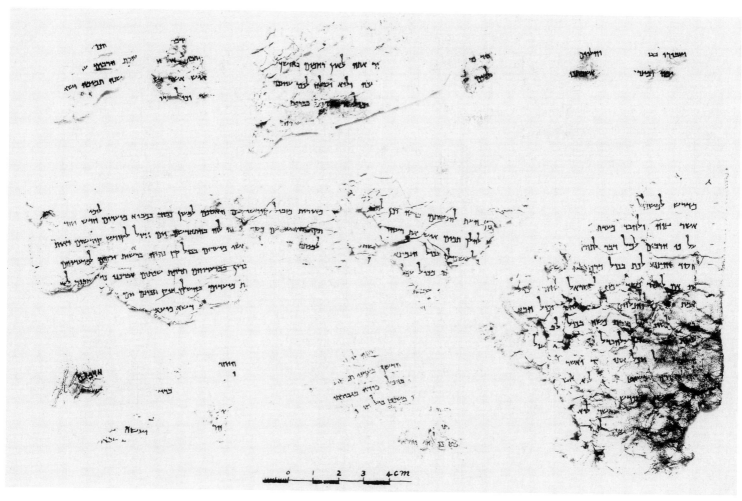

PLATE 329

PLATE 330

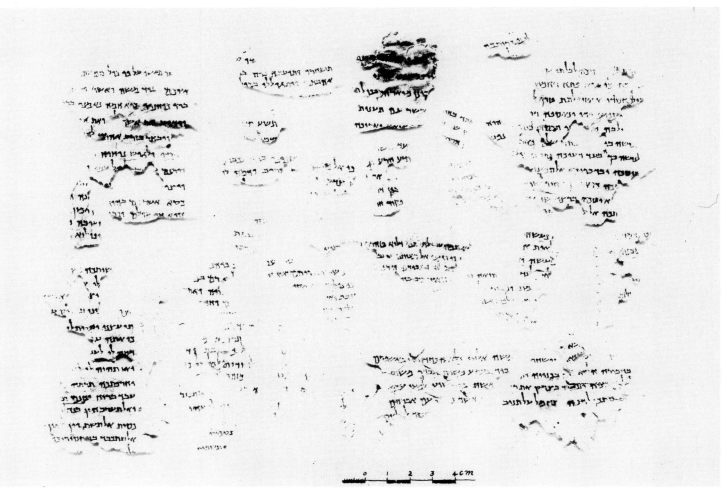

PLATE 331

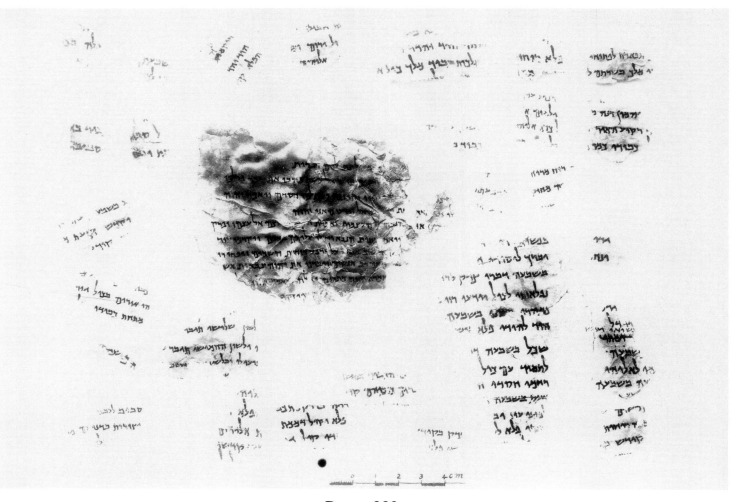

PLATE 332

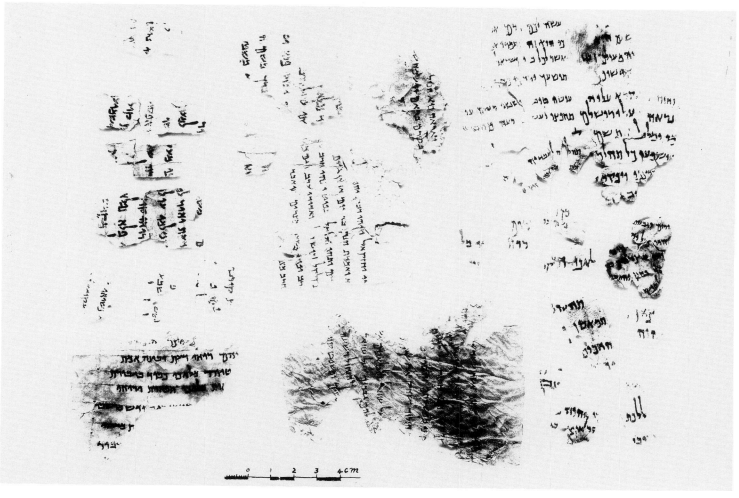

PLATE 333

PLATE 334A

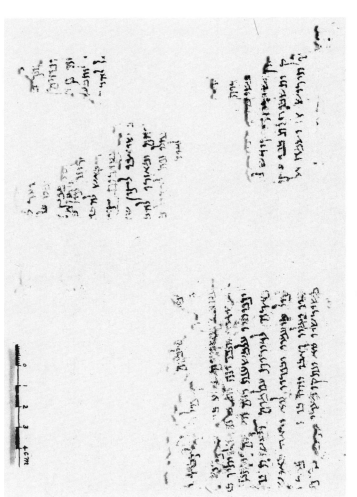

PLATE 334B

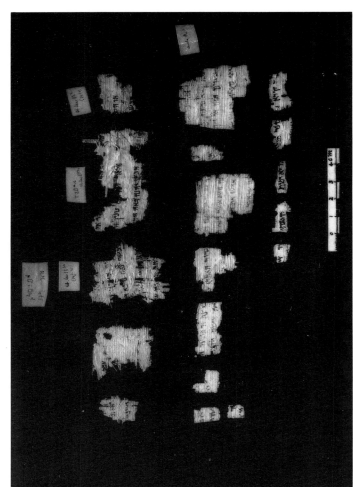

PLATE 335

PLATE 336

PLATE 338

PLATE 337

PLATE 339

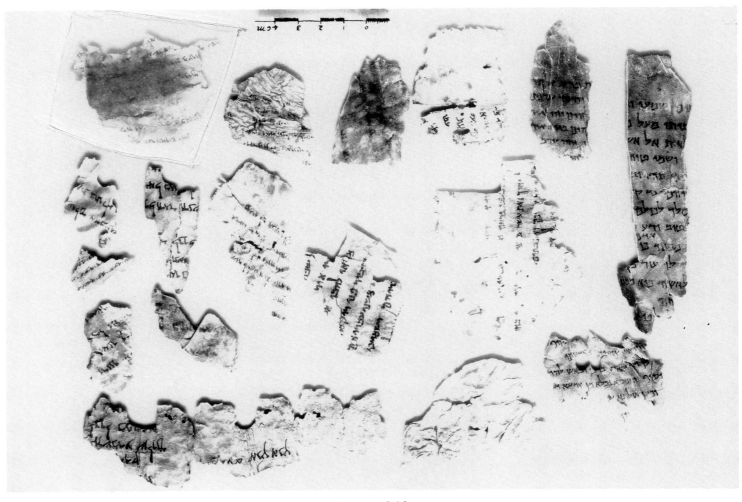

PLATE 340

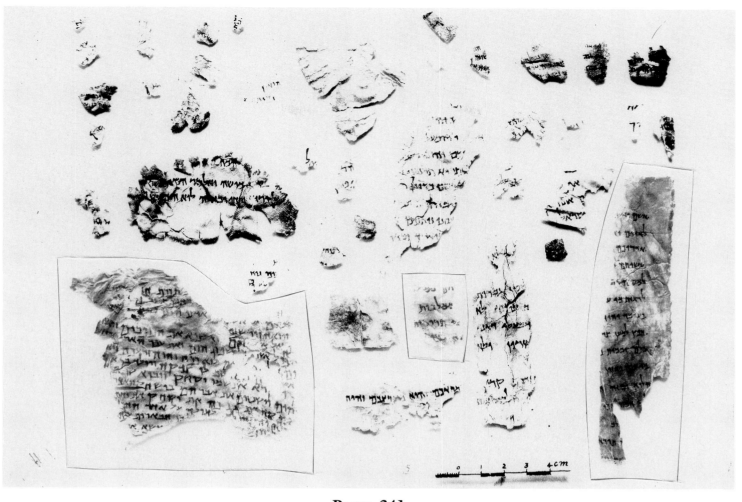

PLATE 341

PLATE 342

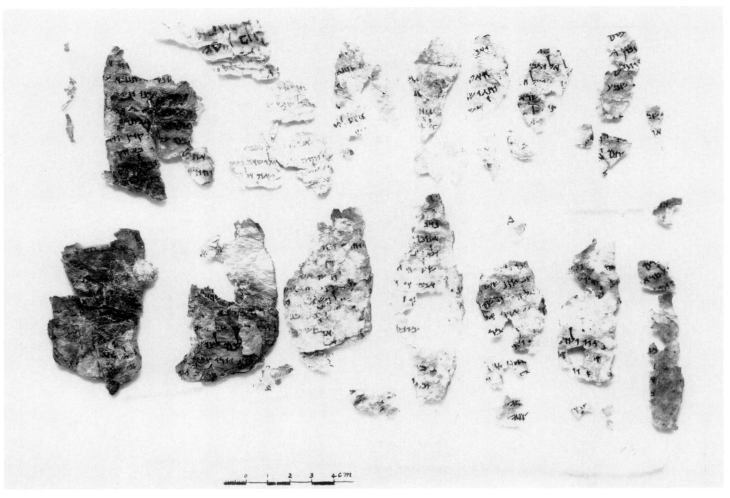

PLATE 343

PLATE 344

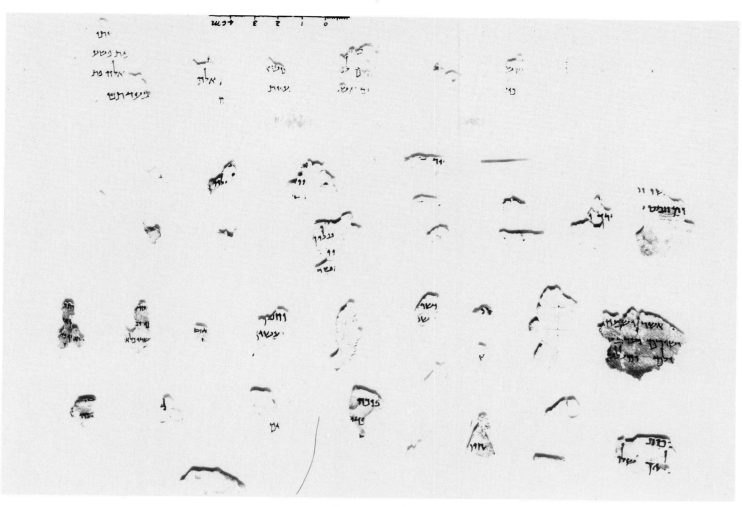

PLATE 345

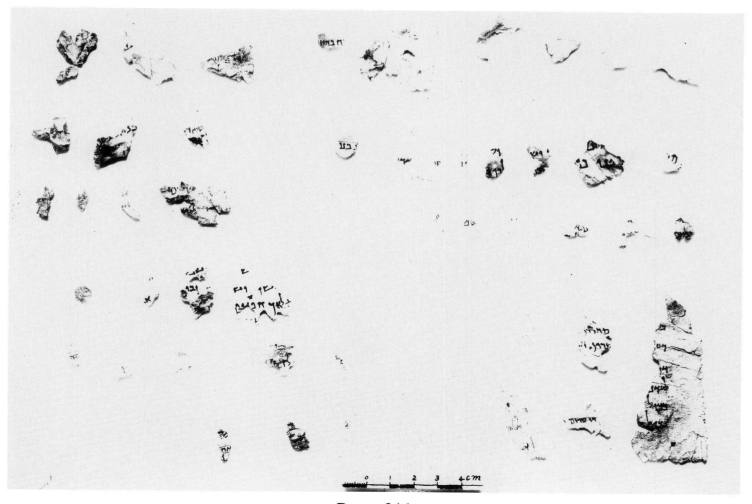

PLATE 346

PLATE 347

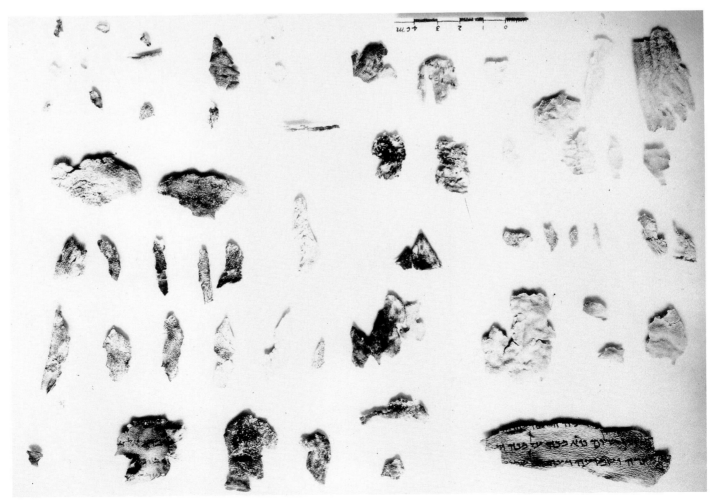

PLATE 348

PLATE 349

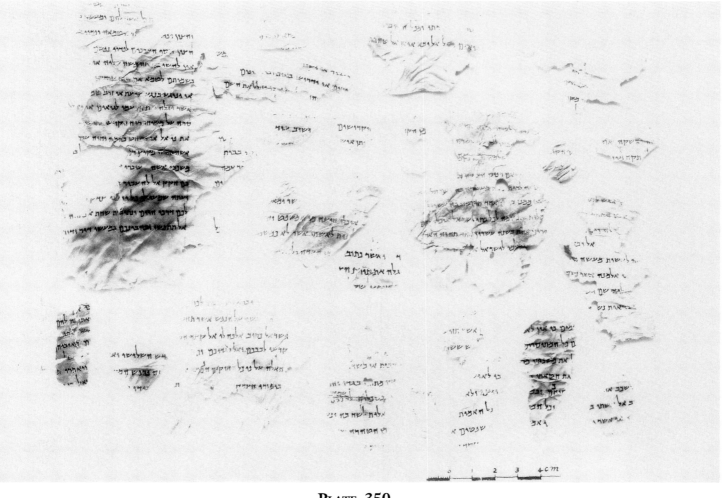

PLATE 350

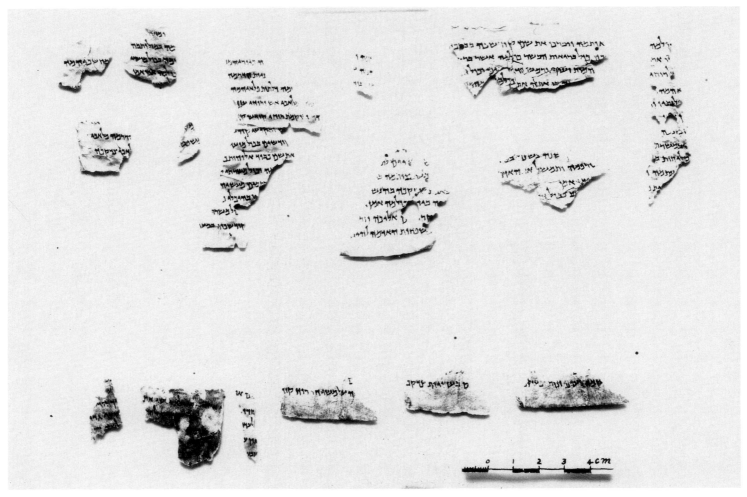

PLATE 351

PLATE 352

PLATE 353

PLATE 354

PLATE 355

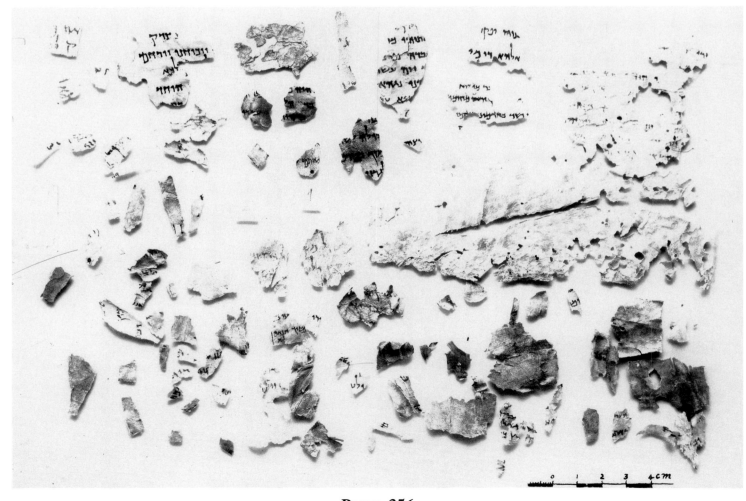

PLATE 356

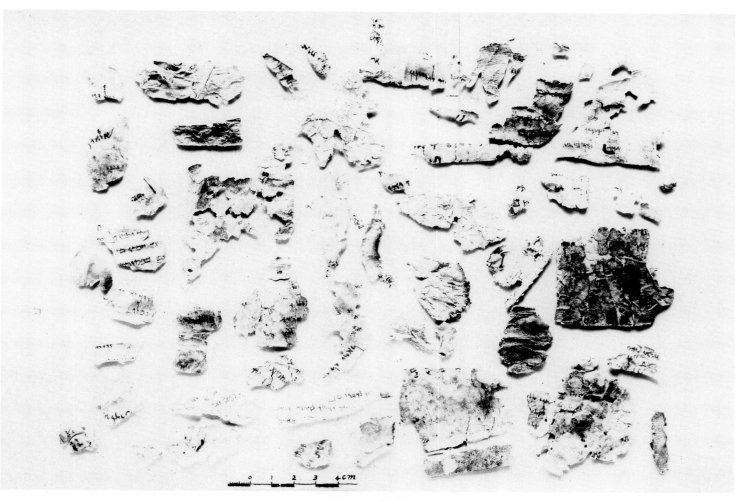

PLATE 357

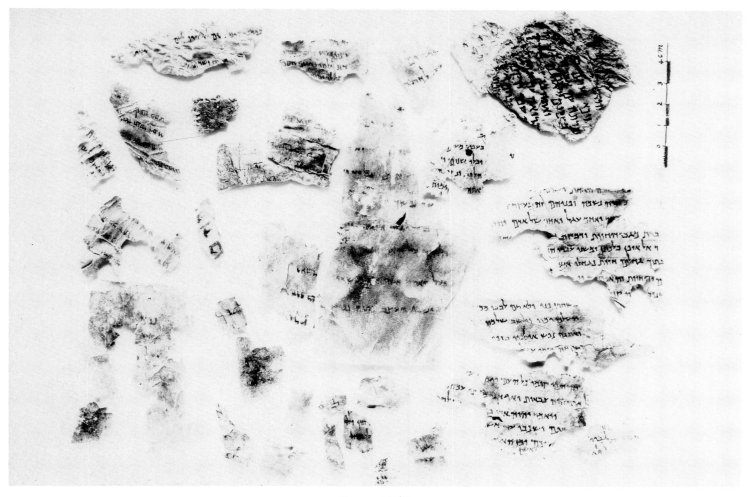

PLATE 358

PLATE 359

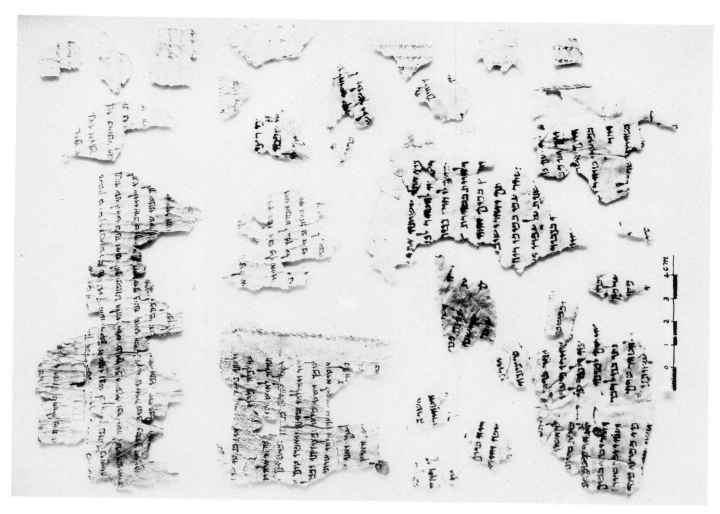

PLATE 360

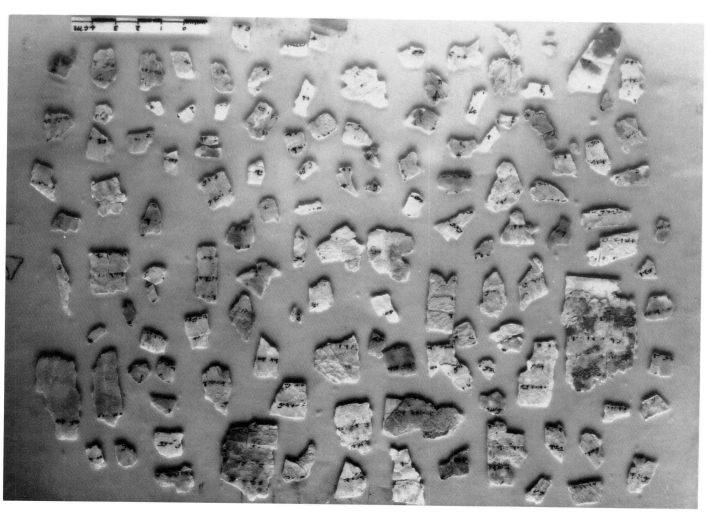

PLATE 361

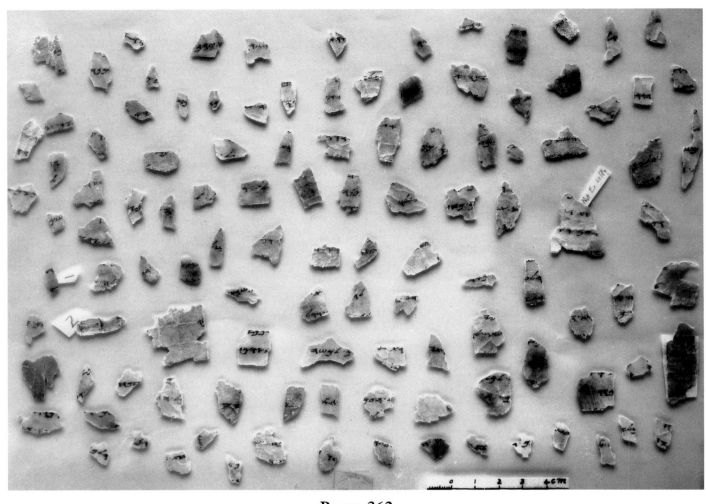

PLATE 362

PLATE 363

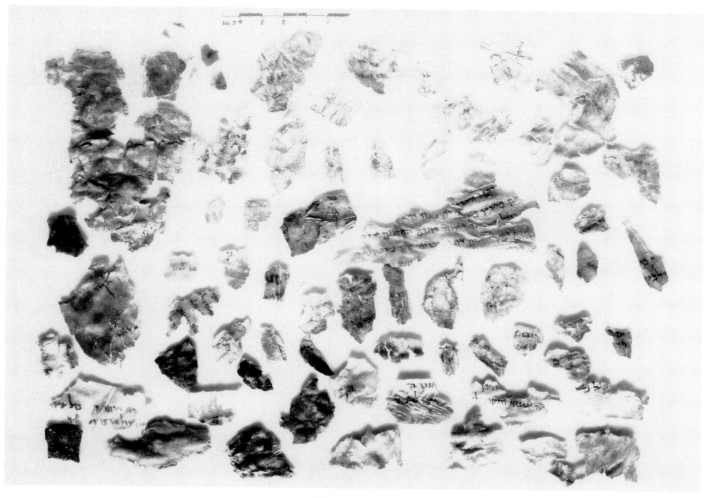

PLATE 364

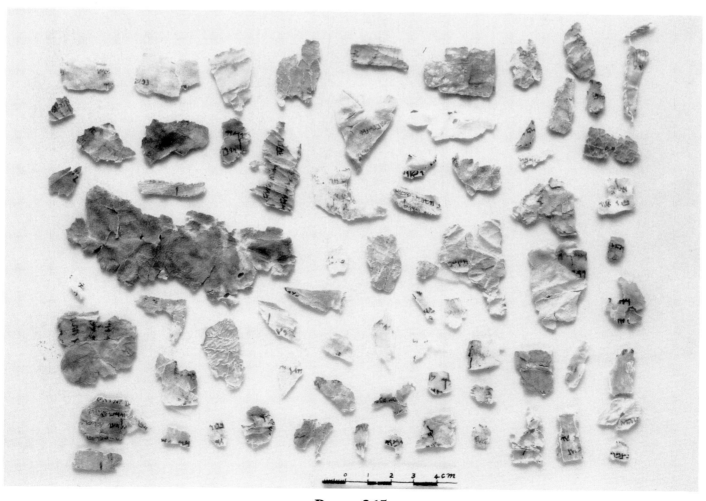

PLATE 365

PLATE 366

PLATE 367

PLATE 368

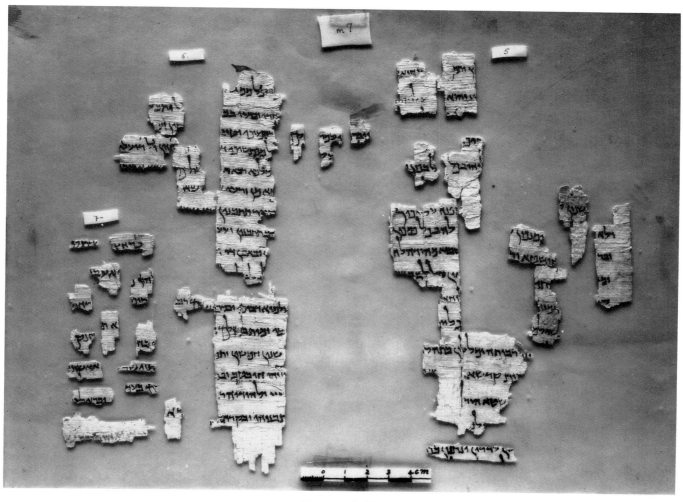

PLATE 369

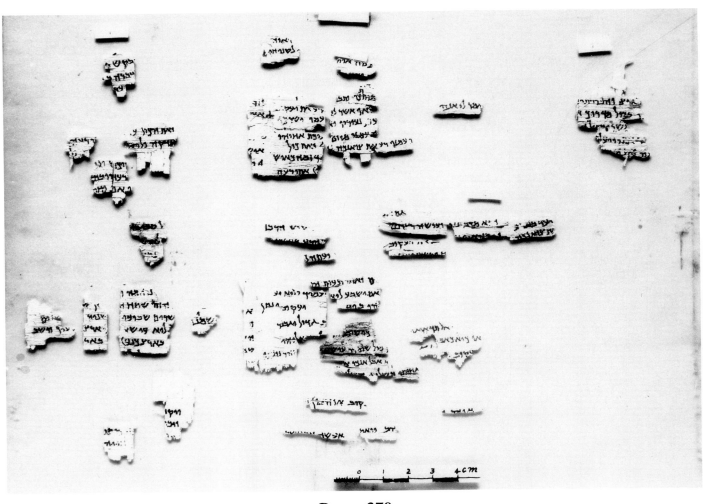

PLATE 370

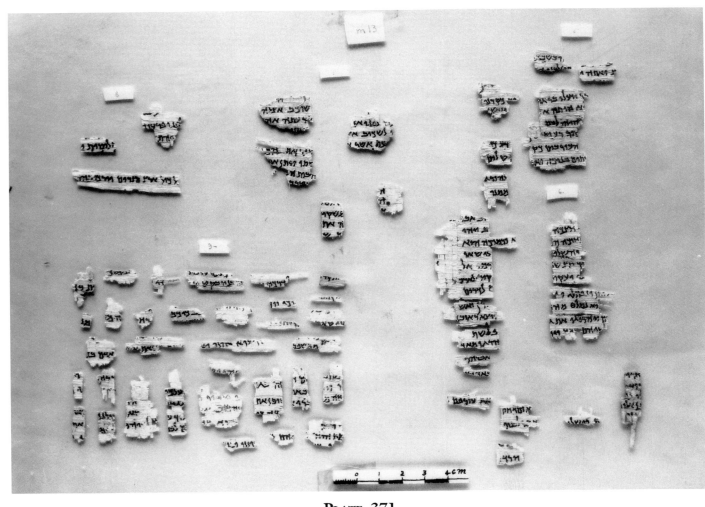

PLATE 371

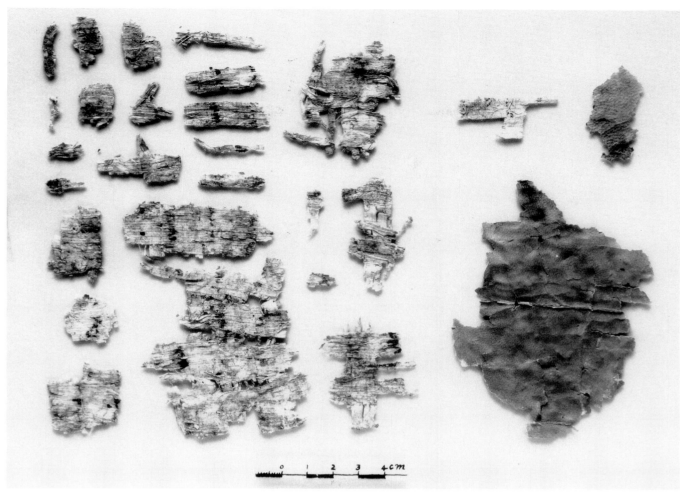

PLATE 372

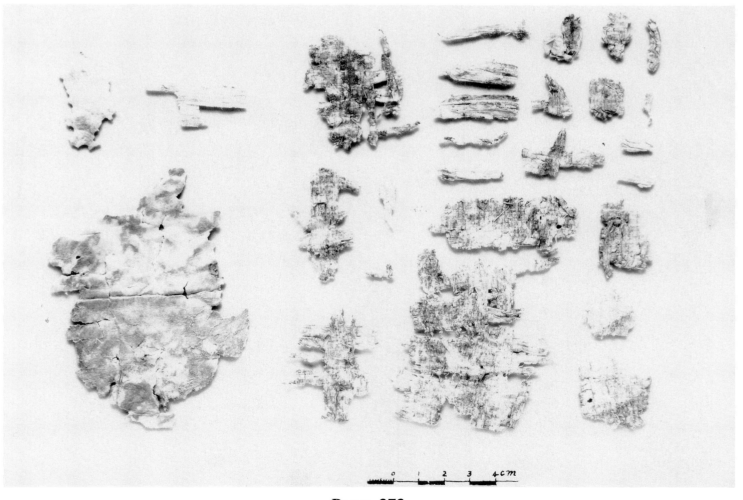

PLATE 373

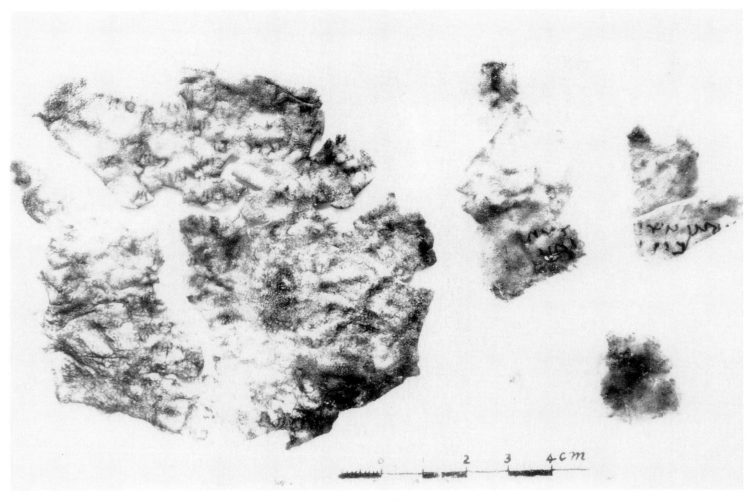

PLATE 374

PLATE 375

PLATE 376

PLATE 377

PLATE 378

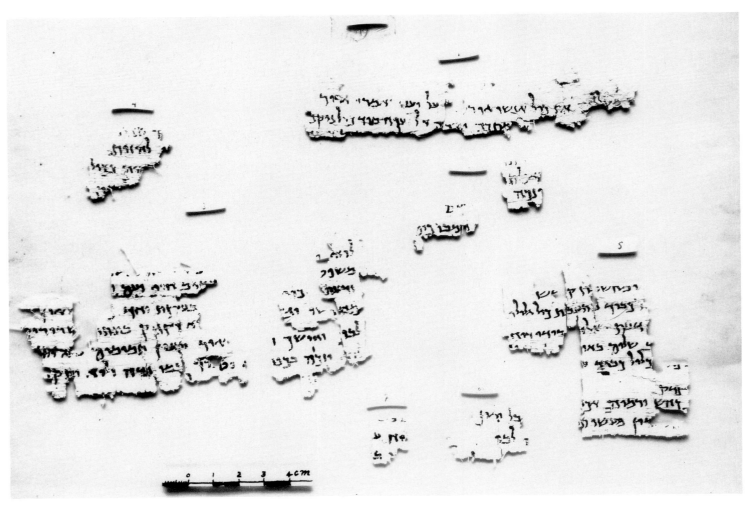

PLATE 379

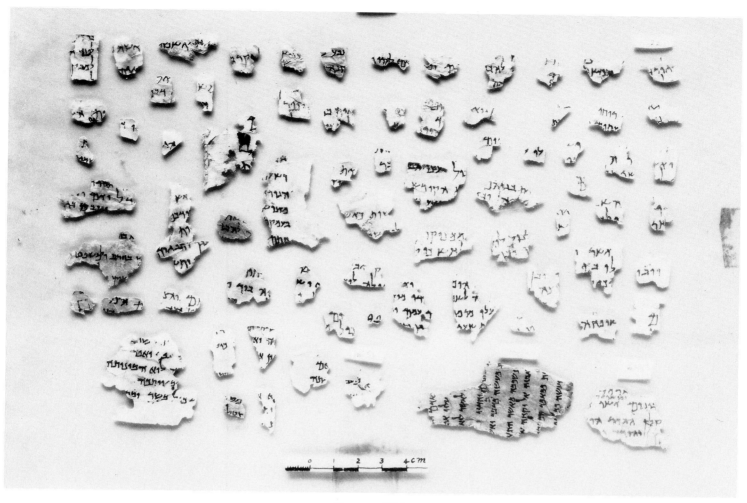

PLATE 380

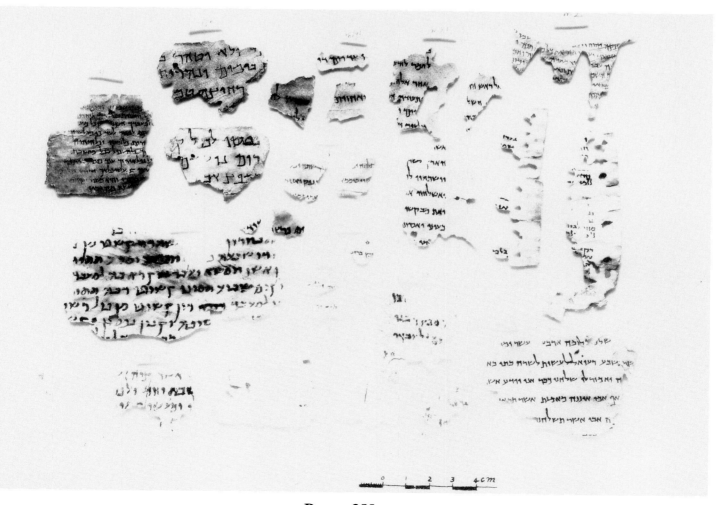

PLATE 381

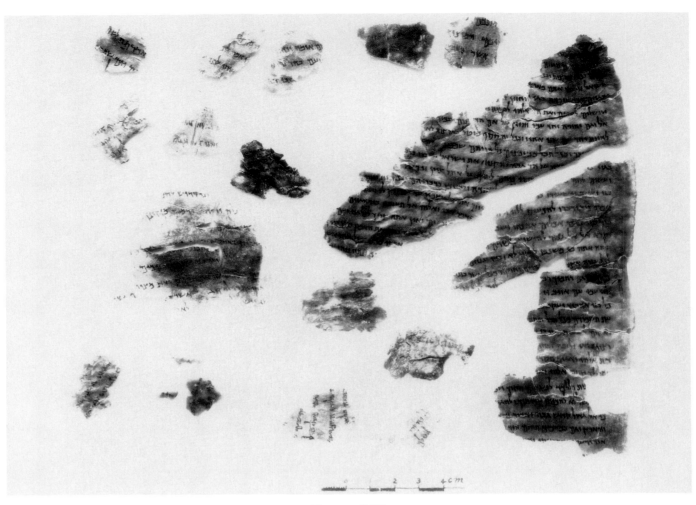

PLATE 382

PLATE 383

PLATE 384

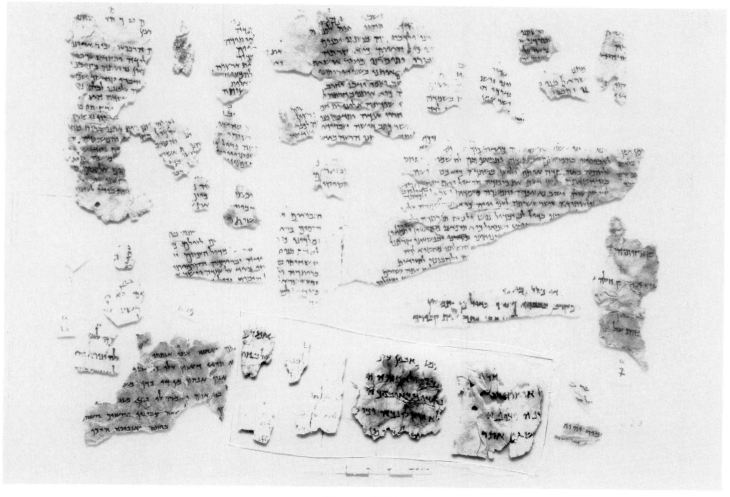

PLATE 385

PLATE 386

PLATE 387

PLATE 389

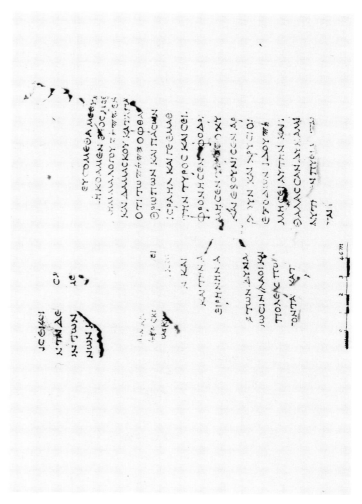

PLATE 390

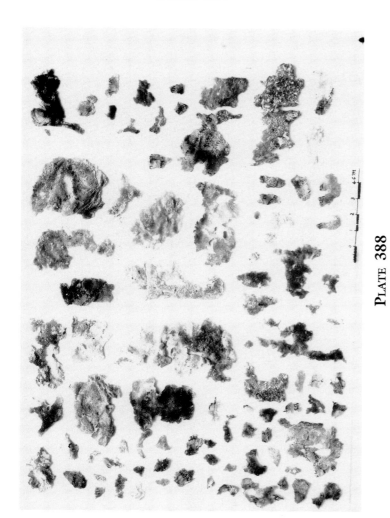

PLATE 388

PLATE 391

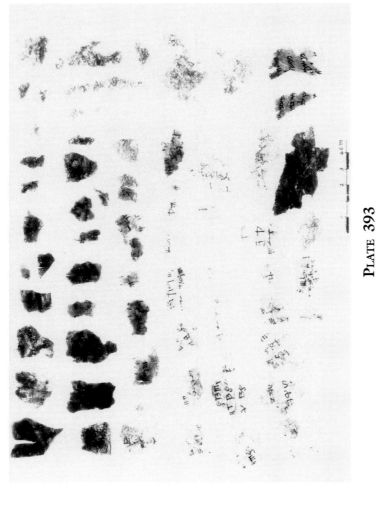

PLATE 393

PLATE 392

PLATE 394

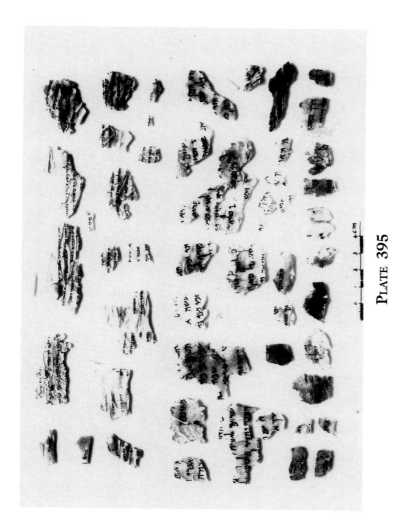

PLATE 395

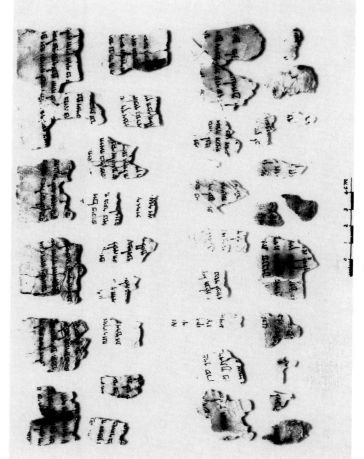

PLATE 396

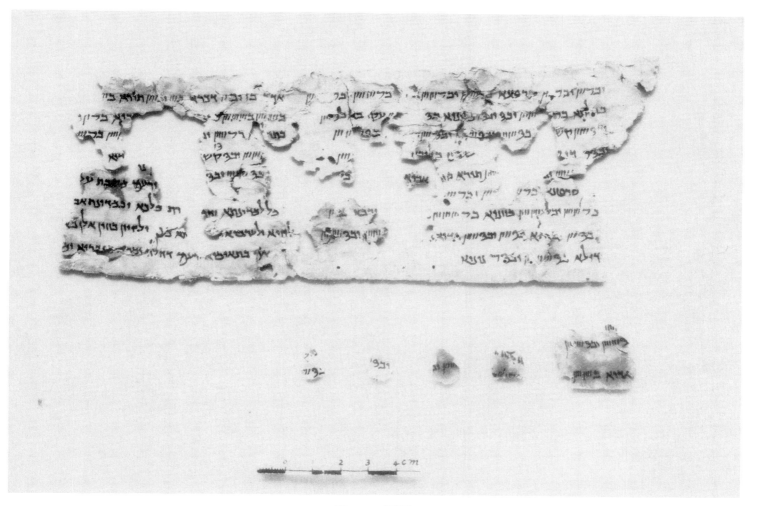

PLATE 397

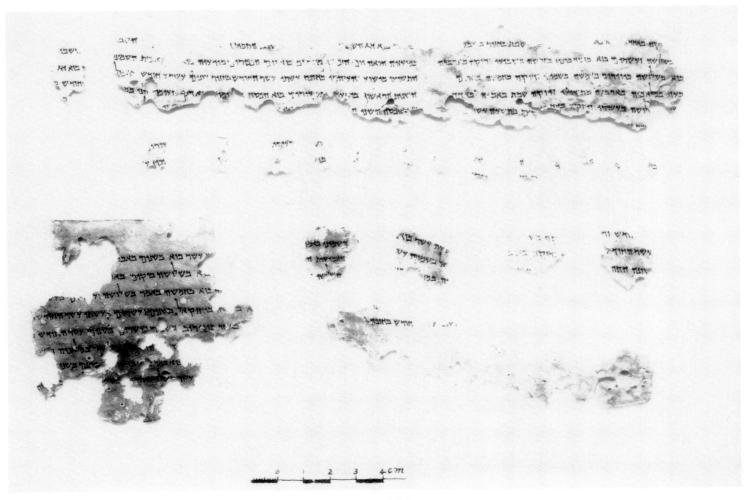

PLATE 398

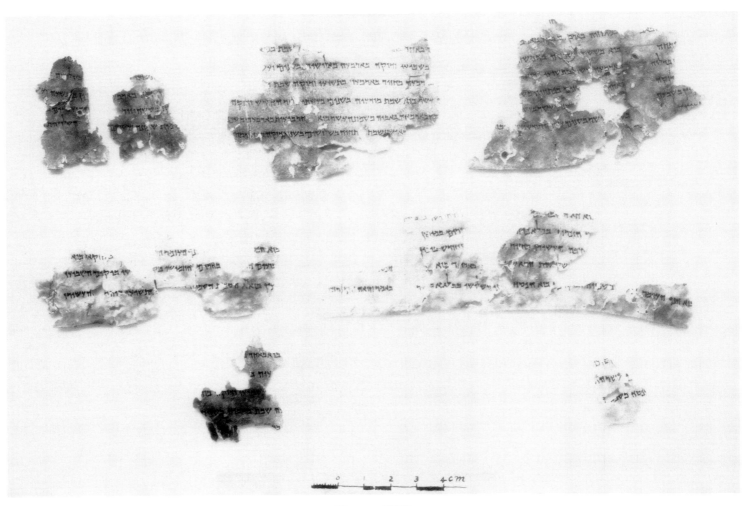

PLATE 399

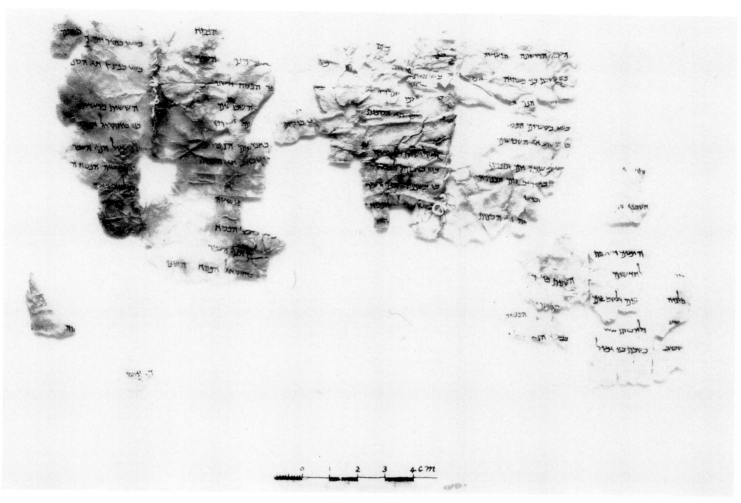

PLATE 400

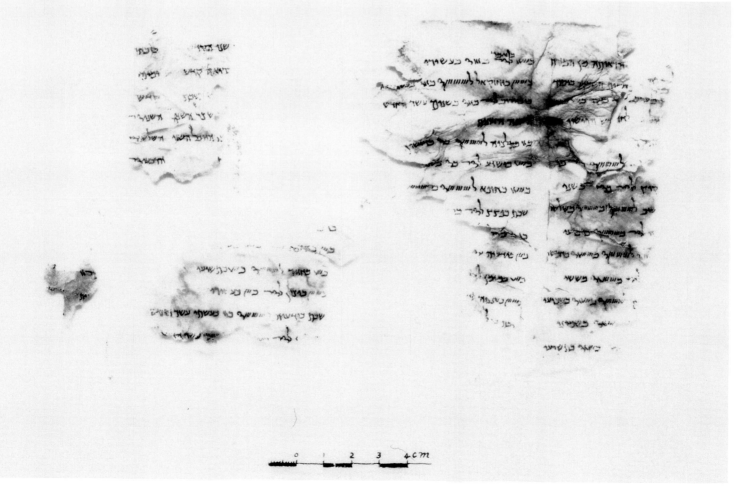

PLATE 401

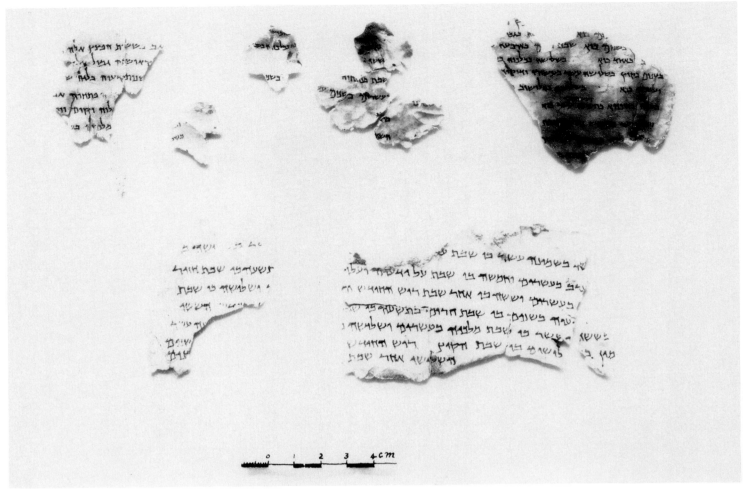

PLATE 402

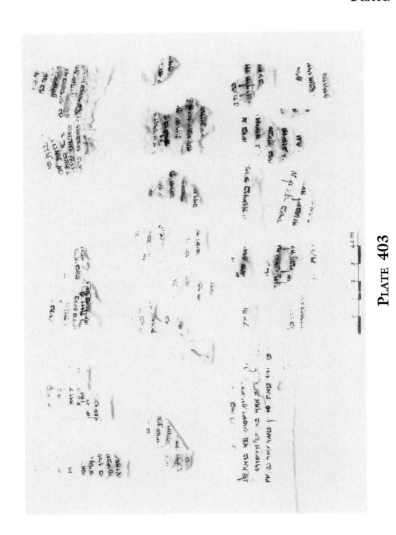

PLATE 403

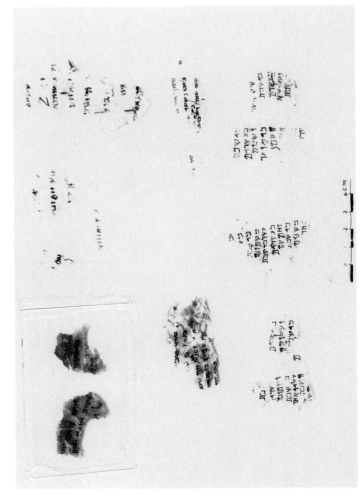

PLATE 404

PLATE 406

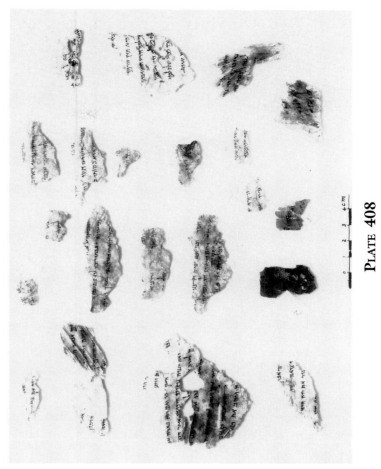

PLATE 408

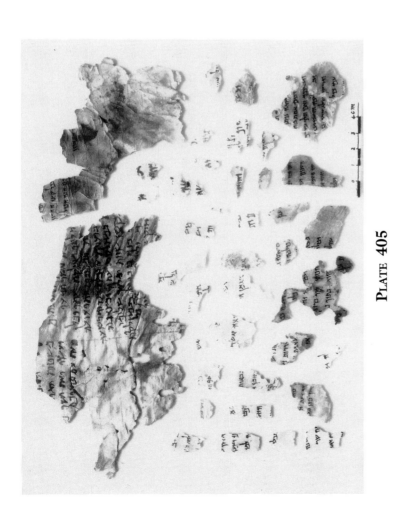

PLATE 405

PLATE 407

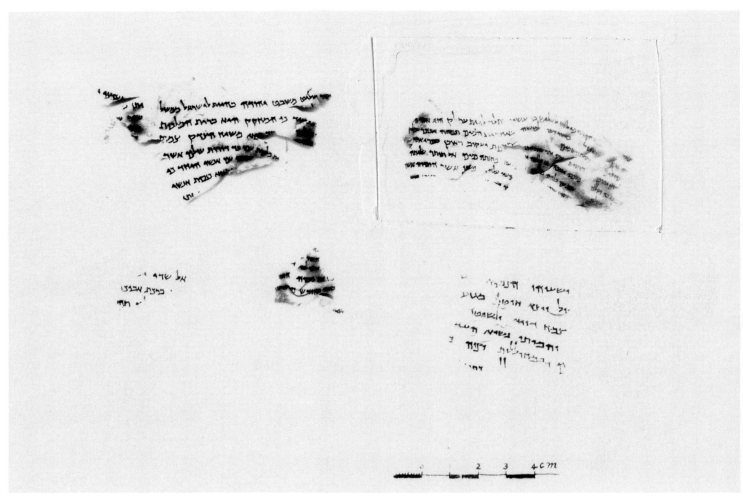

PLATE 409

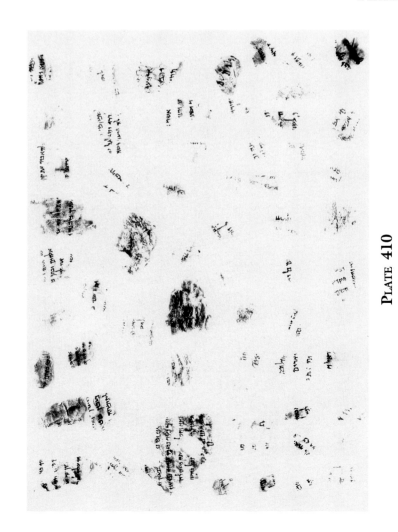

PLATE 410

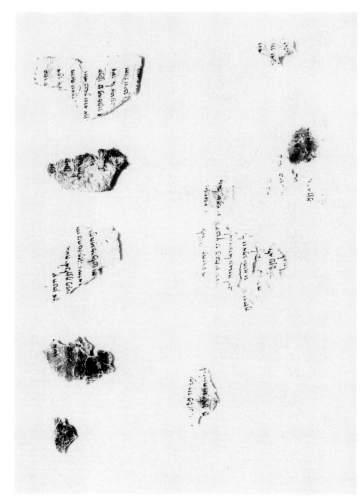

PLATE 411

PLATE 412

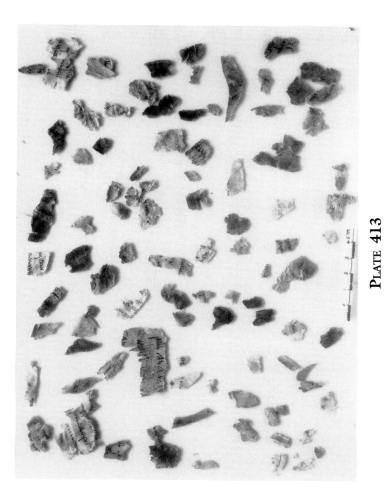

PLATE 413

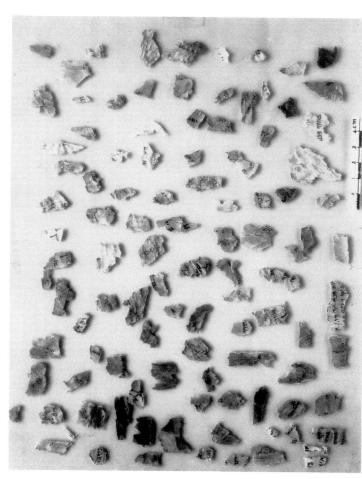

PLATE 414

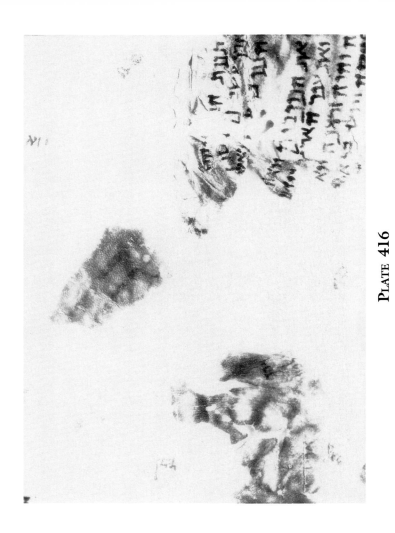

PLATE 416

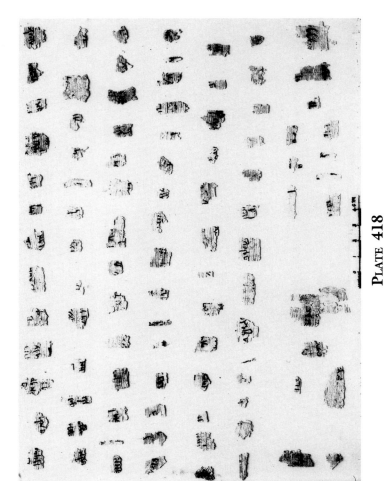

PLATE 418

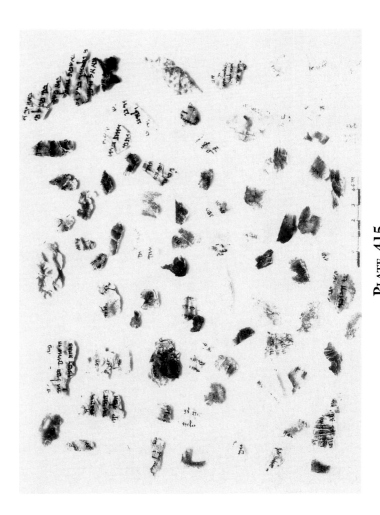

PLATE 415

PLATE 417

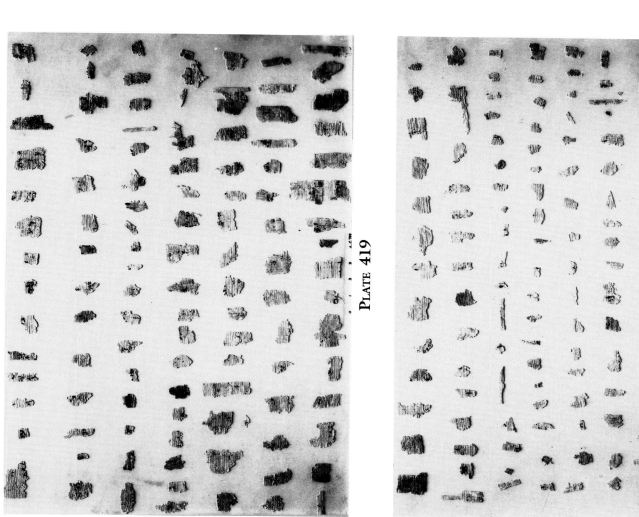

PLATE 419

PLATE 420

PLATE 421

PLATE 422

PLATE 423

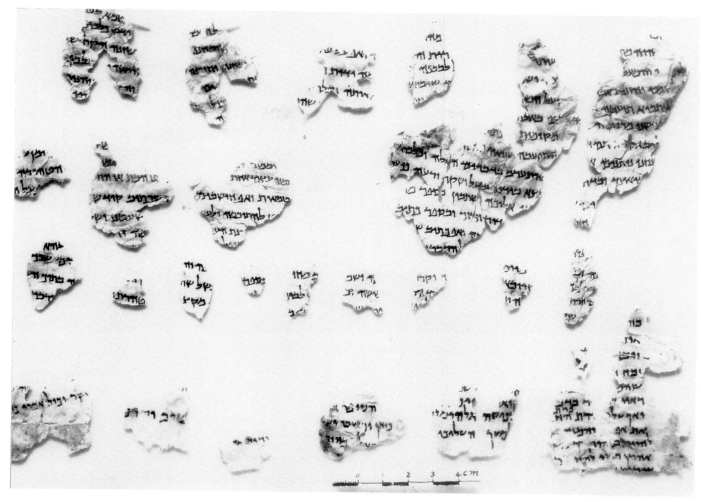

PLATE 424

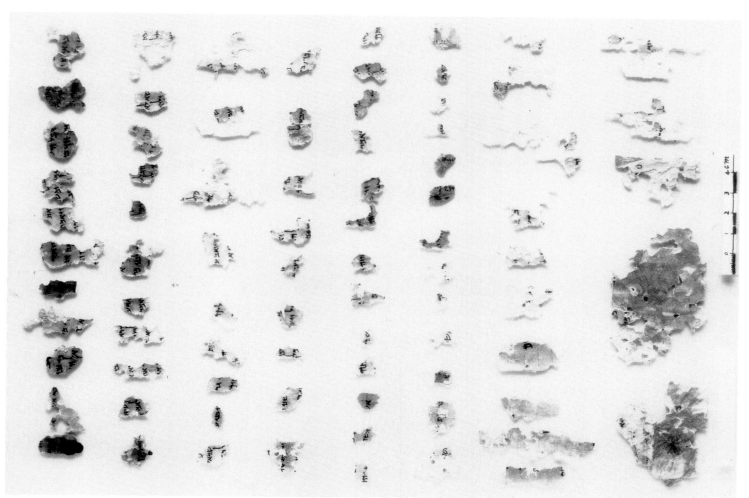

PLATE 425

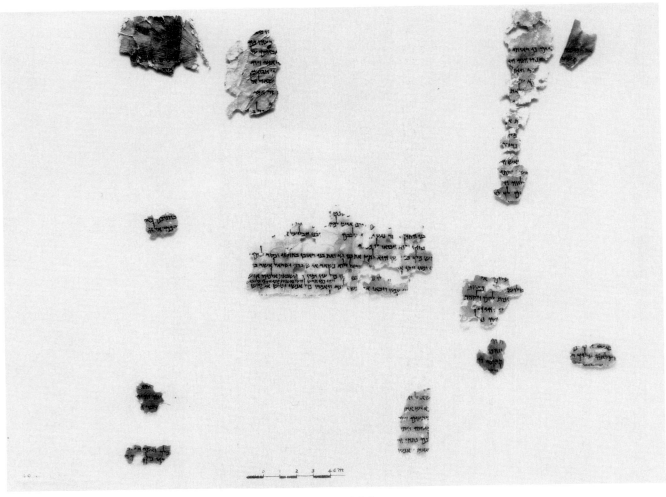

PLATE 426

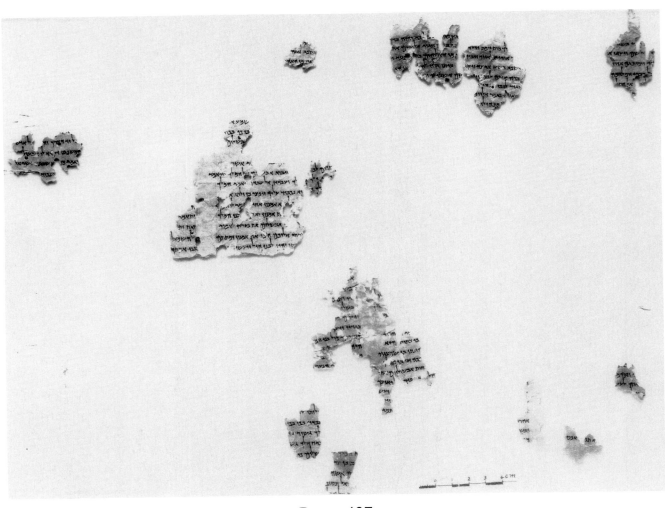

PLATE 427

PLATE 428

PLATE 429

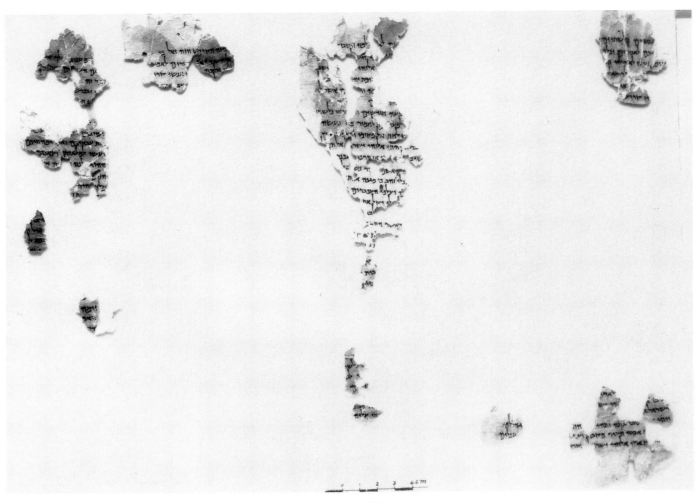

PLATE 430

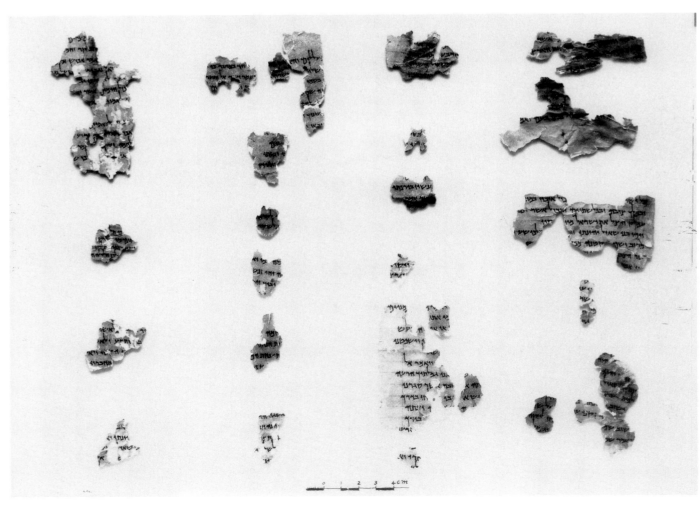

PLATE 431

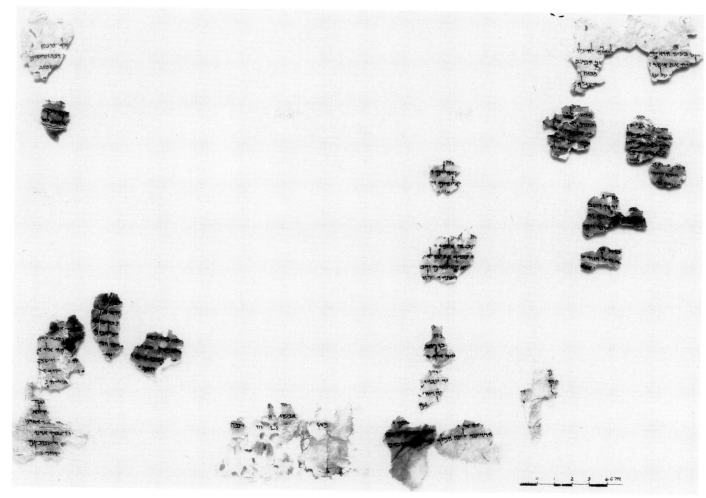

PLATE 432

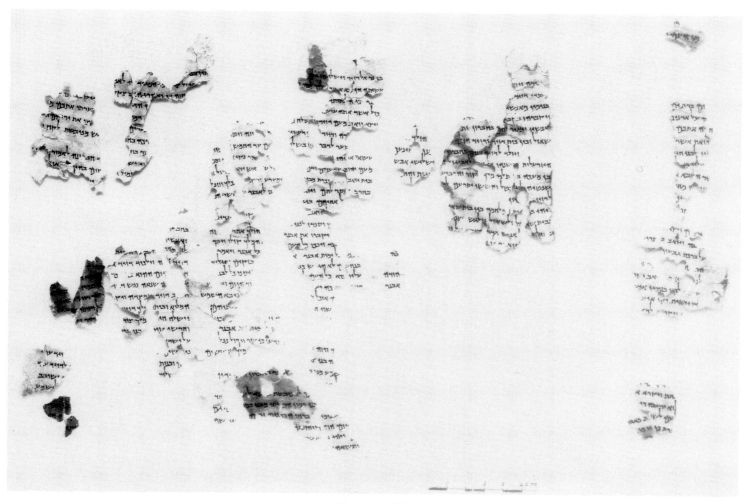

PLATE 433

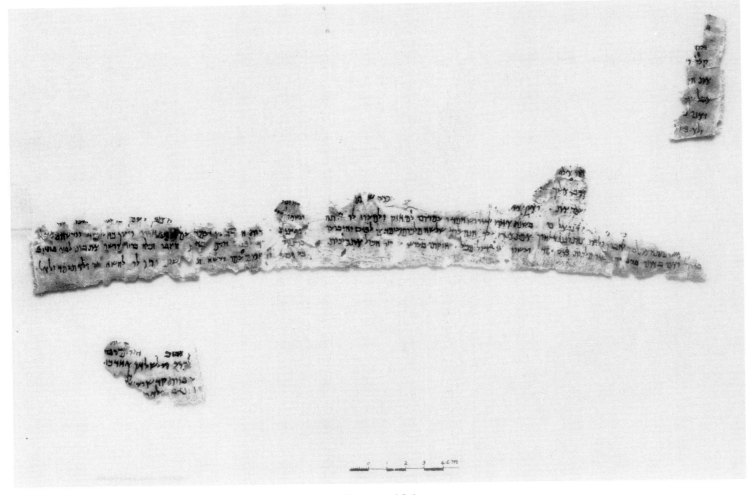

PLATE 434

PLATE 435

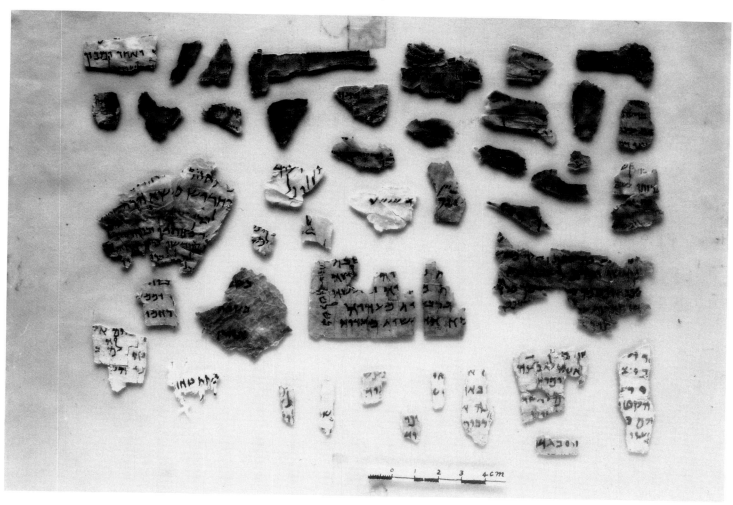

PLATE 436

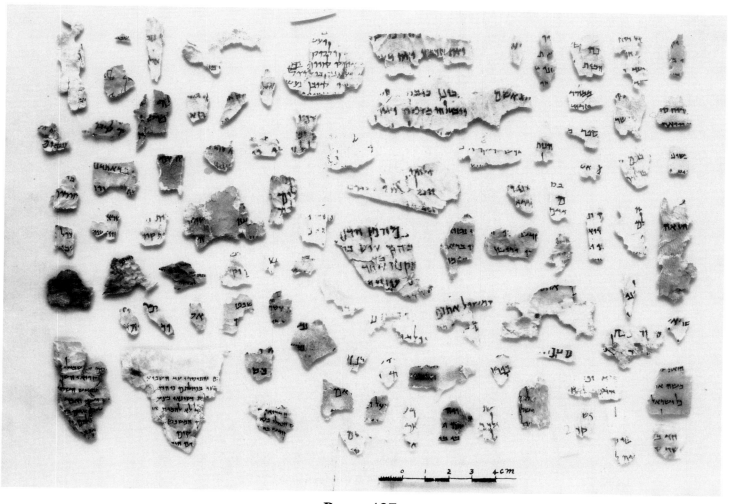

PLATE 437

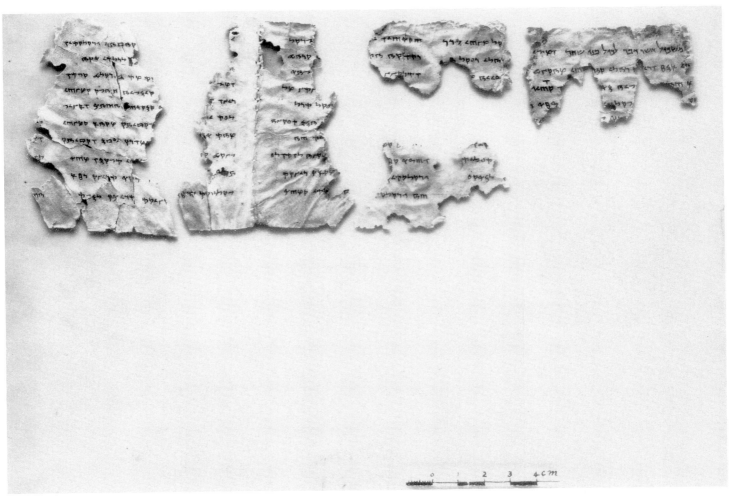

PLATE 438

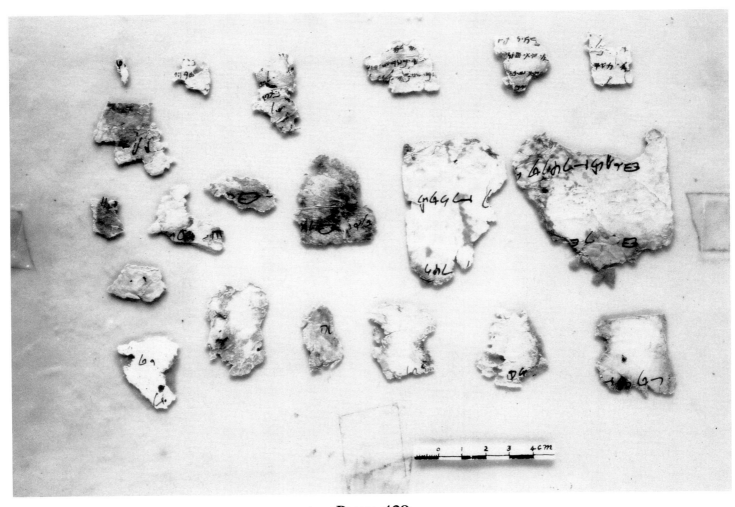

PLATE 439

PLATE 440

PLATE 441

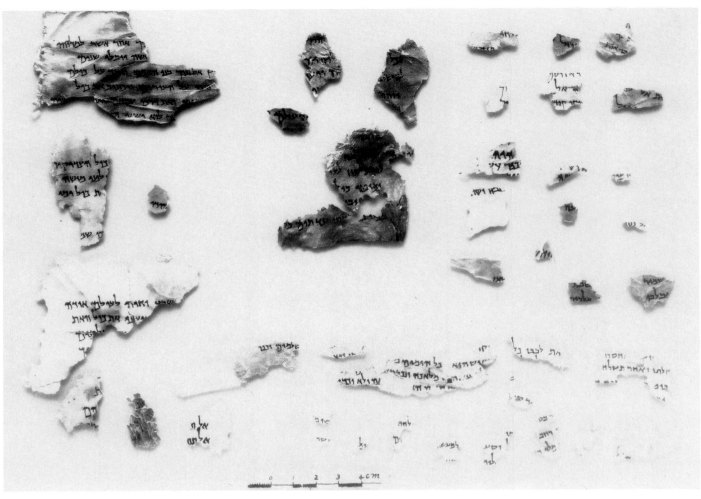

PLATE 442

PLATE 443

PLATE 444

PLATE 445

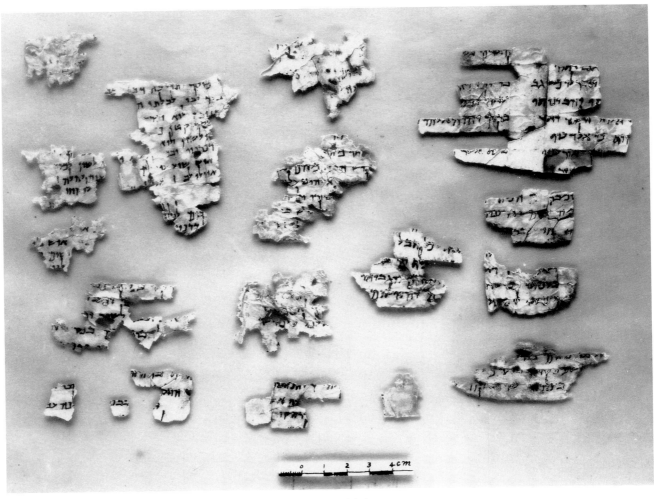

PLATE 446

PLATE 447

PLATE 448

PLATE 449

PLATE 450

PLATE 451

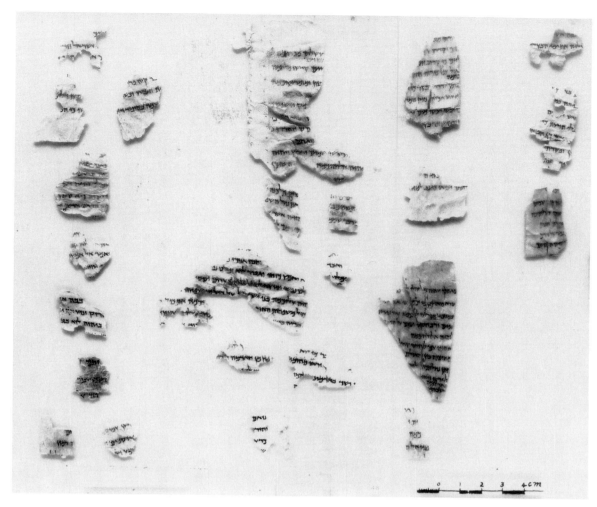

PLATE 452

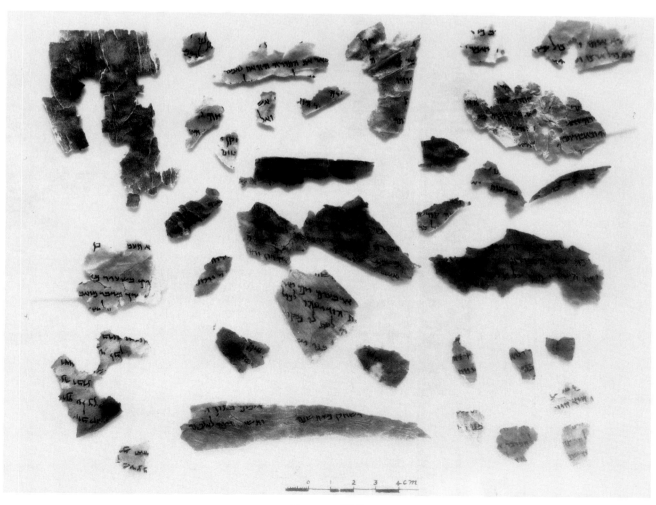

PLATE 453

PLATE 454

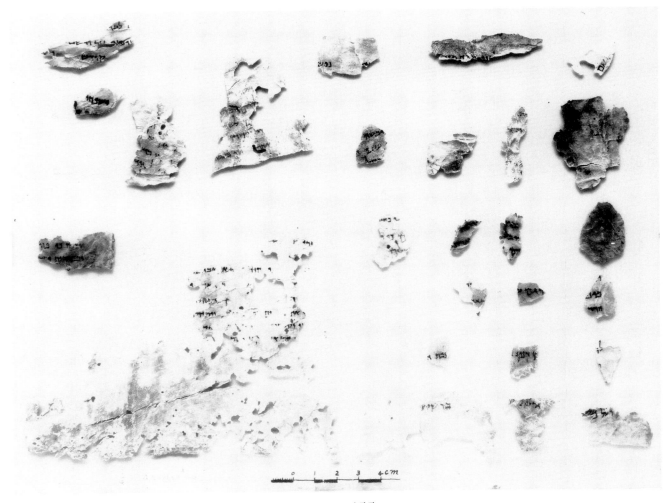

PLATE 455

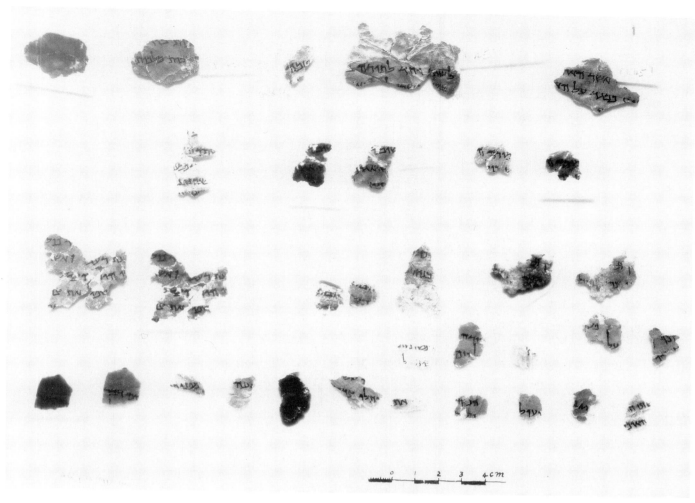

PLATE 456

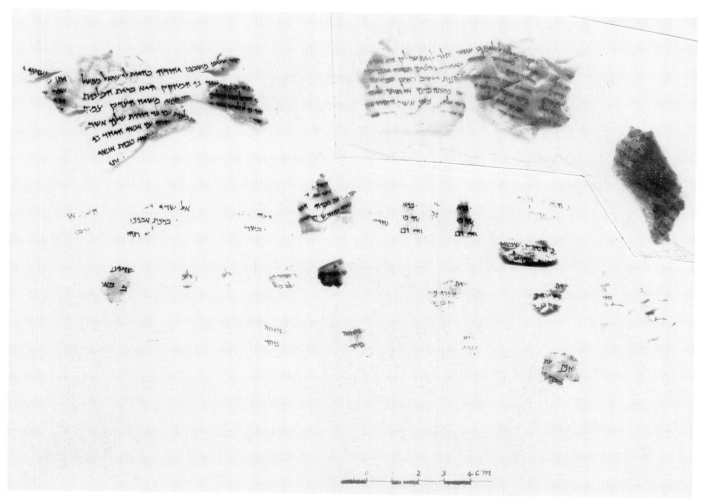

PLATE 457

PLATE 458

PLATE 459

PLATE 460

PLATE 461

PLATE 462

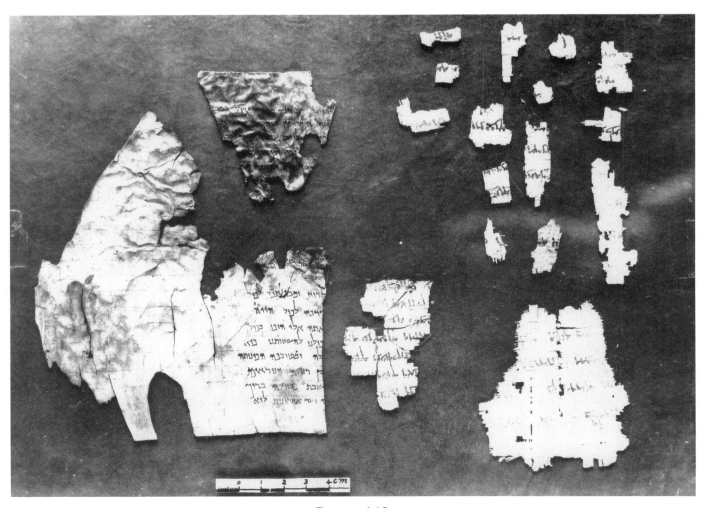

PLATE 463

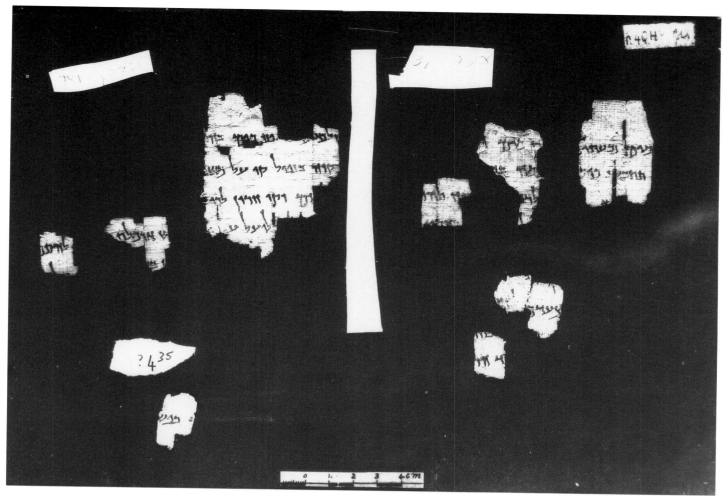

PLATE 464

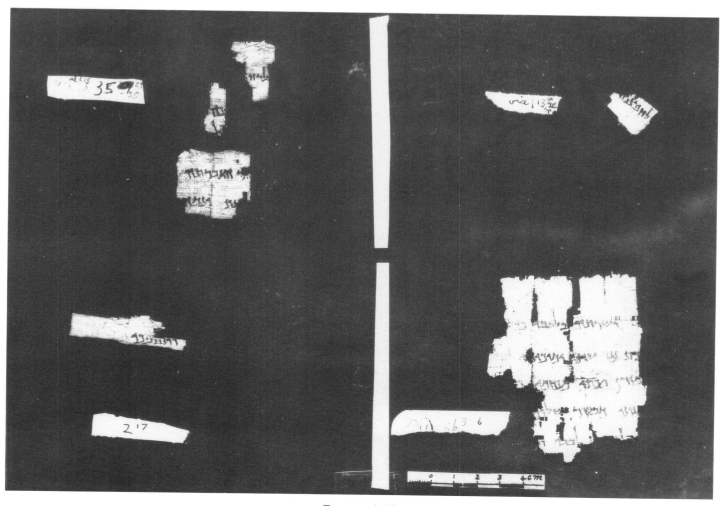

PLATE 465

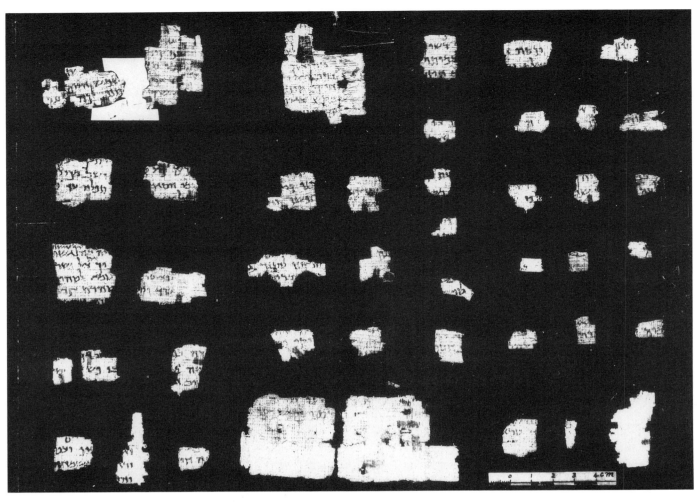

PLATE 466

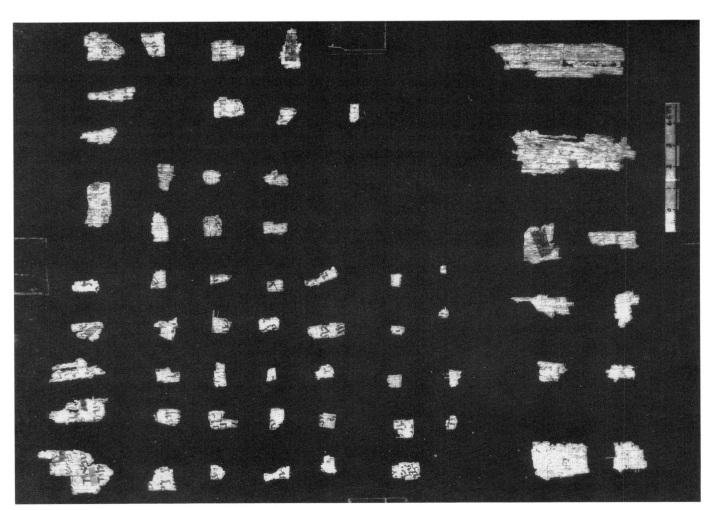

PLATE 467

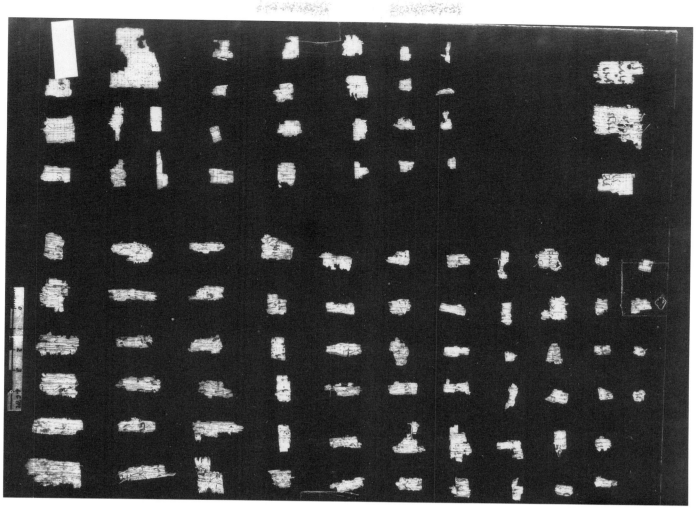

PLATE 469

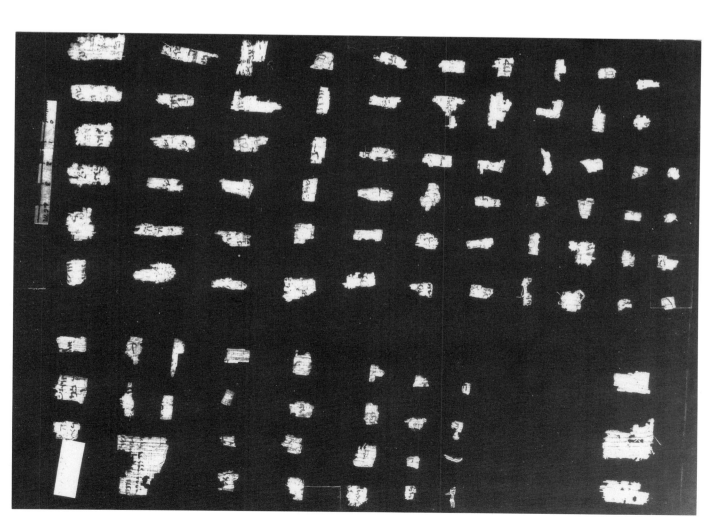

PLATE 468

PLATE 470

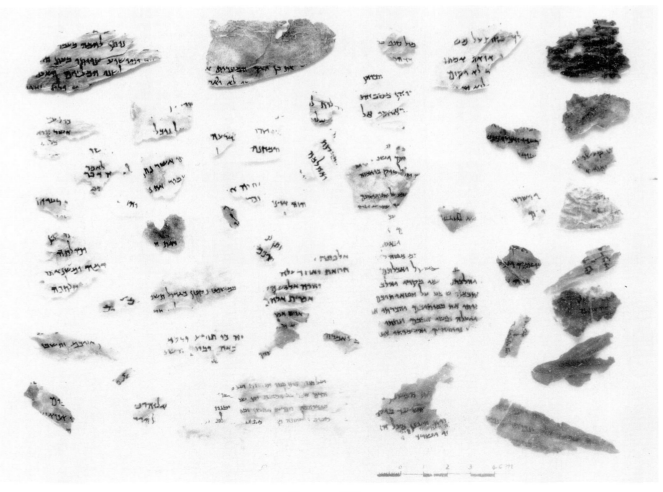

PLATE 471

PLATE 472

PLATE 473

PLATE 474

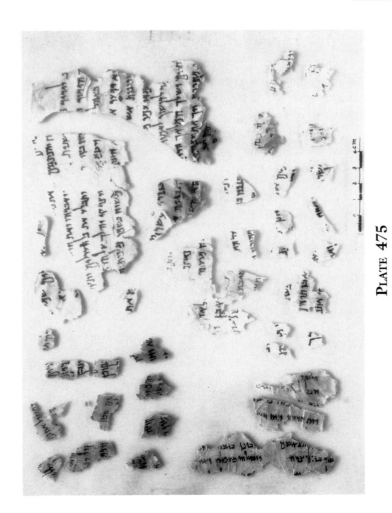

PLATE 475

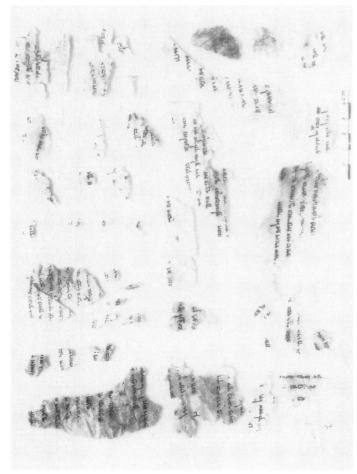

PLATE 476

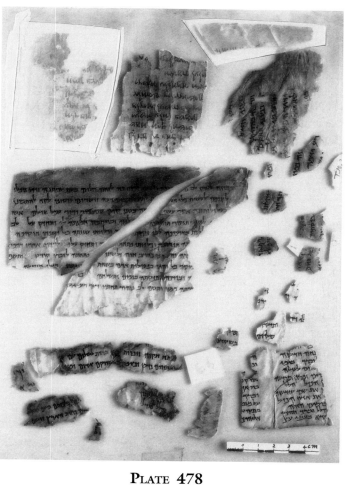

PLATE 478

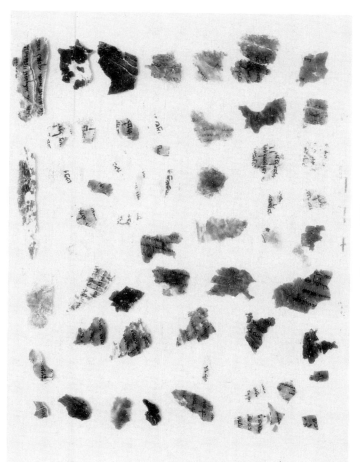

PLATE 480

PLATE 477

PLATE 479

PLATE 481

PLATE 482

PLATE 483

PLATE 484

PLATE 486

PLATE 488

PLATE 485

PLATE 487

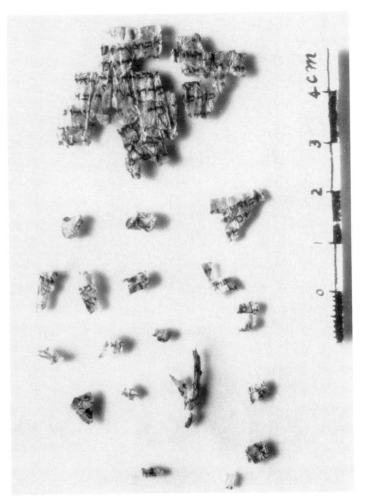

PLATE 489

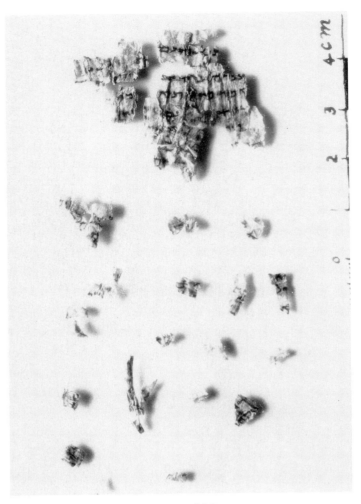

PLATE 490

PLATE 491

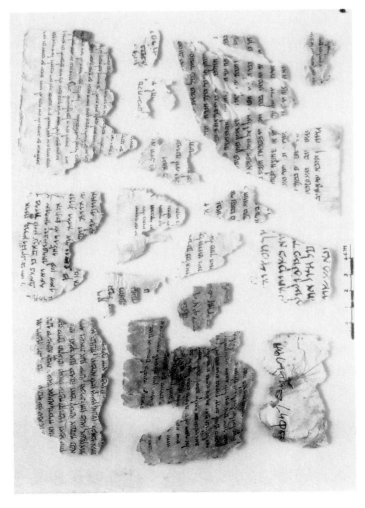

PLATE 492

PLATE 493

PLATE 494

PLATE 495

PLATE 496

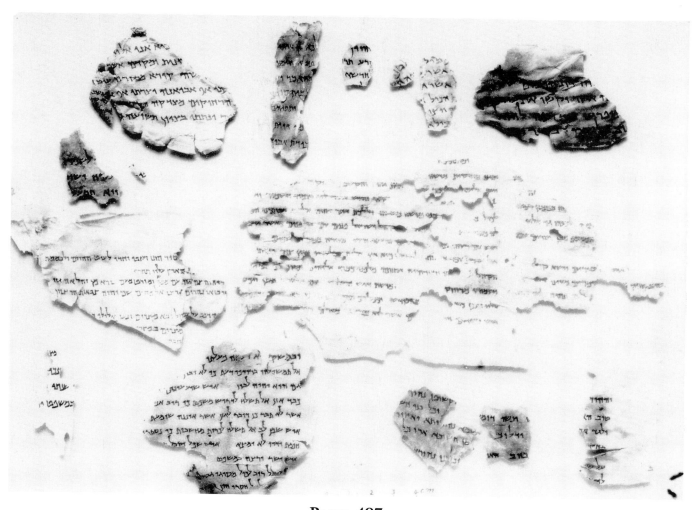

PLATE 497

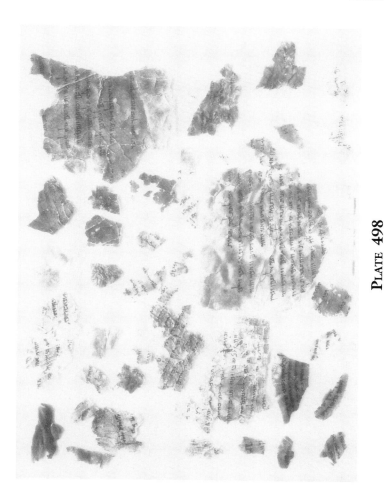

PLATE 498

PLATE 499

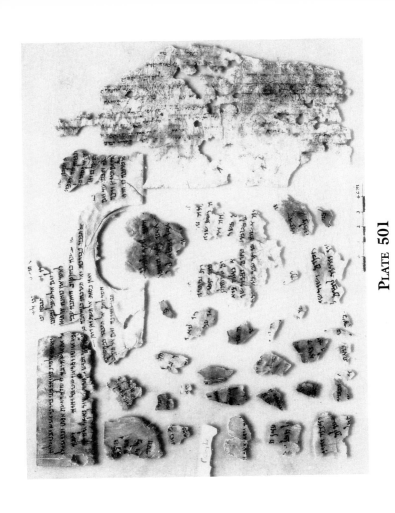

PLATE 501

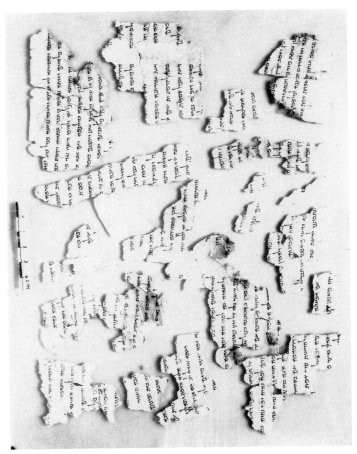

PLATE 503

PLATE 500

PLATE 502

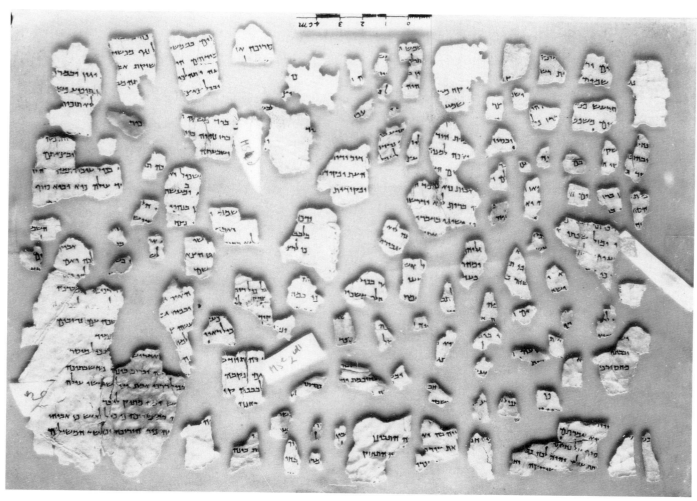

PLATE 504

PLATE 505

PLATE 506

PLATE 507

PLATE 508

PLATE 509

PLATE 510

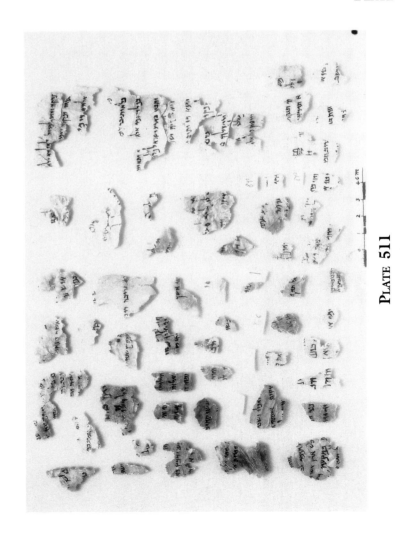

PLATE 511

PLATE 512

PLATE 513

PLATE 514

PLATE 515

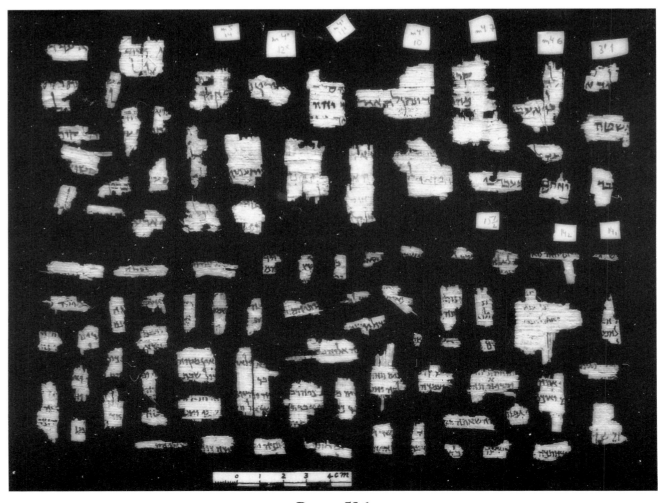

PLATE 516

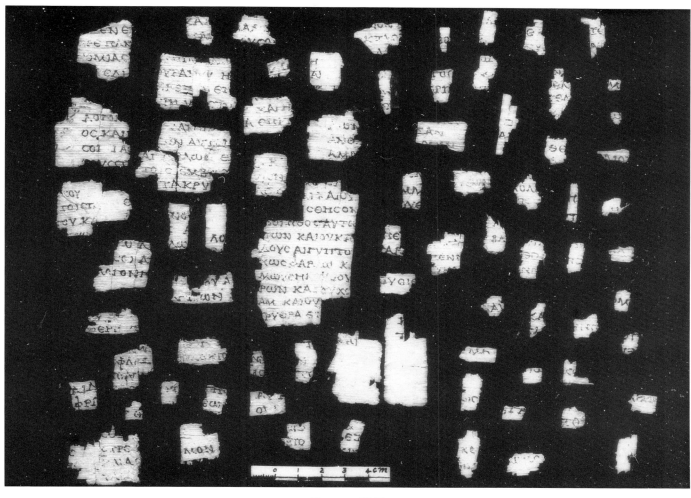

PLATE 517

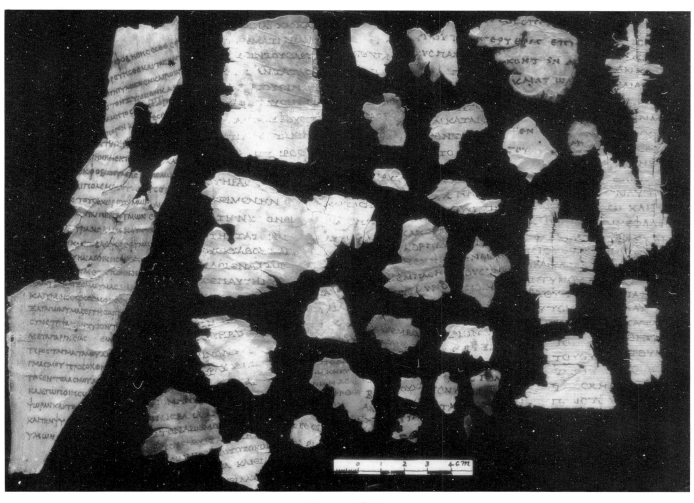

PLATE 518

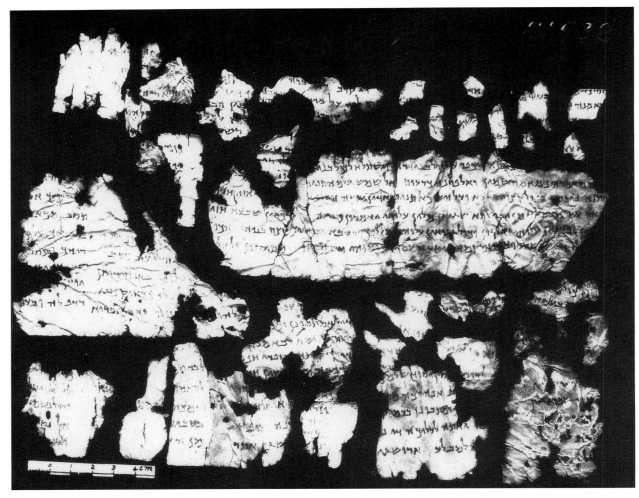

PLATE 519

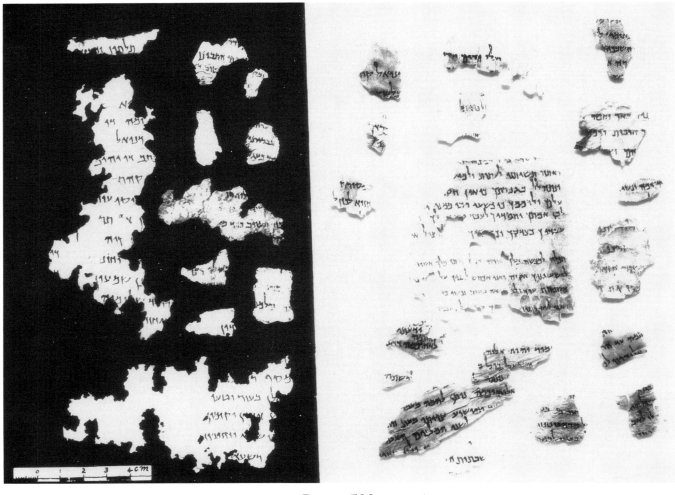

PLATE 520

PLATE 521

PLATE 522

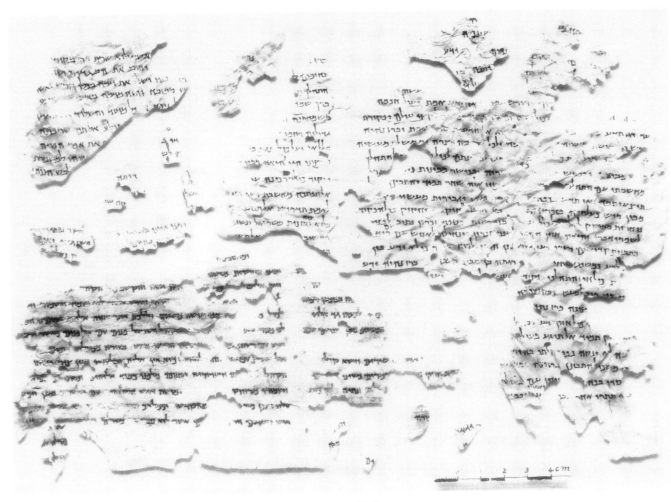

PLATE 523

PLATE 524

PLATE 525

PLATE 526

PLATE 527

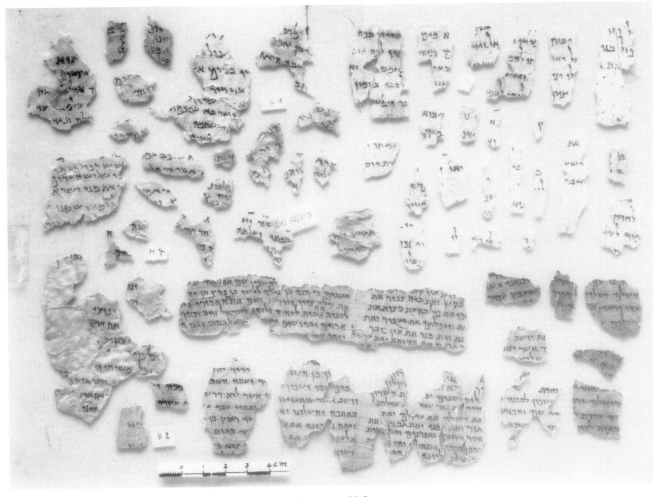

PLATE 528

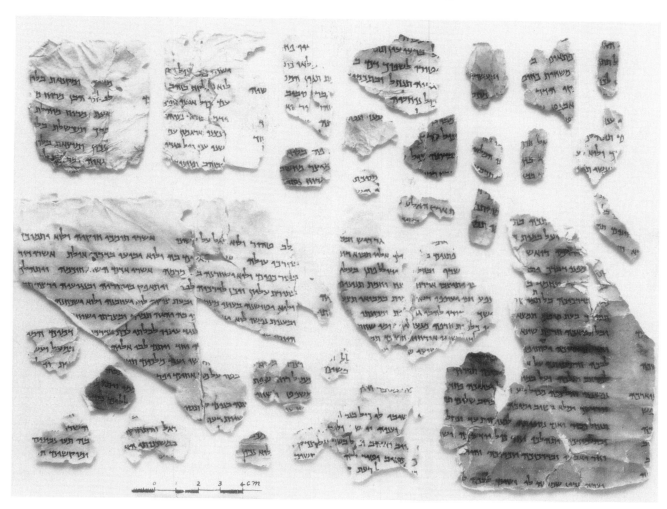

PLATE 529

PLATE 530

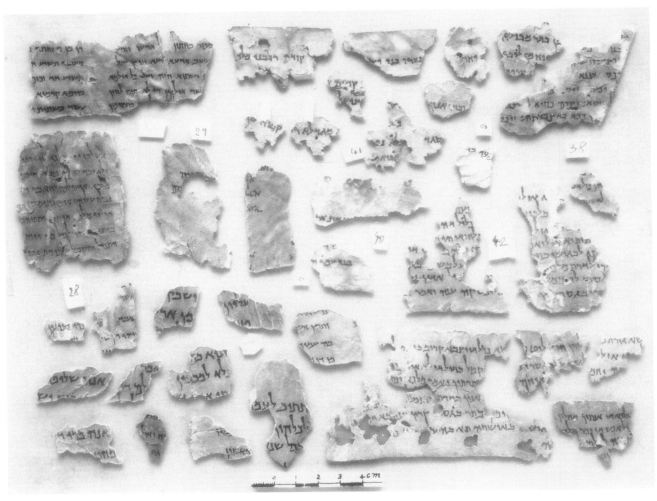

PLATE 531

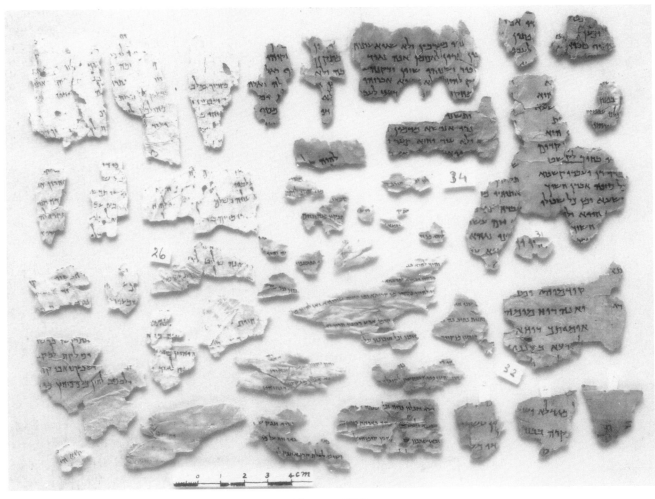

PLATE 532

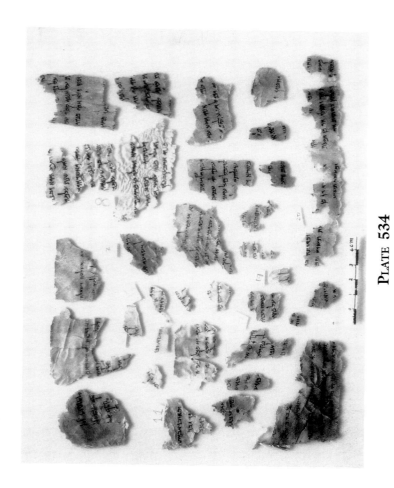

PLATE 534

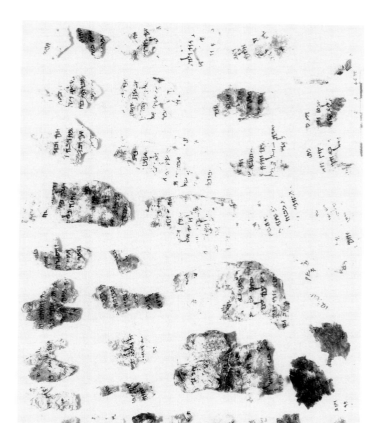

PLATE 536

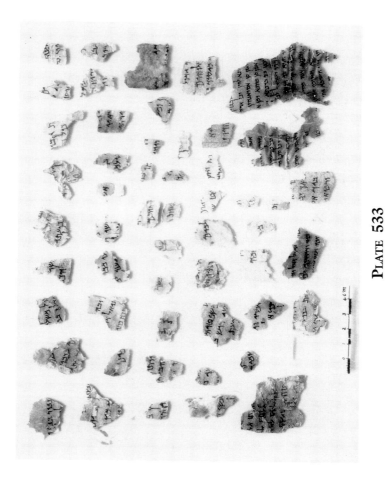

PLATE 533

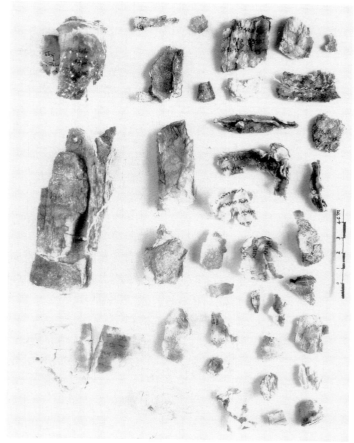

PLATE 535

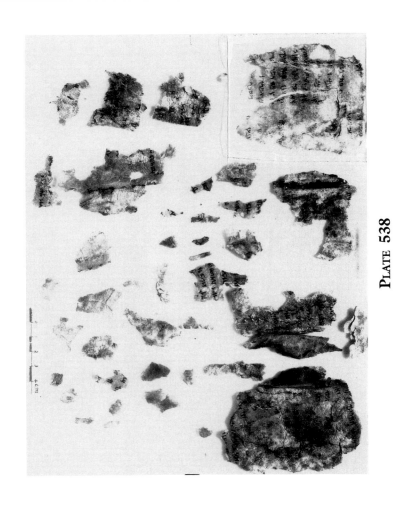

PLATE 538

PLATE 540

PLATE 537

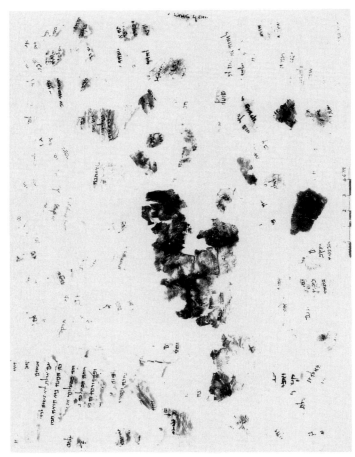

PLATE 539

PLATE 541

PLATE 542

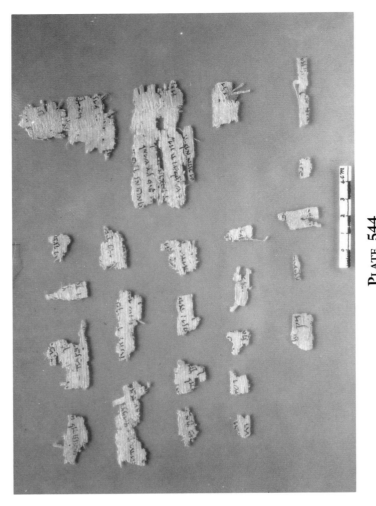

PLATE 544

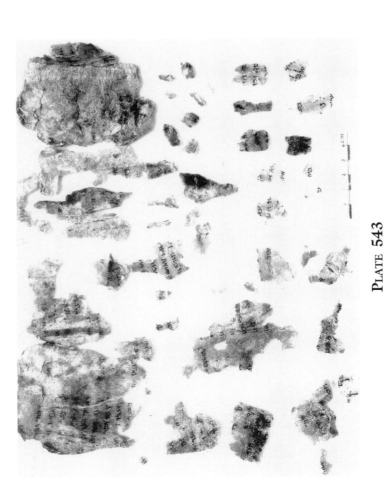

PLATE 543

PLATE 546

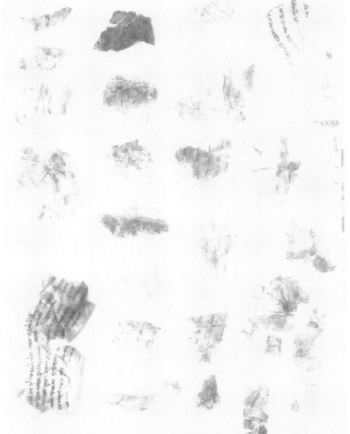

PLATE 545

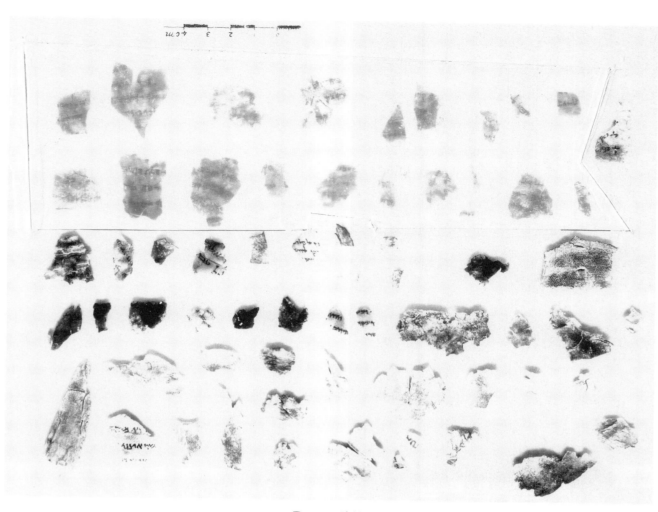

PLATE 547

PLATE 548

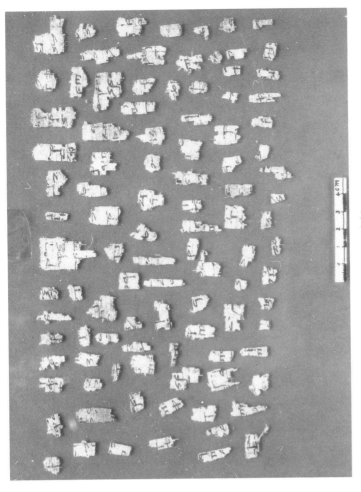

PLATE 558

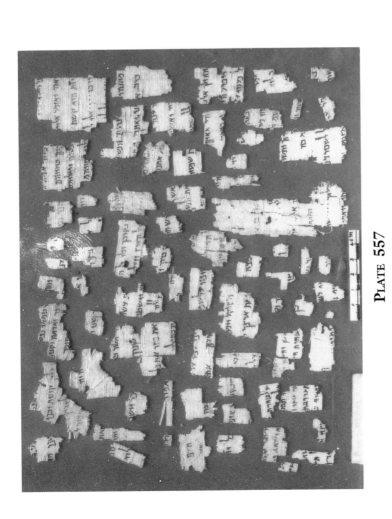

PLATE 557

PLATE 559

PLATE 560

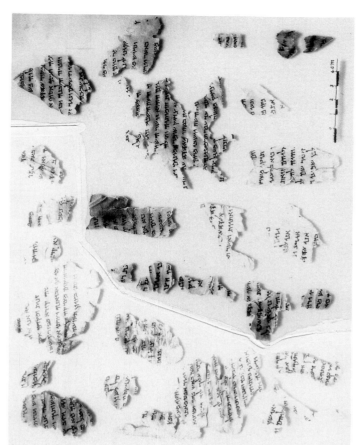

PLATE 564

PLATE 562

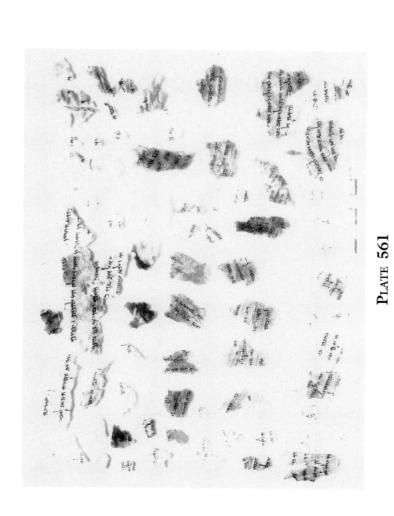

PLATE 561

PLATE 563

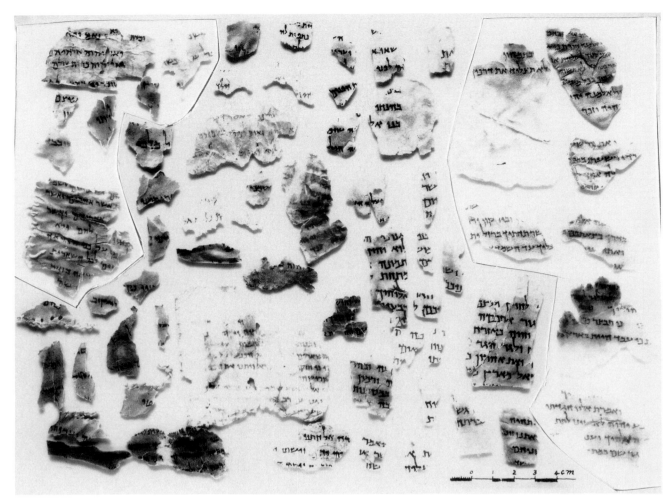

PLATE 565

PLATE 566

PLATE 567

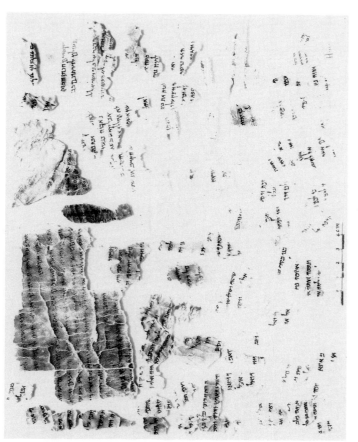

PLATE 568

PLATE 569

PLATE 571

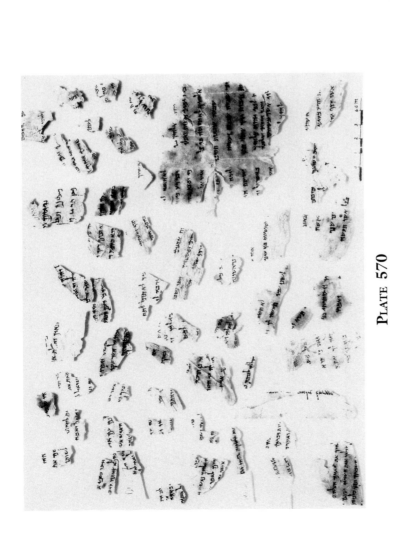

PLATE 570

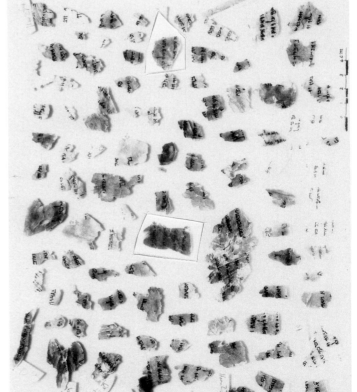

PLATE 573

PLATE 572

PLATE 575

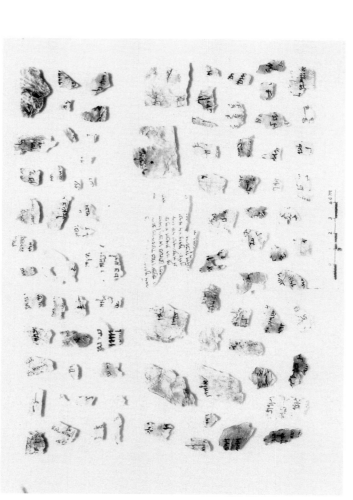

PLATE 574

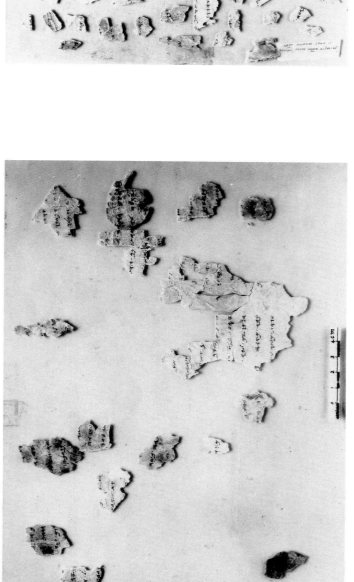

PLATE 577

PLATE 576

PLATE 578

PLATE 579

PLATE 580

PLATE 581

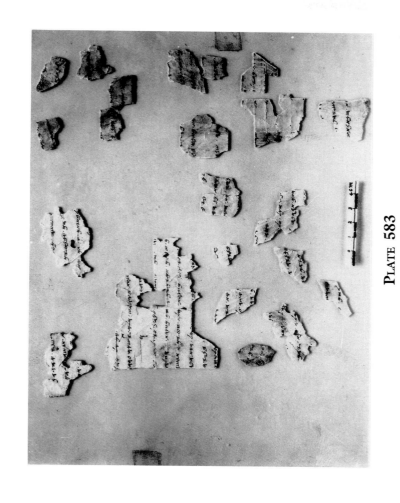

PLATE 583

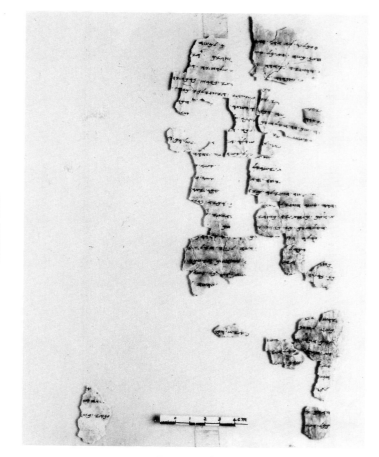

PLATE 585

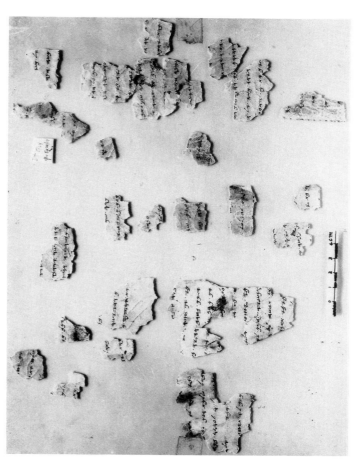

PLATE 582

PLATE 584

PLATE 586

PLATE 587

PLATE 588

PLATE 591

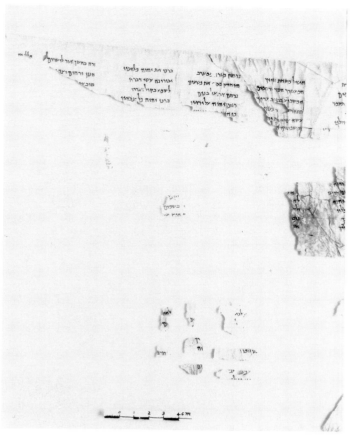

PLATE 590

PLATE 589

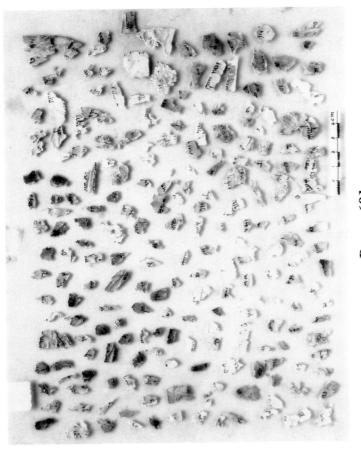

PLATE 601

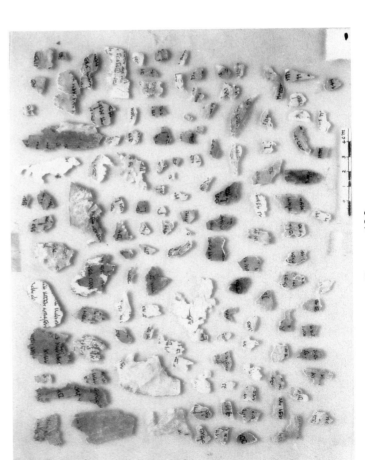

PLATE 603

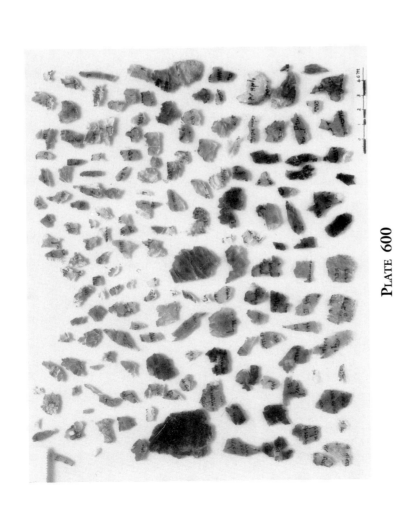

PLATE 600

PLATE 602

PLATE 604

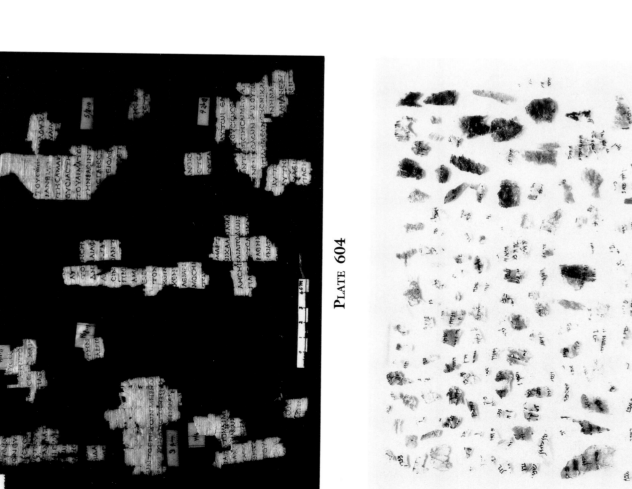

PLATE 605

PLATE 606

PLATE 607

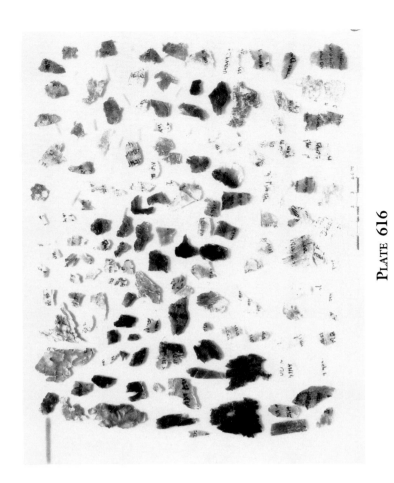

PLATE 616

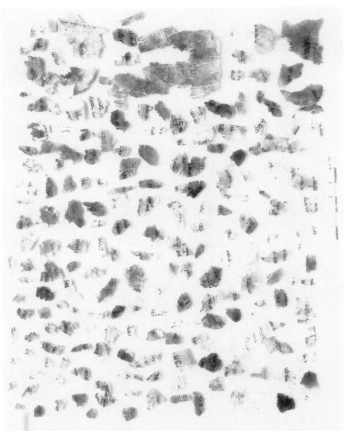

PLATE 617

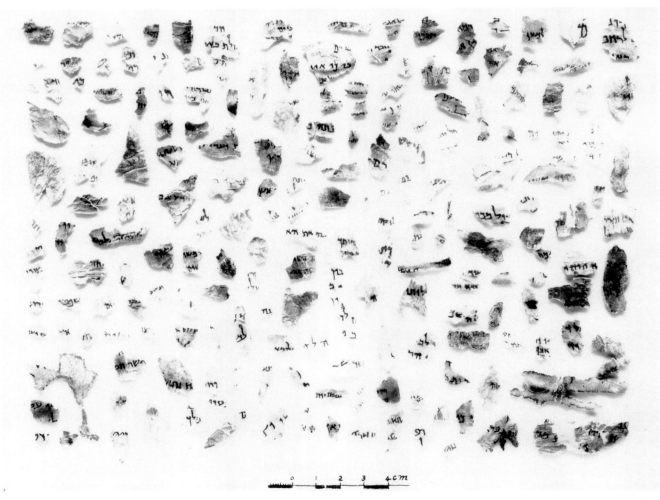

PLATE 618

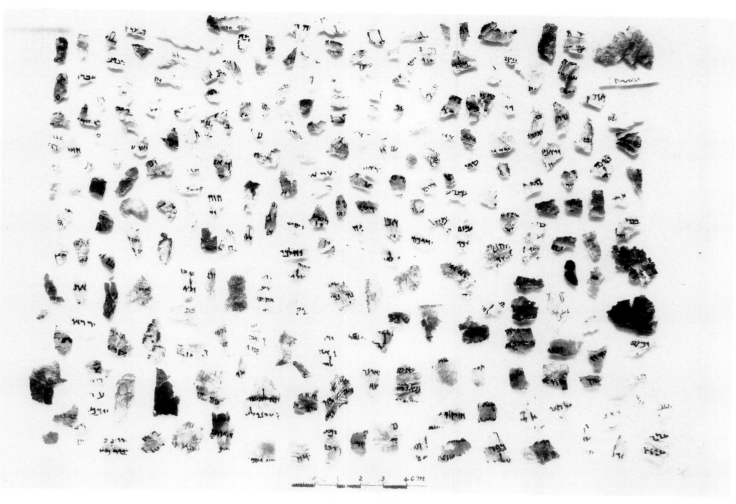

PLATE 619

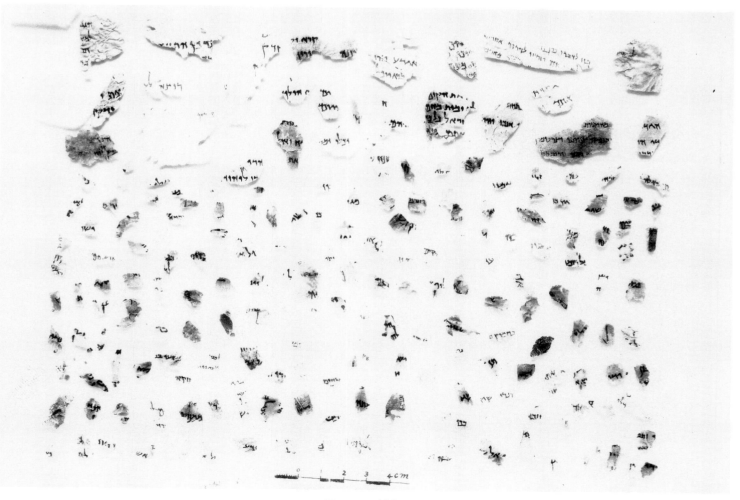

PLATE 620

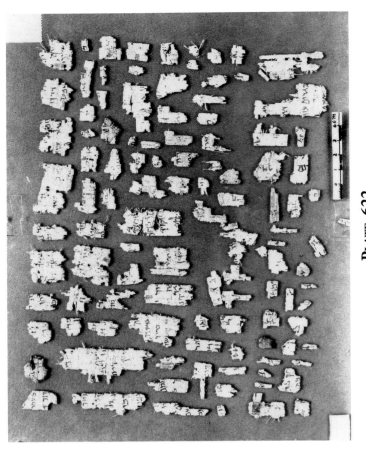

PLATE 622

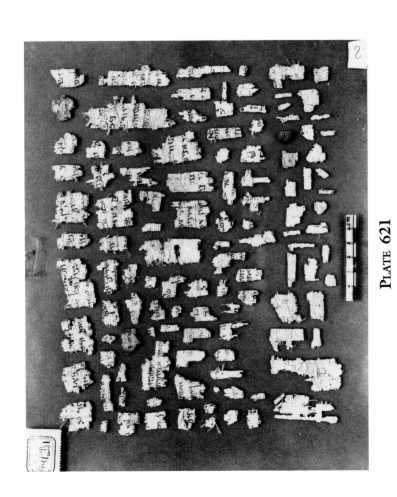

PLATE 621

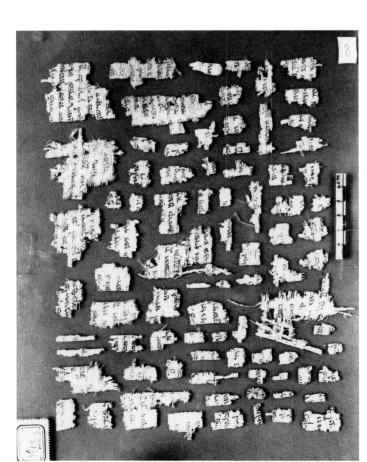

PLATE 624

PLATE 623

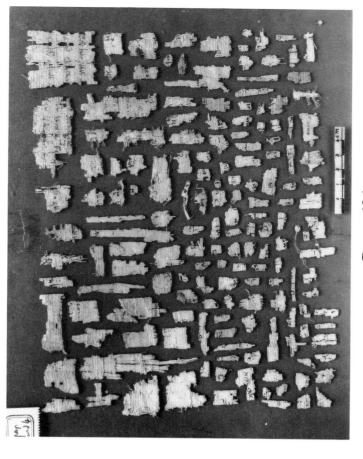

PLATE 626

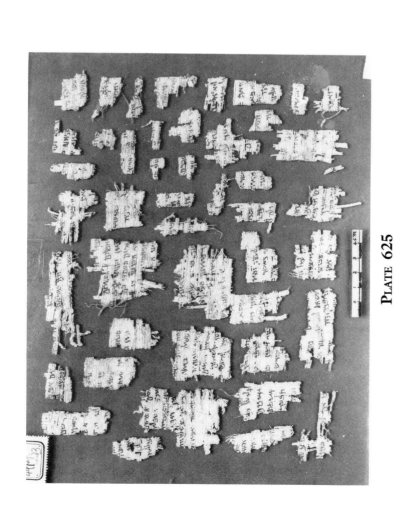

PLATE 625

PLATE 627

PLATE 628

PLATE 630

PLATE 632

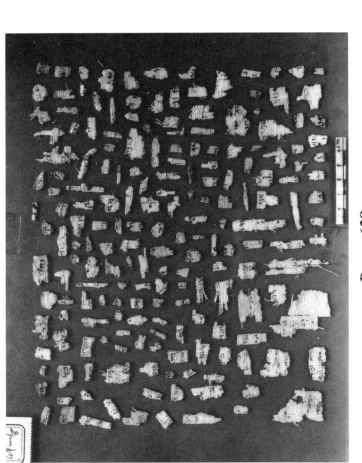

PLATE 629

PLATE 631

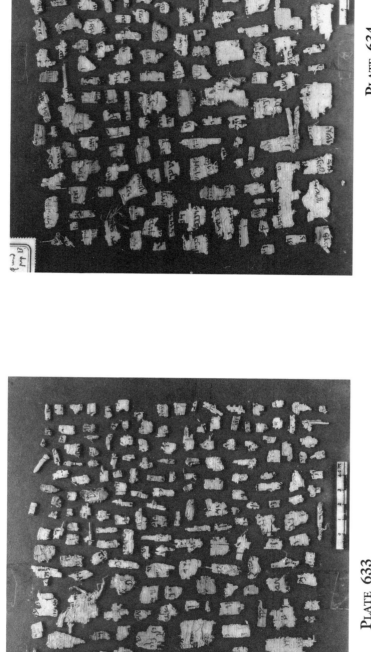

PLATE 633

PLATE 634

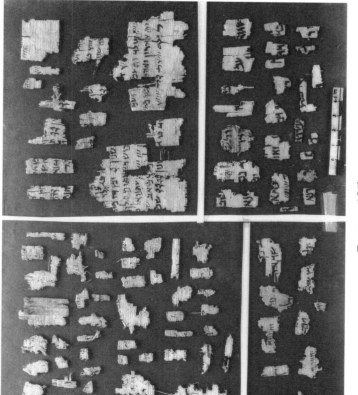

PLATE 635

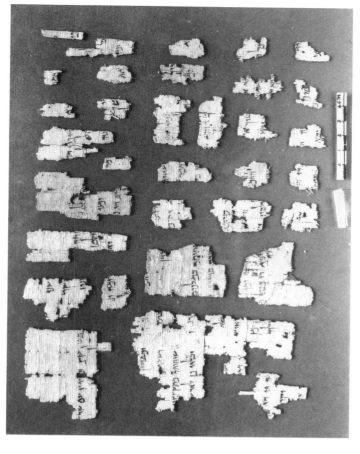

PLATE 636

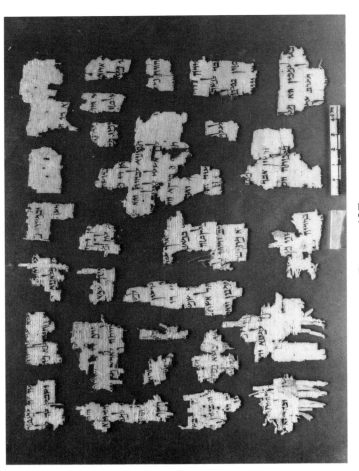

PLATE 637

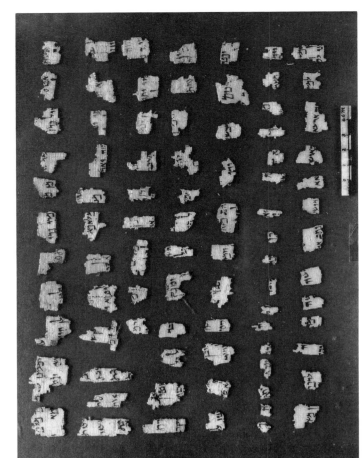

PLATE 638

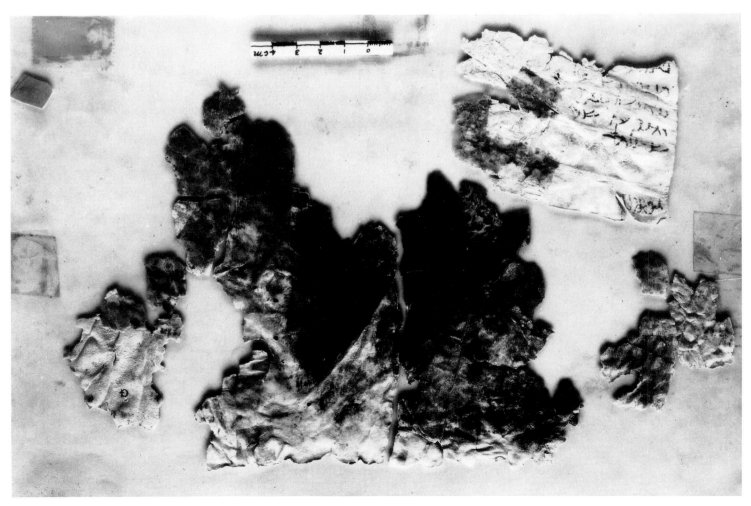

PLATE 639

PLATE 640

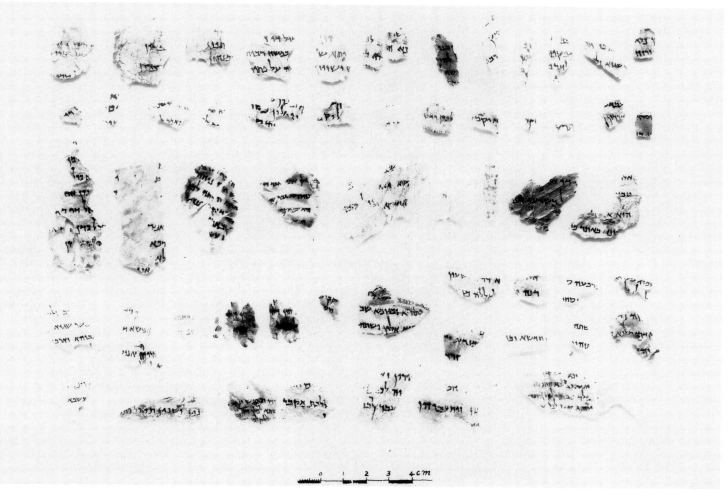

PLATE 641

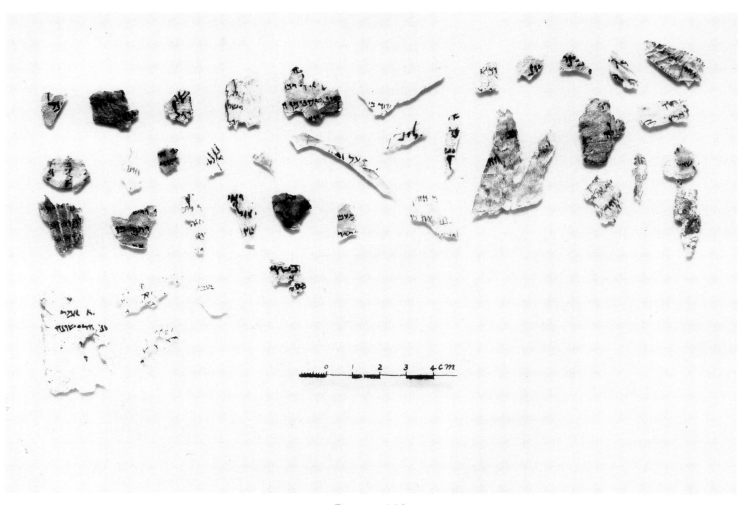

PLATE 642

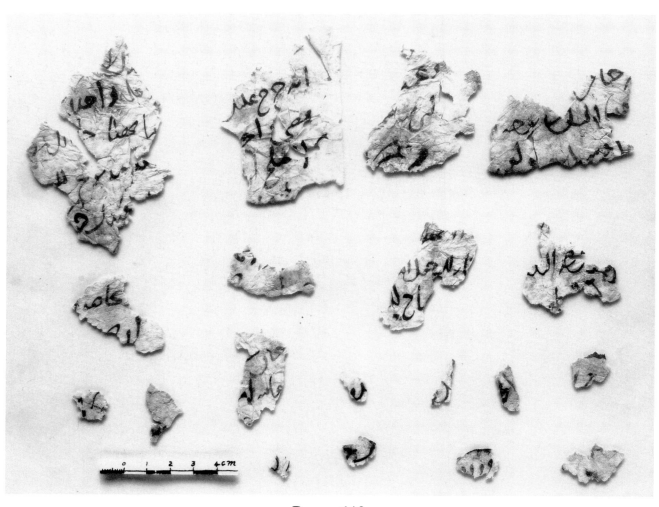

PLATE 643

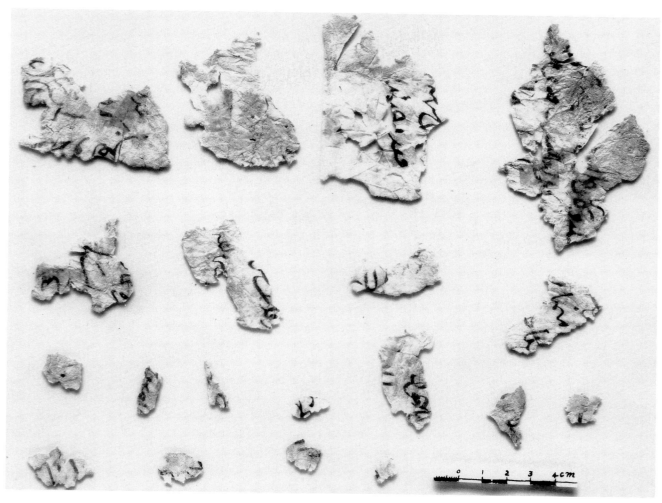

PLATE 644

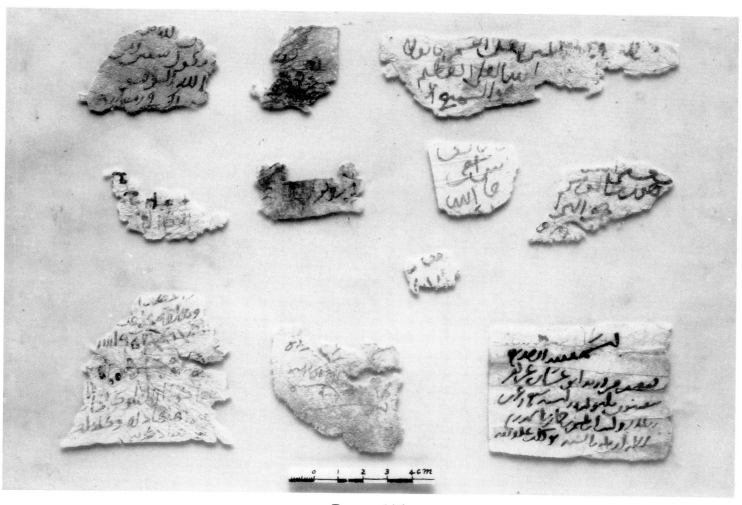

PLATE 645

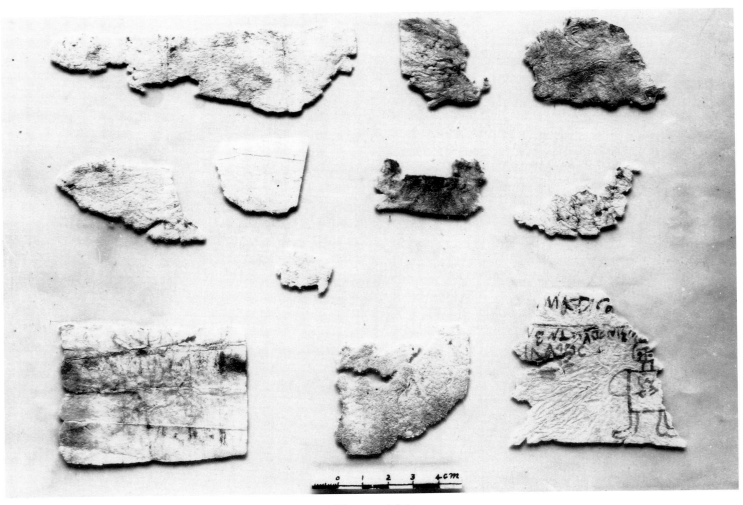

PLATE 646

PLATE 647

PLATE 648

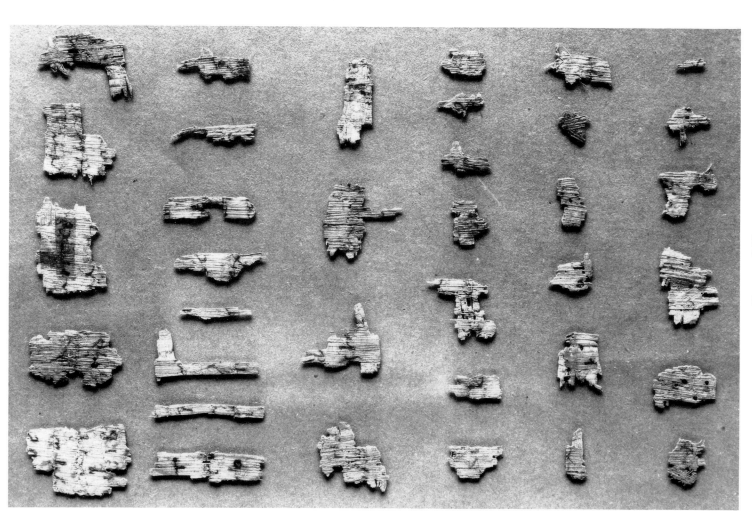

PLATE 649

PLATE 650

PLATE 651

PLATE 652

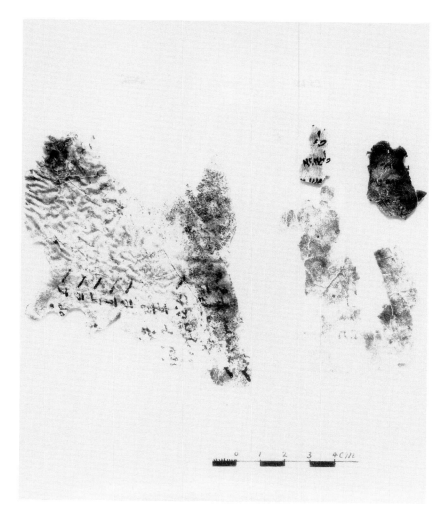

PLATE 653

PLATE 654

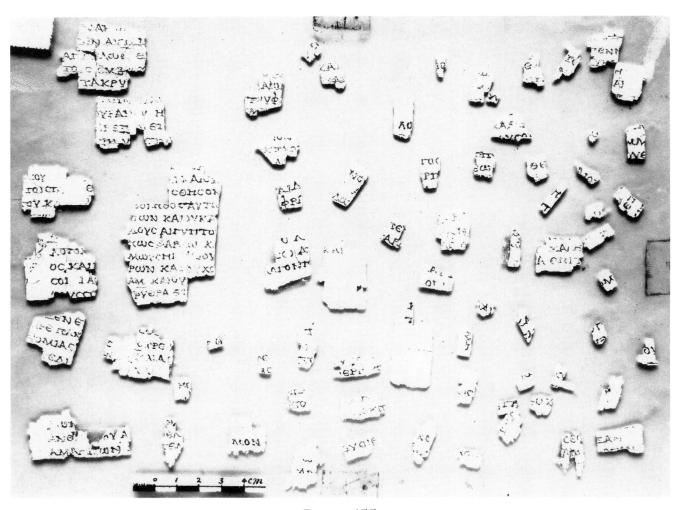

PLATE 655

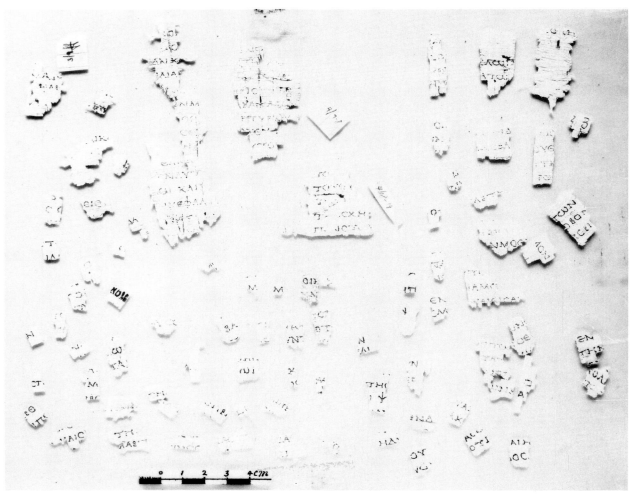

PLATE 656

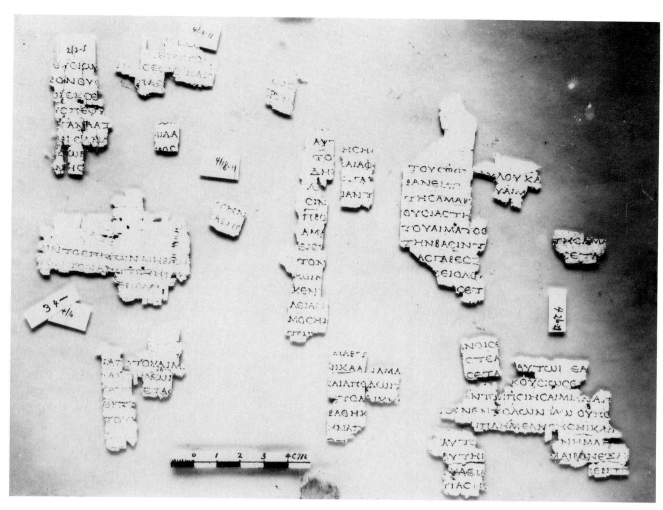

PLATE 657

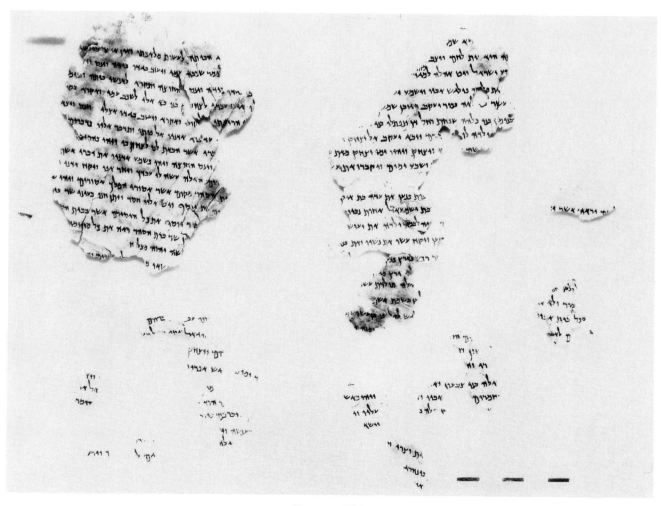

PLATE 658

PLATE 659

PLATE 660

PLATE 661

PLATE 662

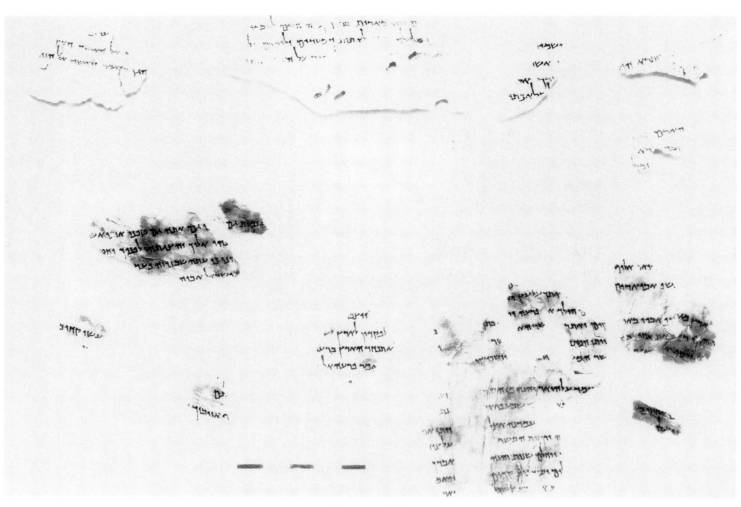

PLATE 663

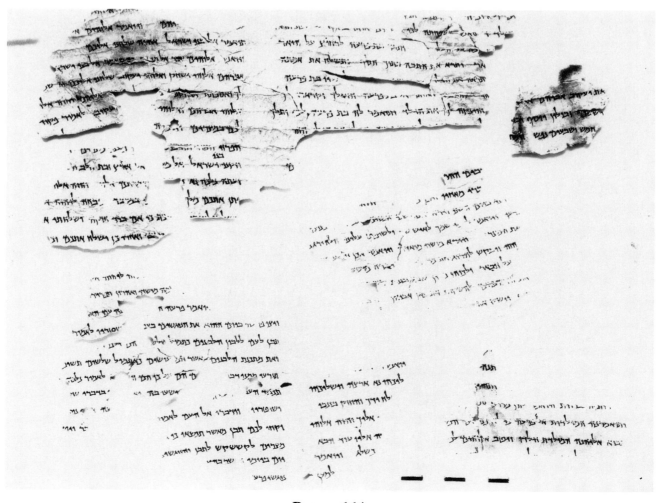

PLATE 664

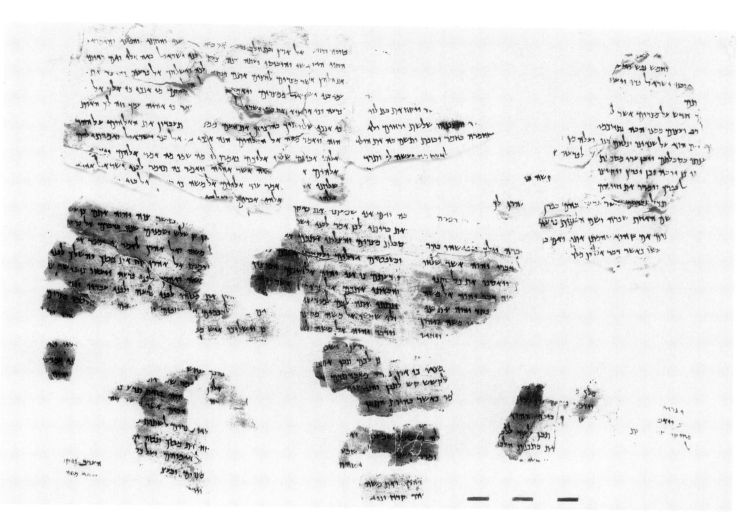

PLATE 665

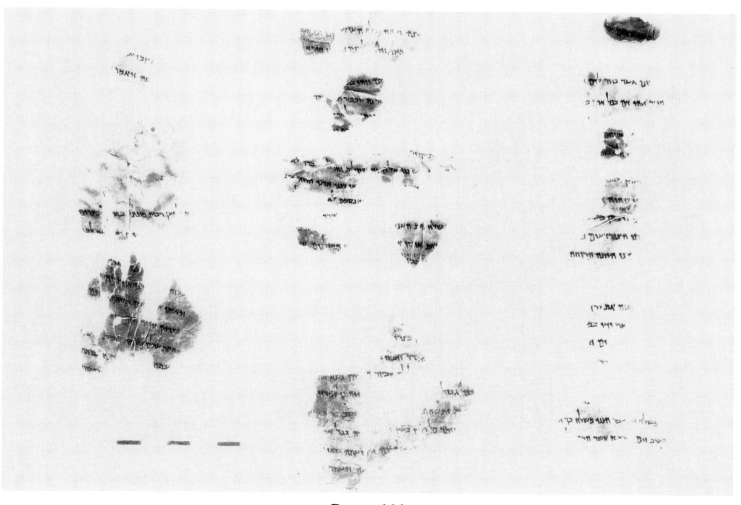

PLATE 666

PLATE 667

PLATE 668

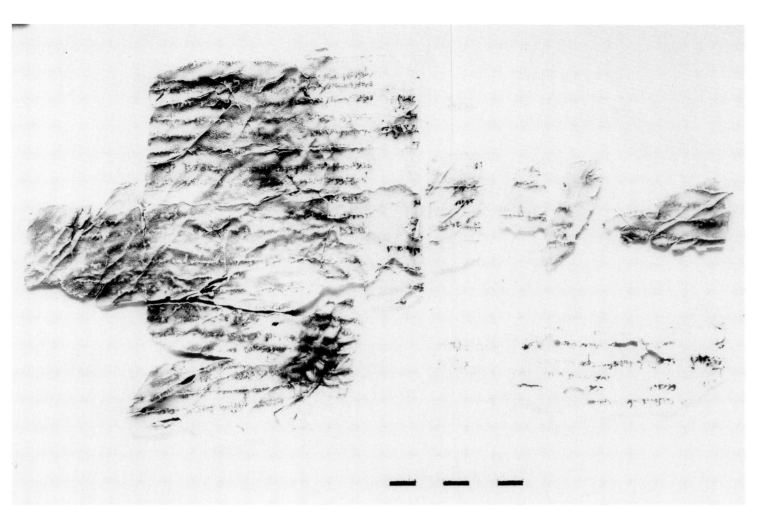

PLATE 669

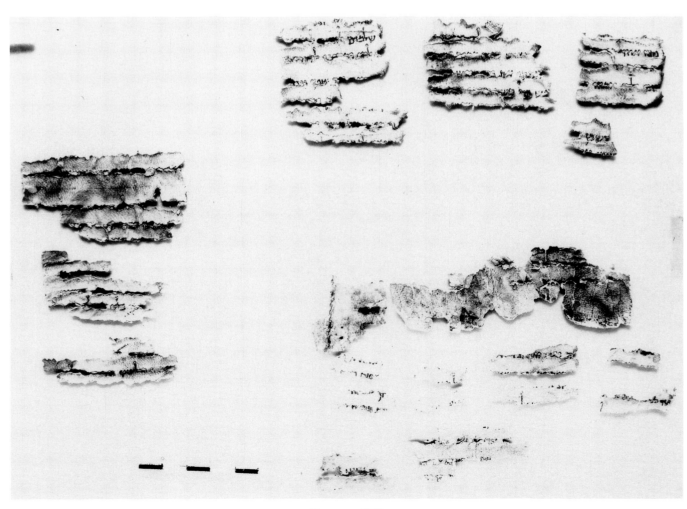

PLATE 670

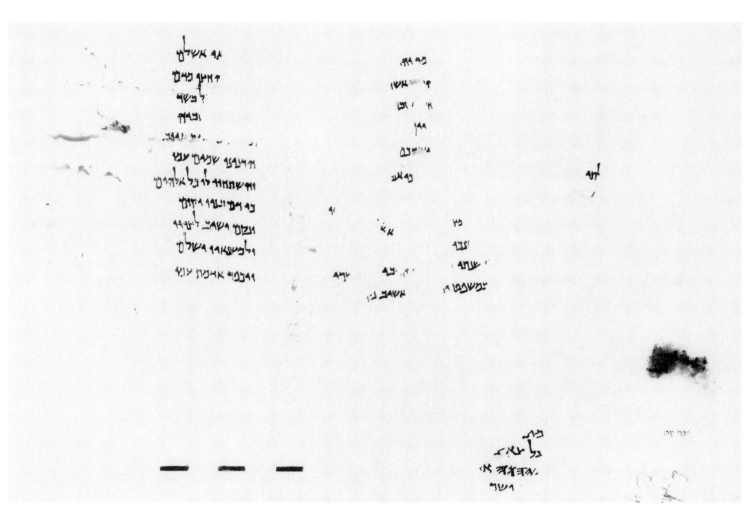

Plate 671

Plate 672

PLATE 673

PLATE 674

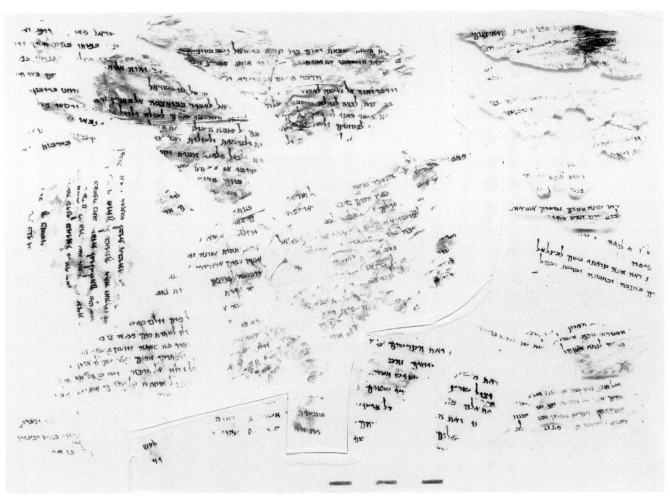

PLATE 675

PLATE 676

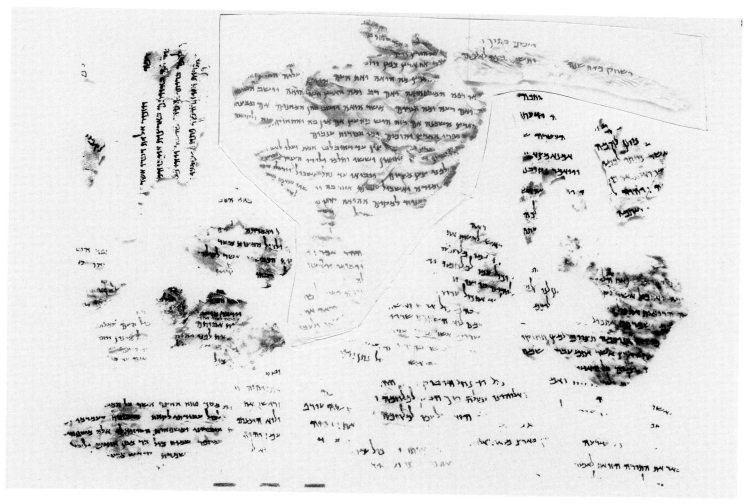

PLATE 677

PLATE 678

PLATE 679

PLATE 680

PLATE 681

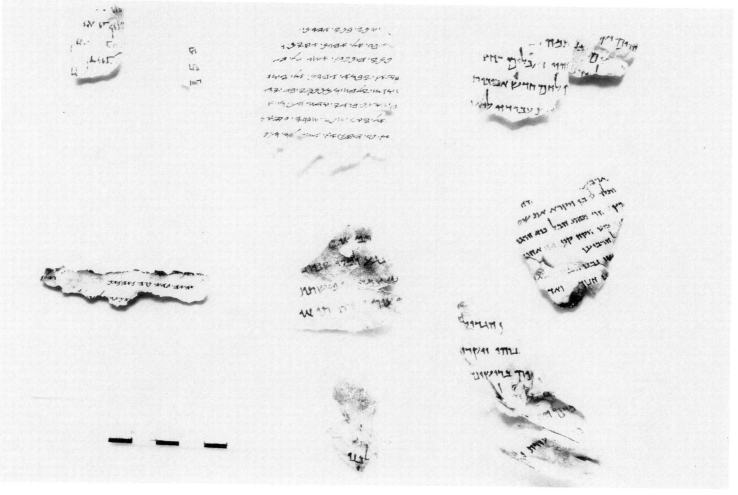

PLATE 682

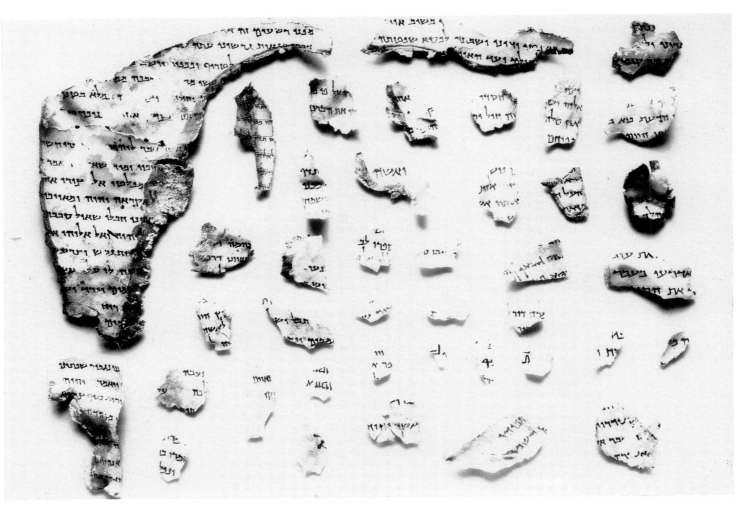

PLATE 683

PLATE 684

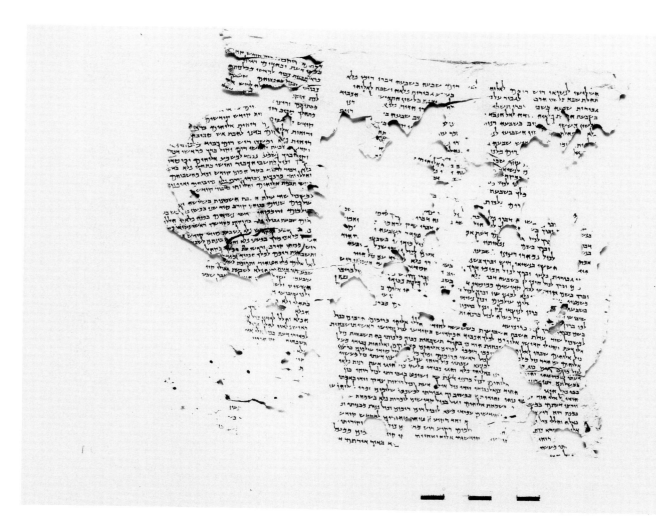

PLATE 685

PLATE 686

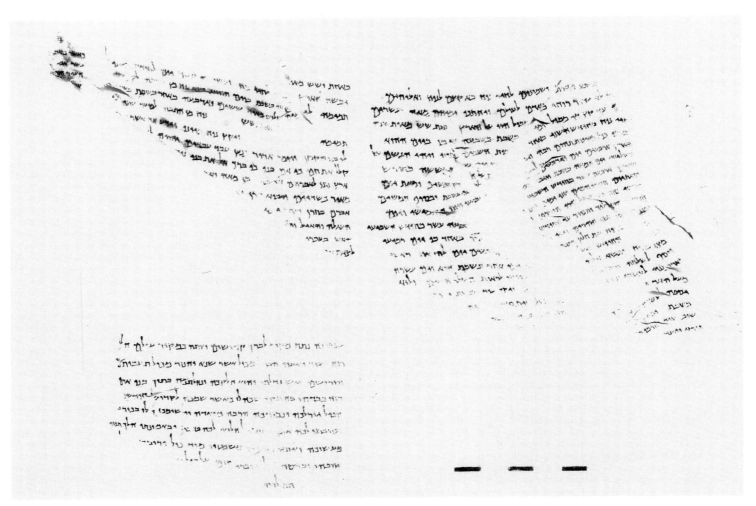

PLATE 687

PLATE 688

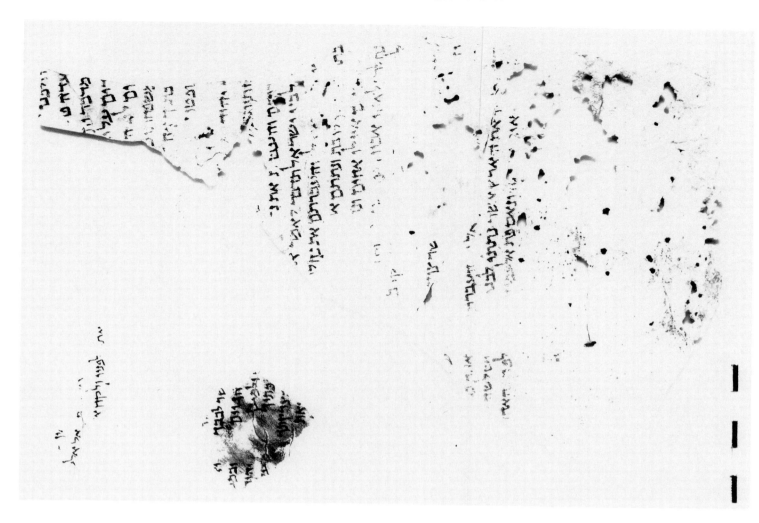

PLATE 689

PLATE 690

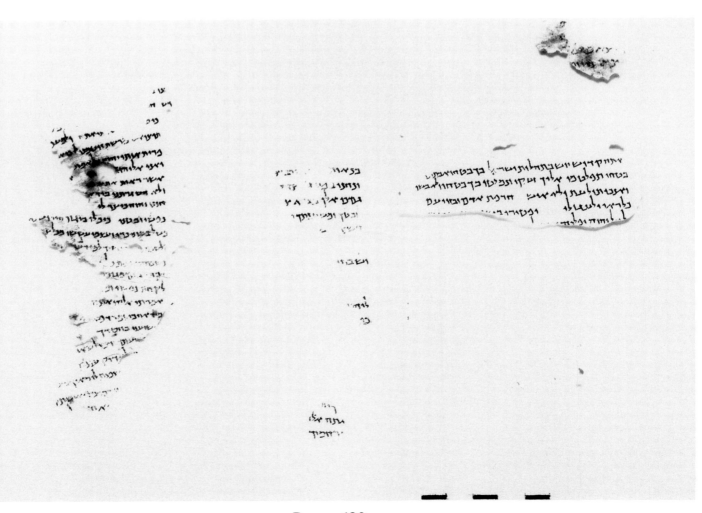

PLATE 691

PLATE 692

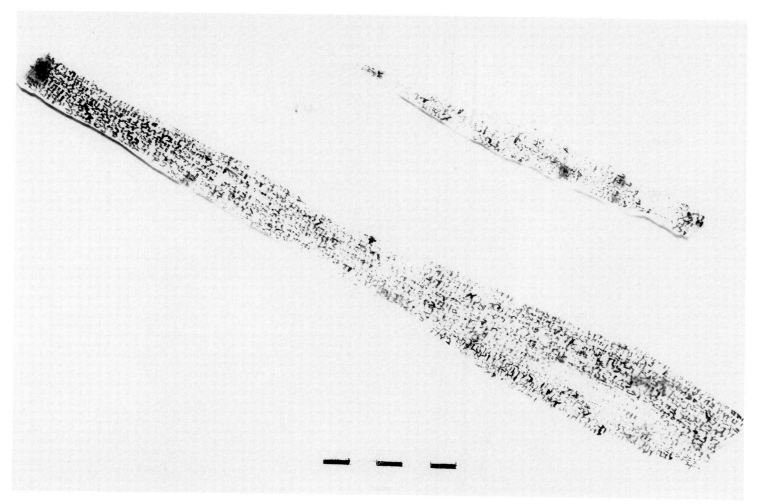

PLATE 693

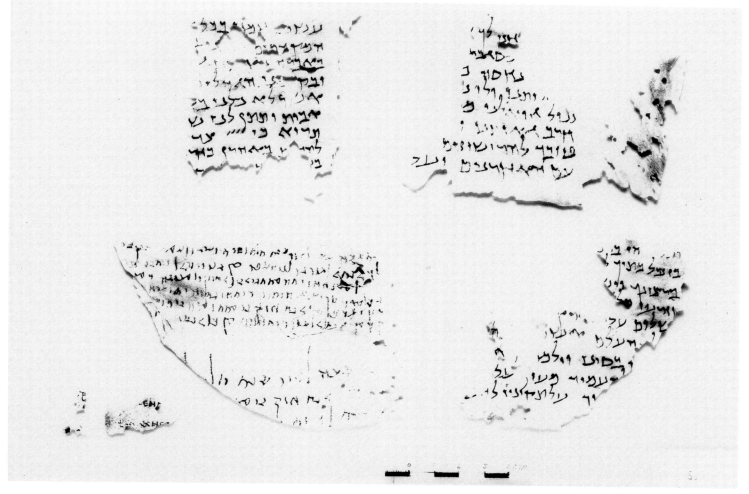

PLATE 694

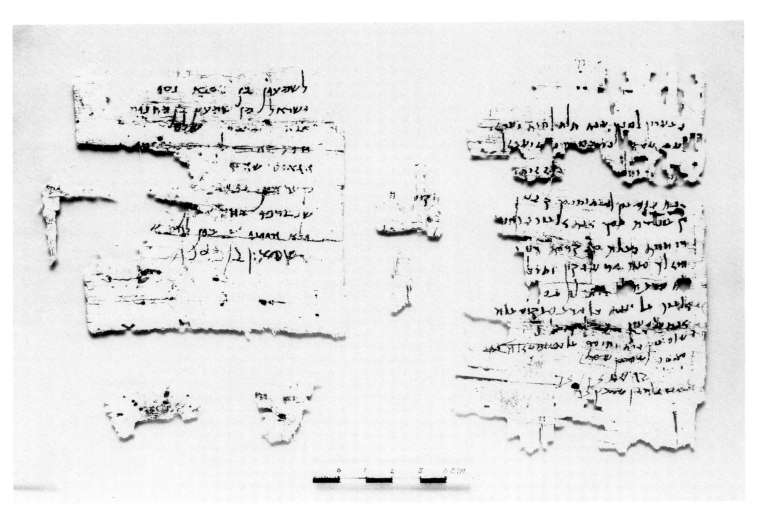

PLATE 695

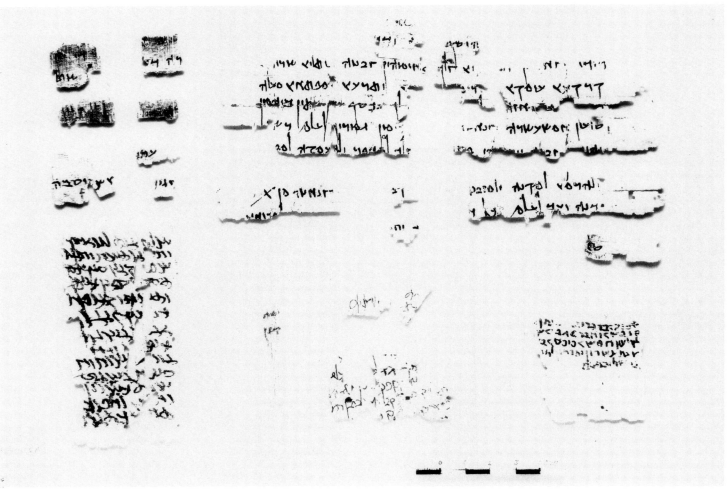

PLATE 696

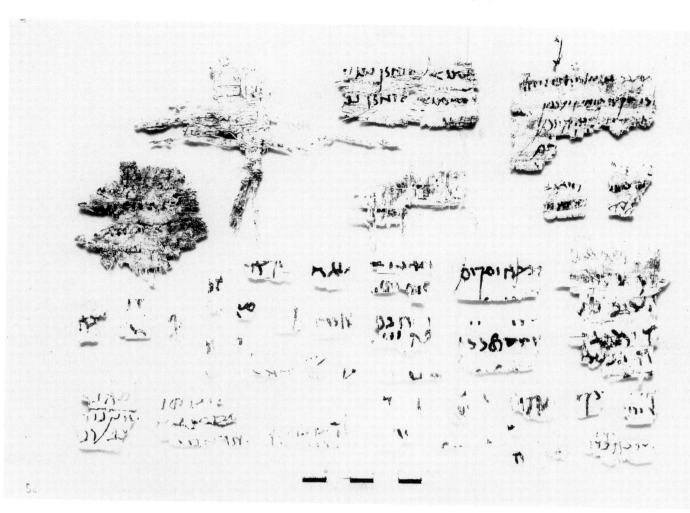

PLATE 697

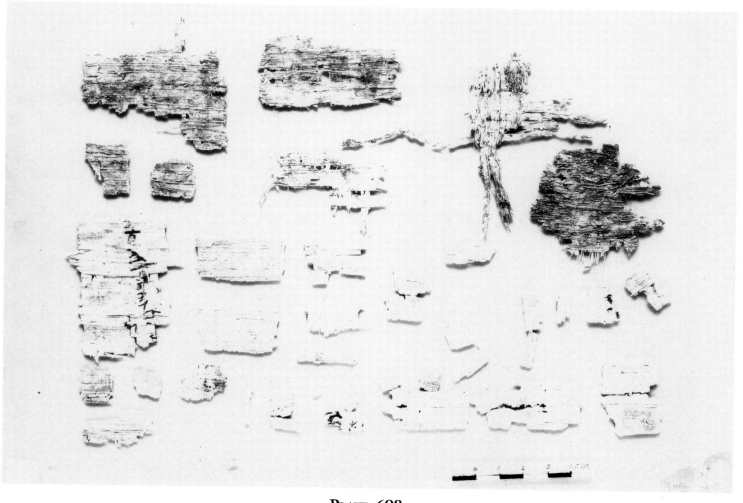

PLATE 698

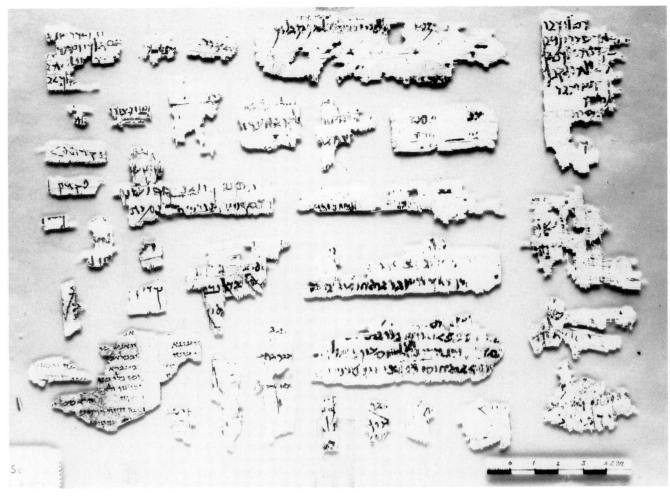

PLATE 699

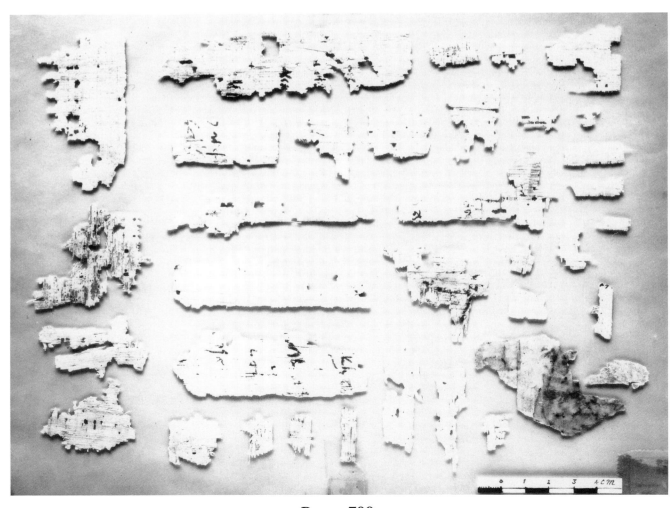

PLATE 700

PLATE 701

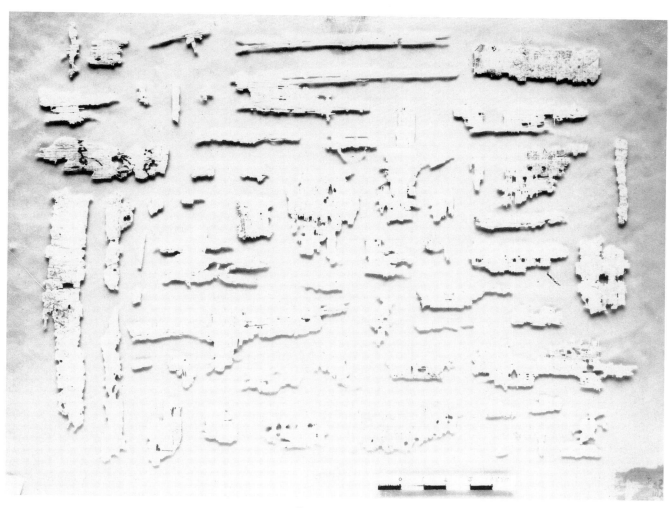

PLATE 702

PLATE 703

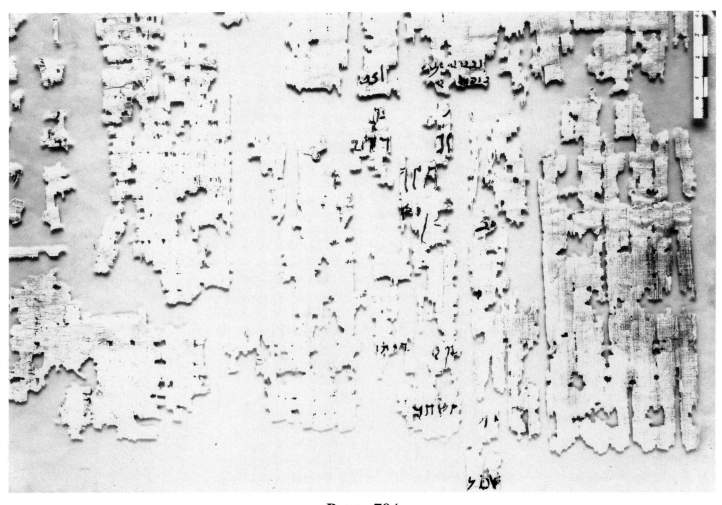

PLATE 704

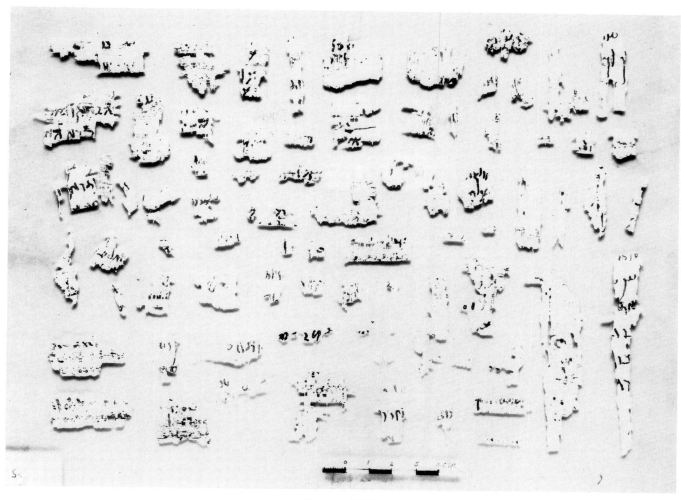

PLATE 705

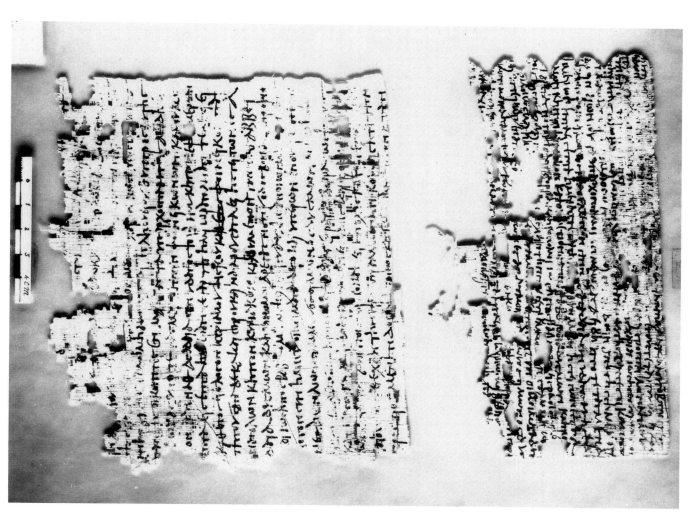

PLATE 706

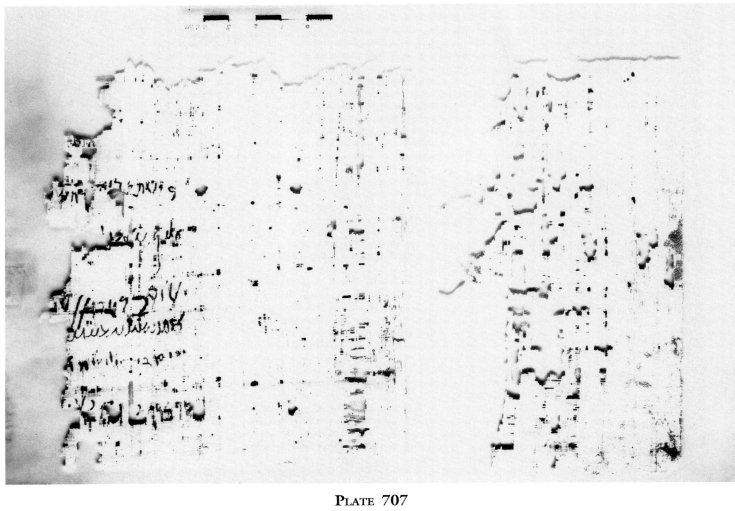

PLATE 707

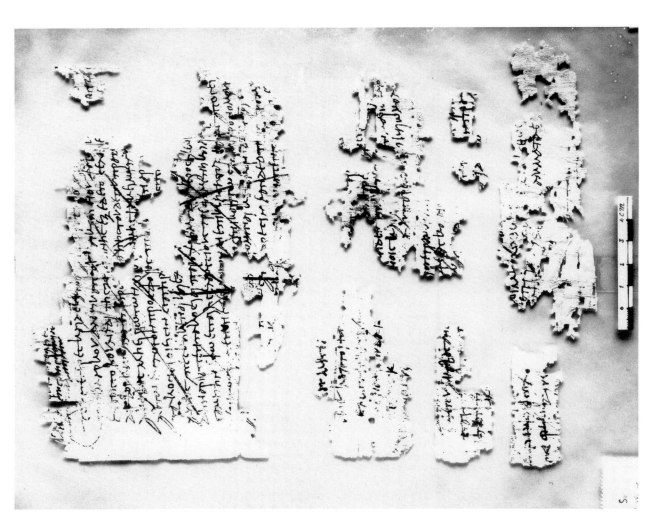

PLATE 708

PLATE 709

PLATE 710

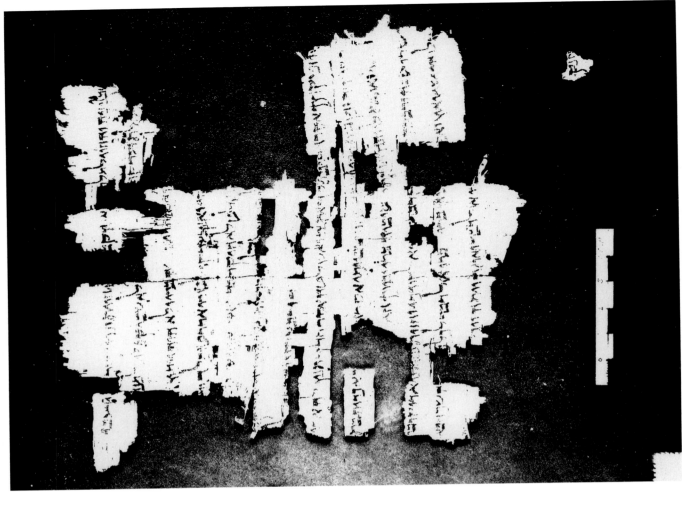

PLATE 712

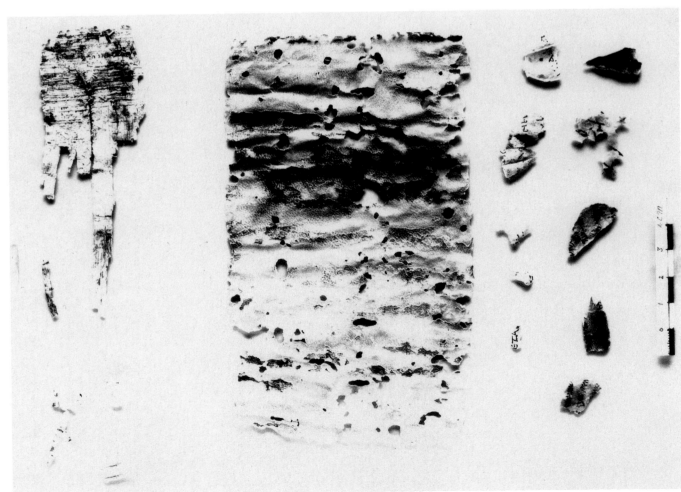

PLATE 711

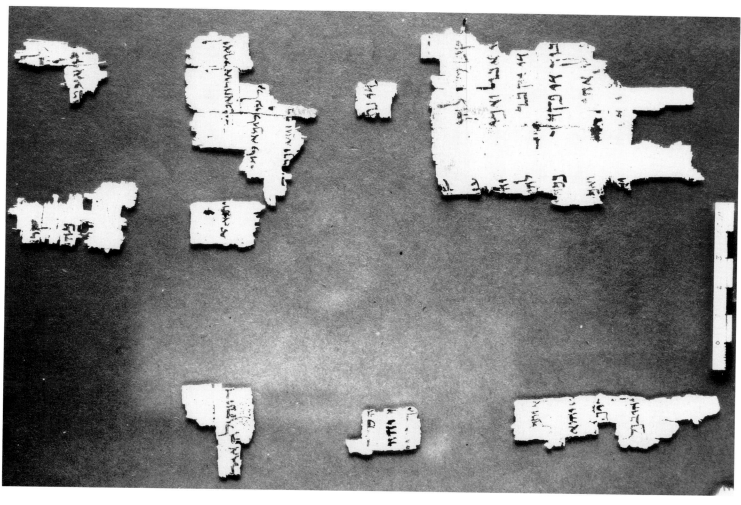

PLATE 714

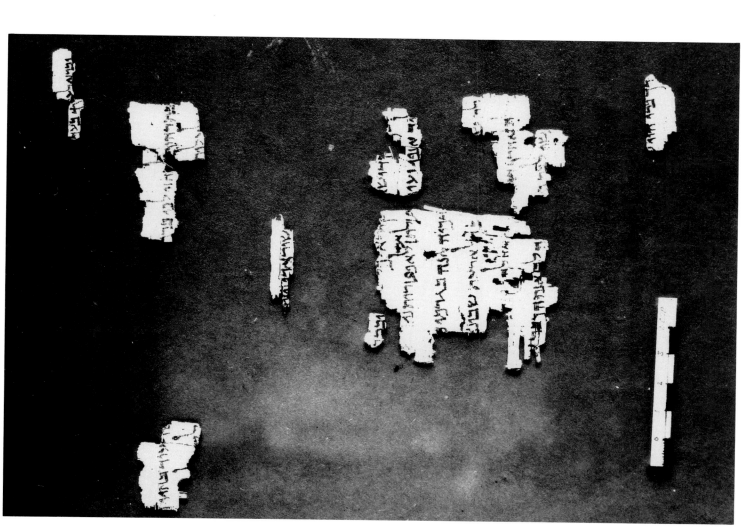

PLATE 713

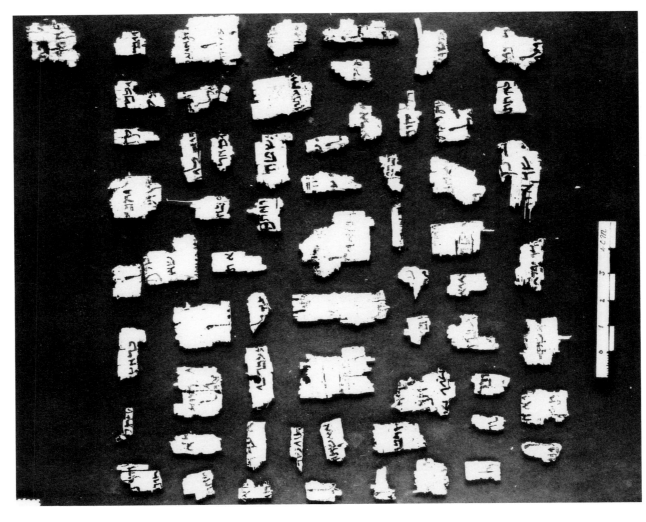

PLATE 716

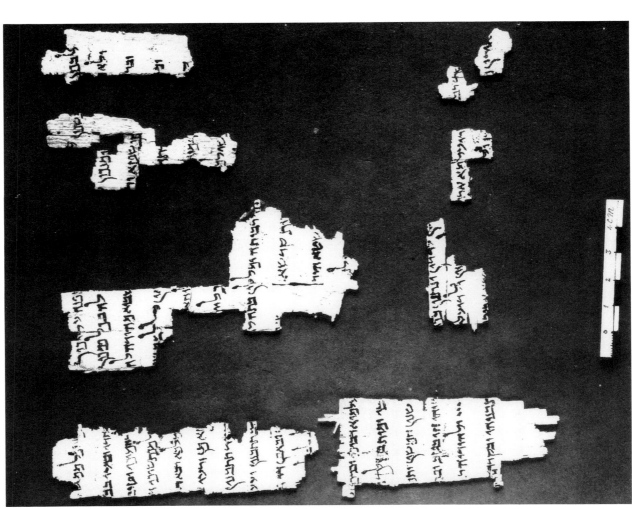

PLATE 715

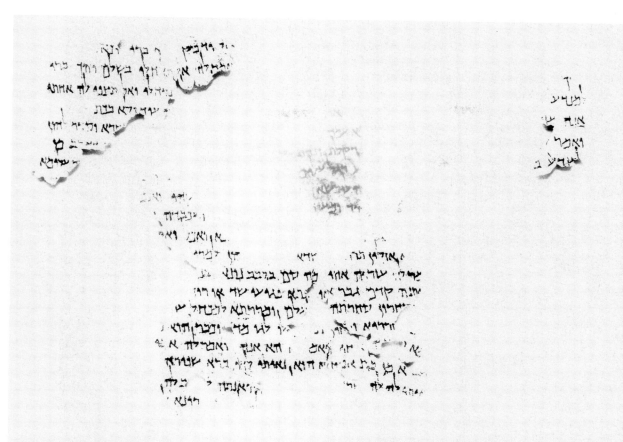

PLATE 717

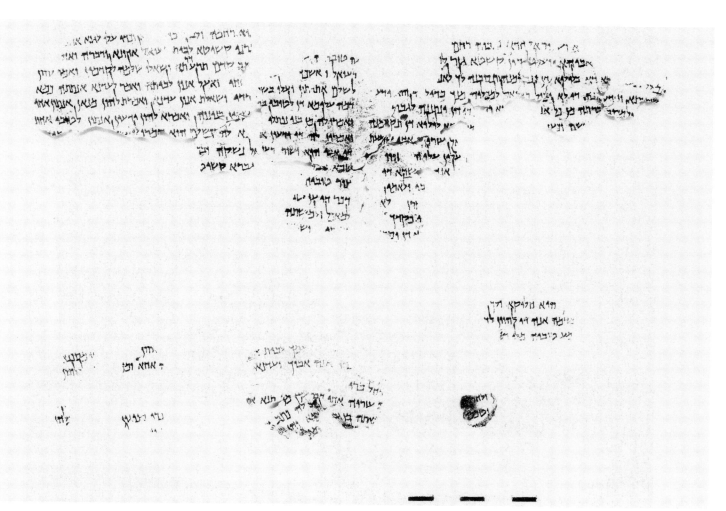

PLATE 718

PLATE 719

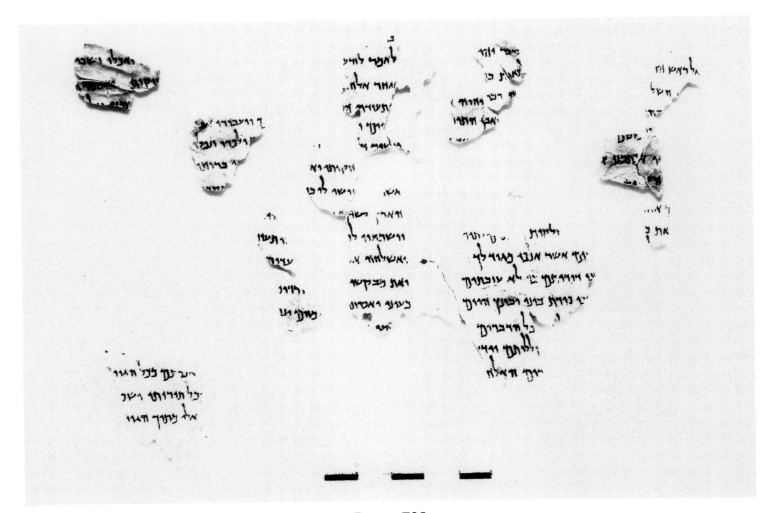

PLATE 720

PLATE 722

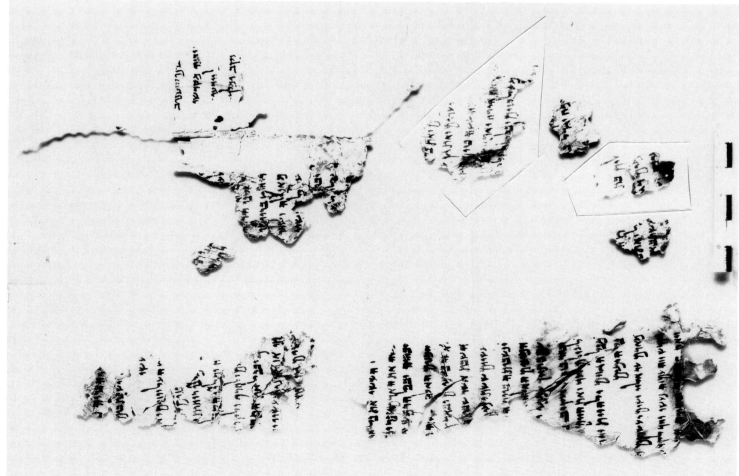

PLATE 721

PLATE 723

PLATE 724

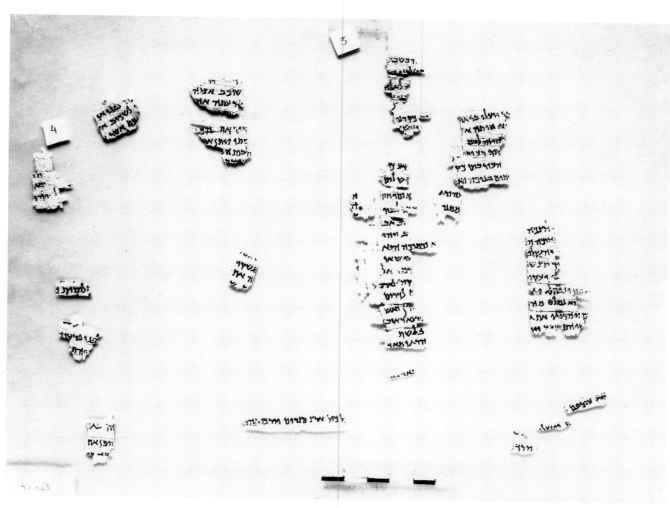

PLATE 725

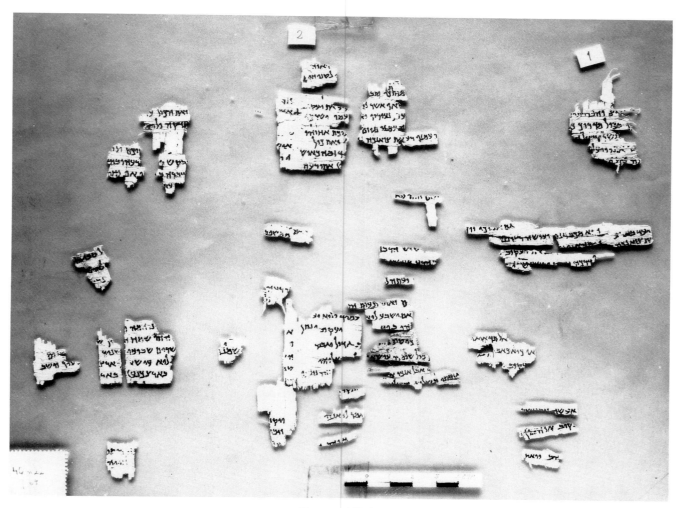

PLATE 726

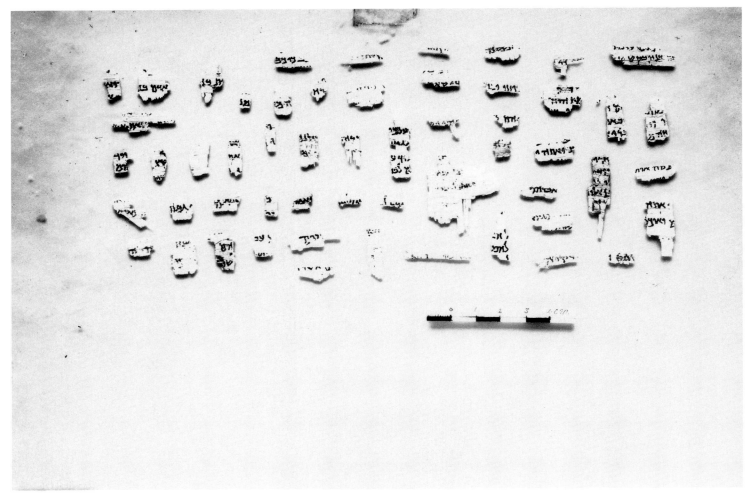

PLATE 727

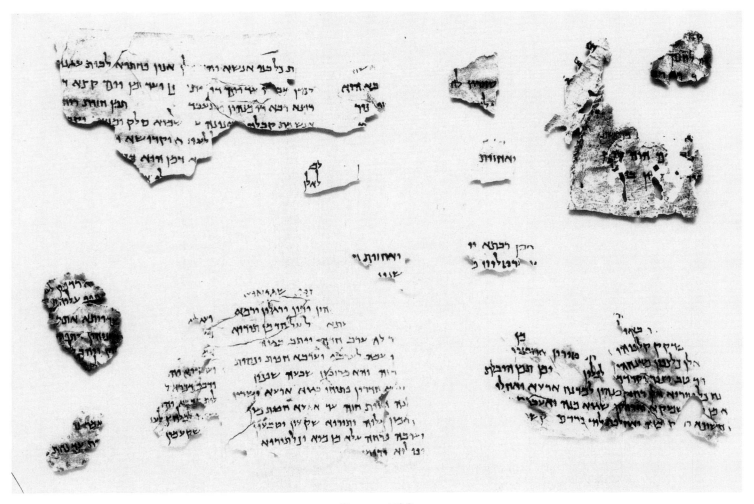

PLATE 728

PLATE 733

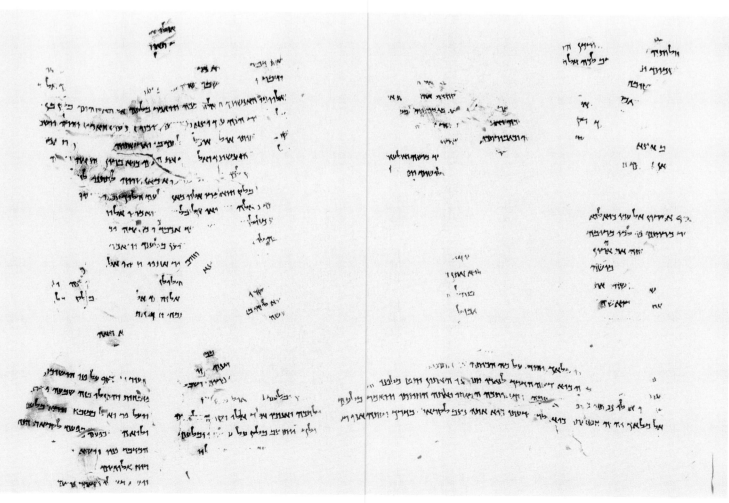

PLATE 734

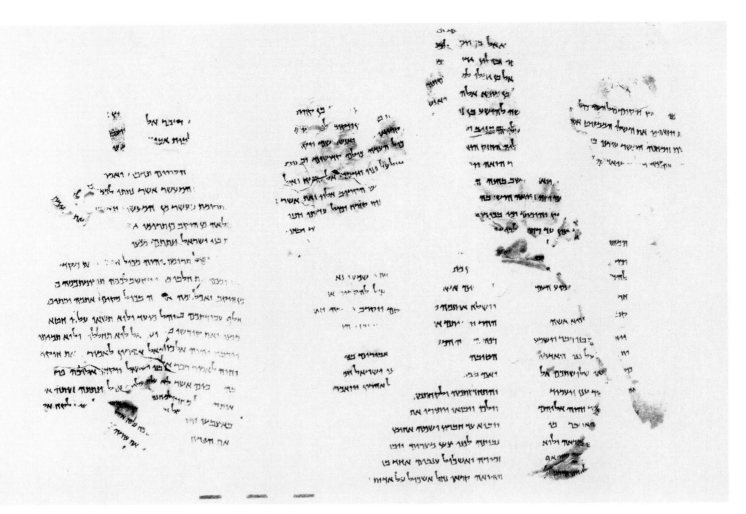

PLATE 735

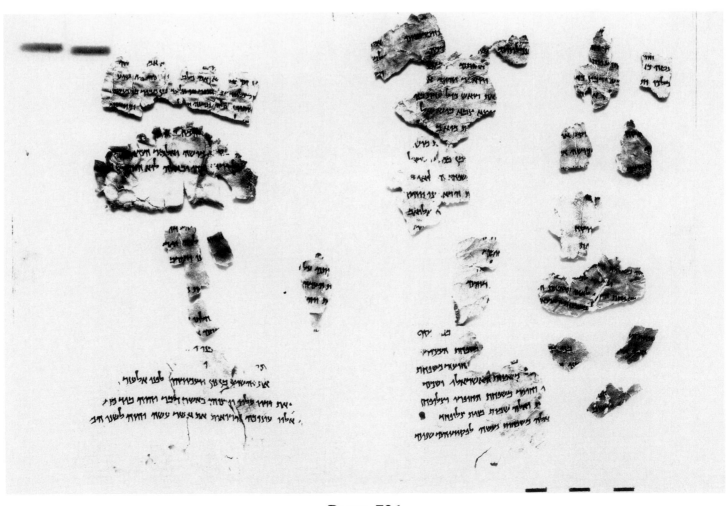

PLATE 736

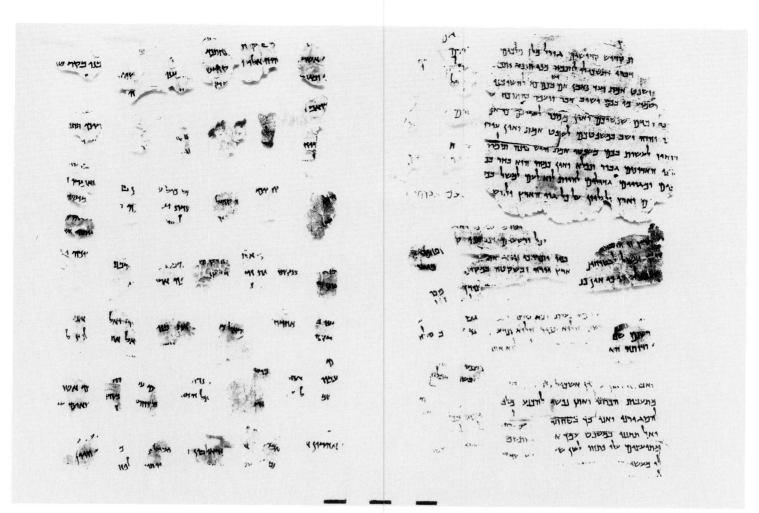

PLATE 737

PLATE 738

PLATE 739

PLATE 740

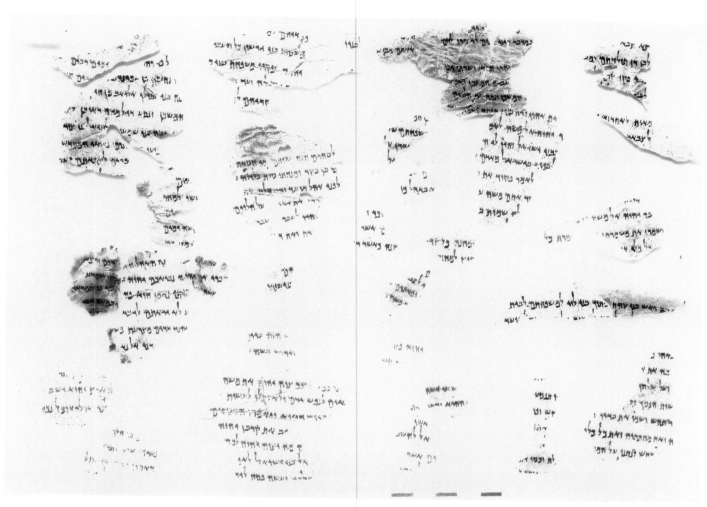

PLATE 741

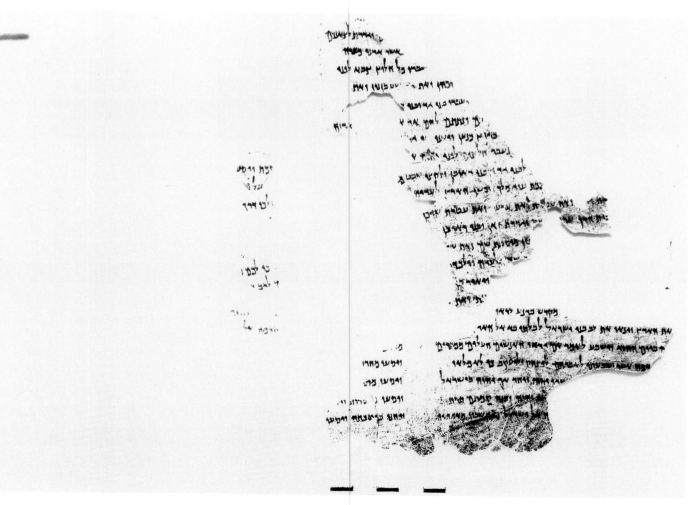

PLATE 742

PLATE 743

PLATE 744

PLATE 745

PLATE 746

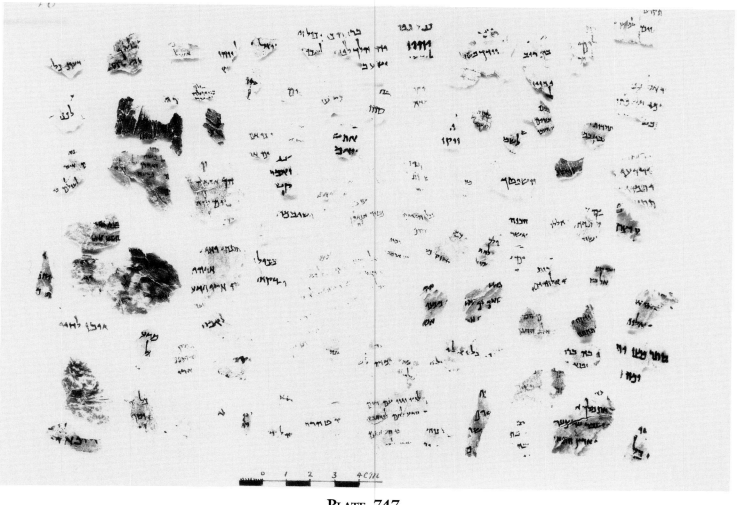

PLATE 747

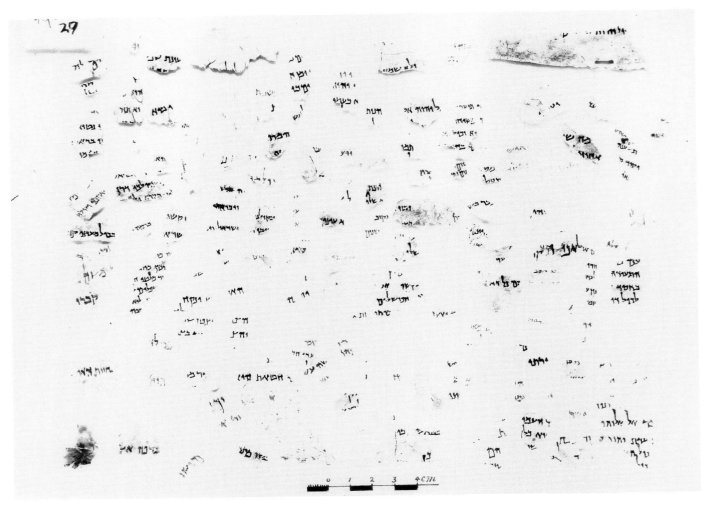

PLATE 748

PLATE 749

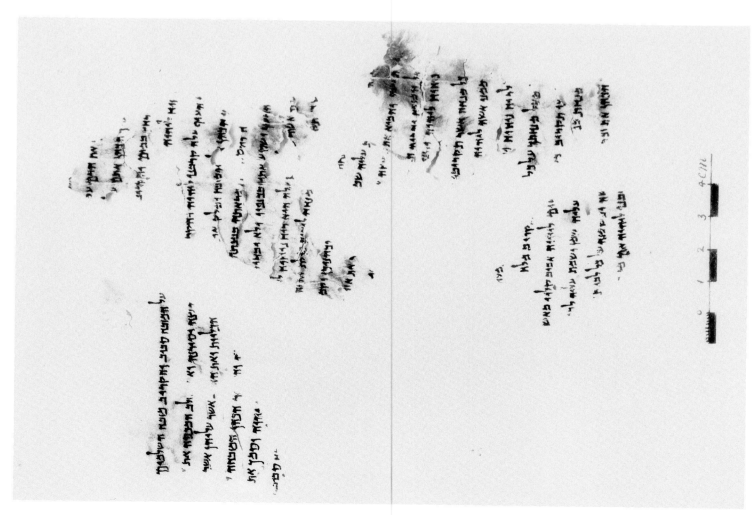

PLATE 750

PLATE 751

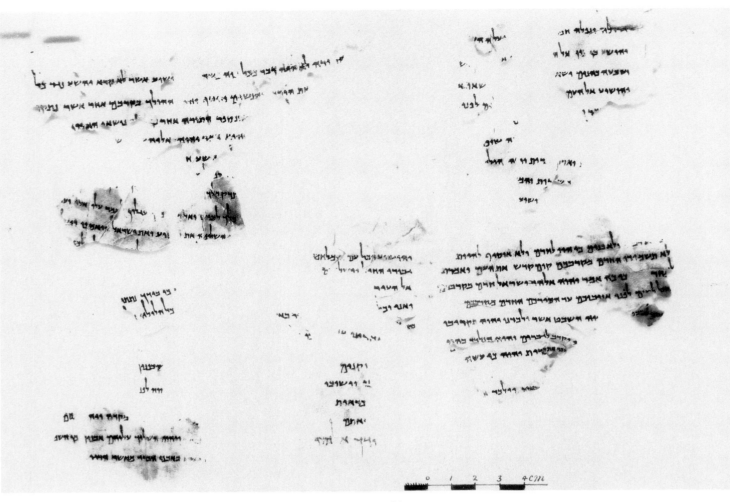

Plate 752

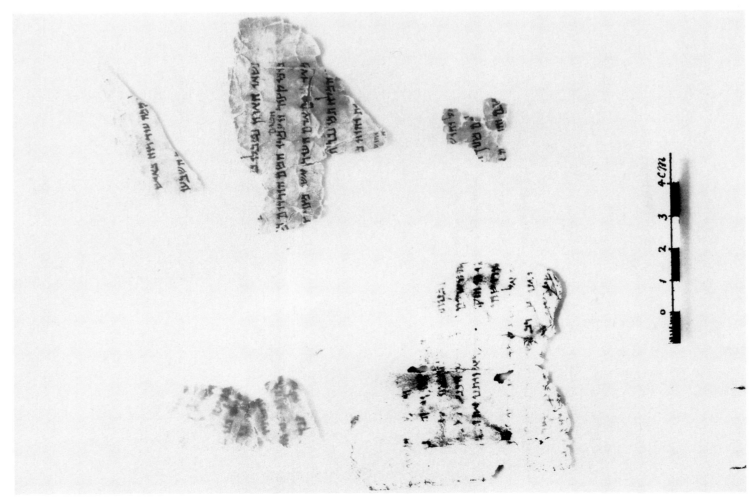

Plate 753

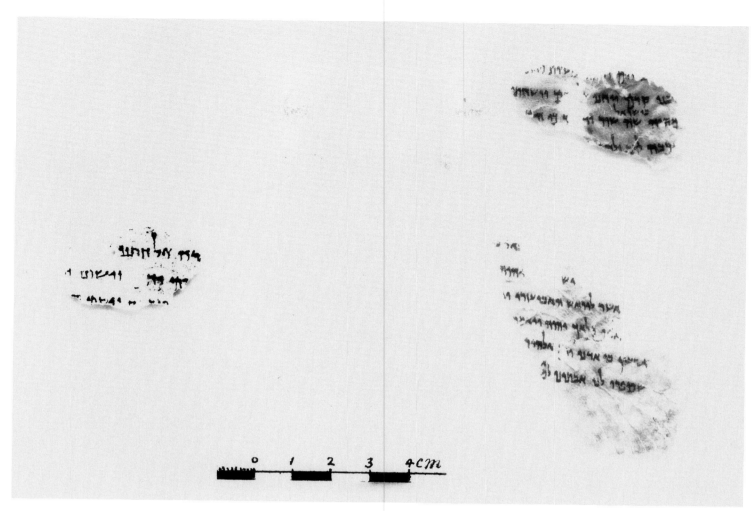

PLATE 754

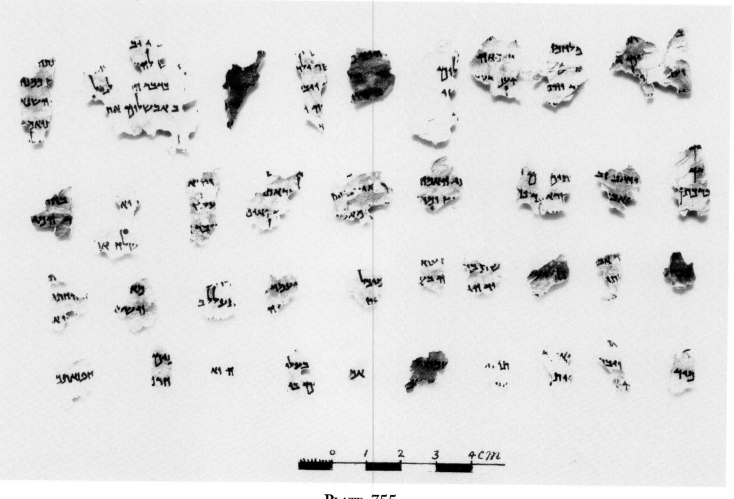

PLATE 755

PLATE 756

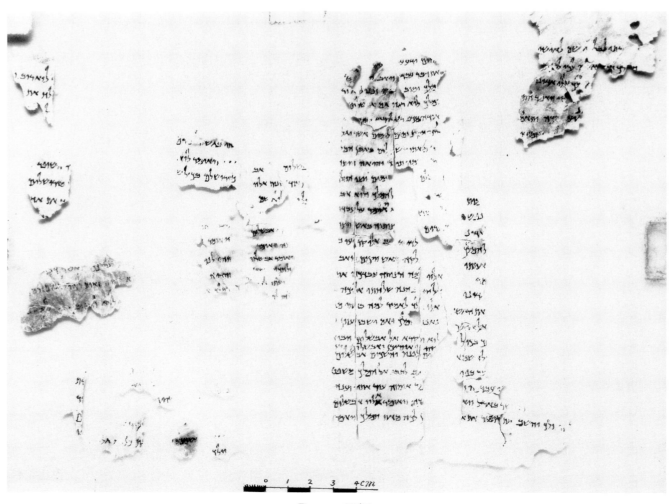

PLATE 757

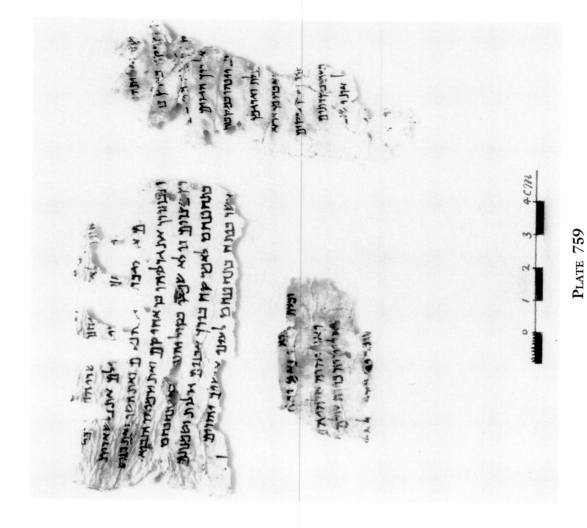

PLATE 759

PLATE 758

PLATE 760

PLATE 761

PLATE 762

PLATE 763

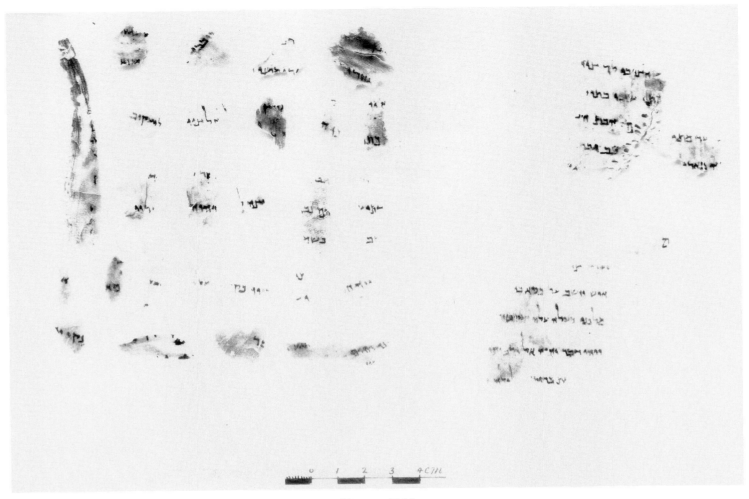

PLATE 764

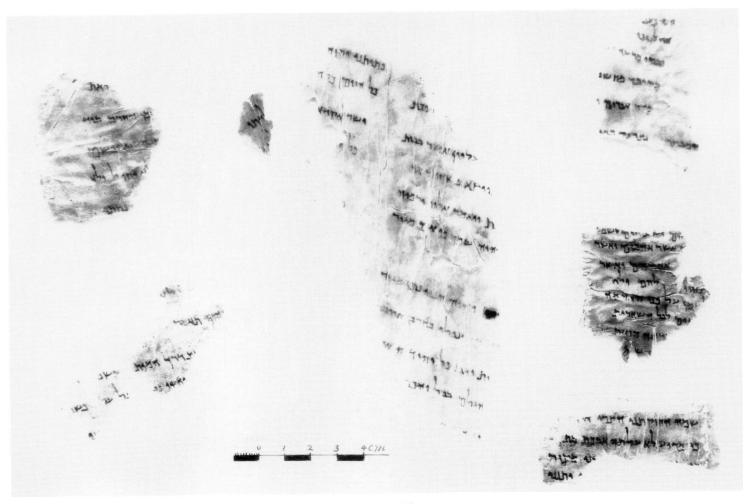

PLATE 765

PLATE 766

PLATE 767

PLATE 768

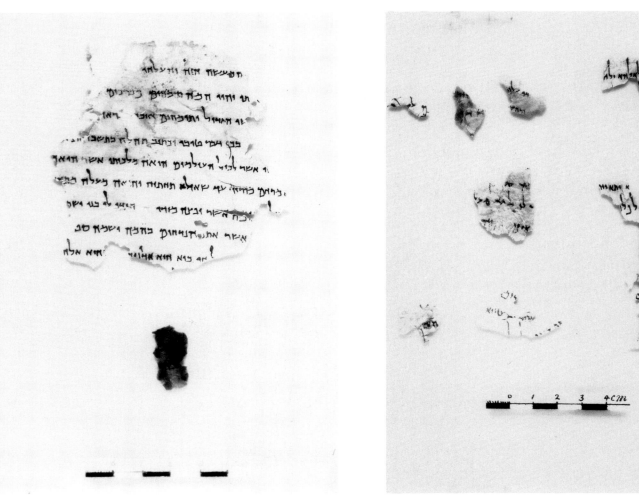

PLATE 769

PLATE 770

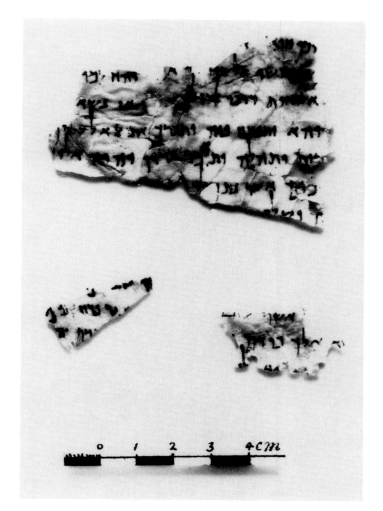

PLATE 771

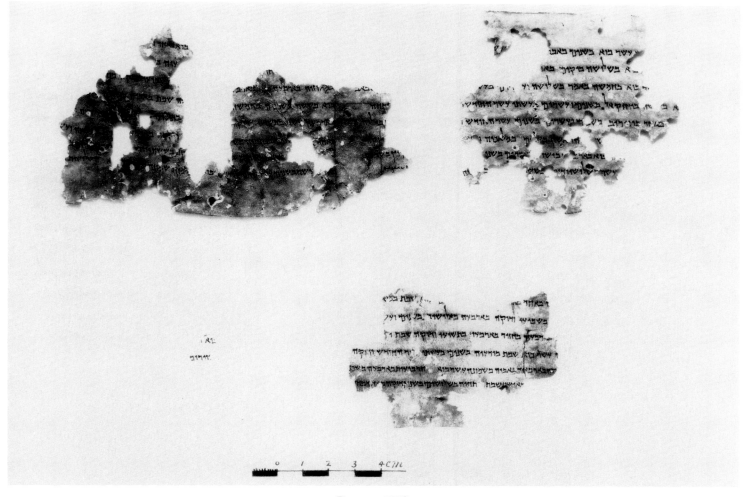

PLATE 772

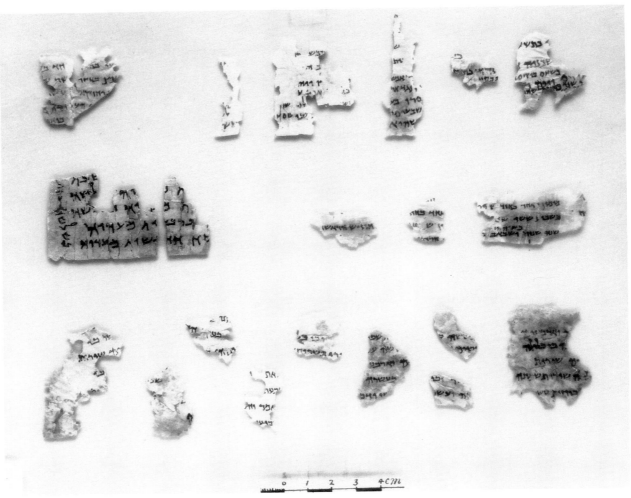

PLATE 777

PLATE 778

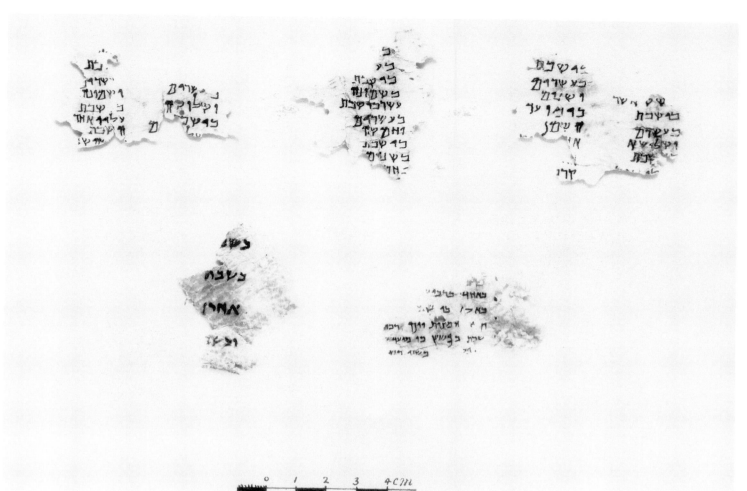

PLATE 779

PLATE 780

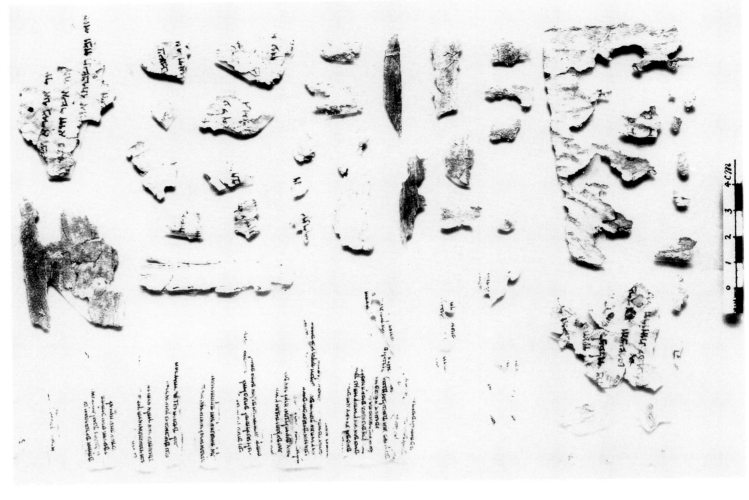

PLATE 782

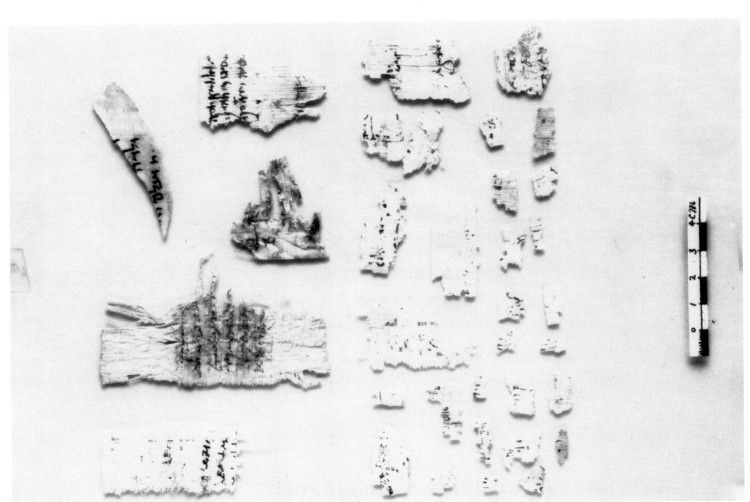

PLATE 781

PLATE 783

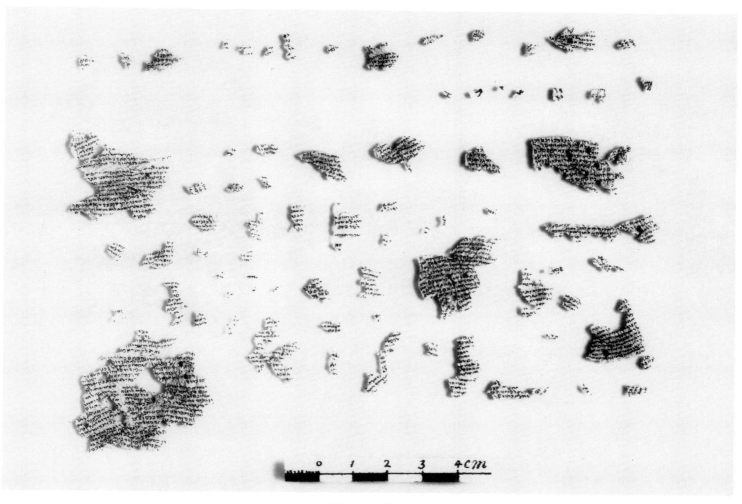

PLATE 784

PLATE 786

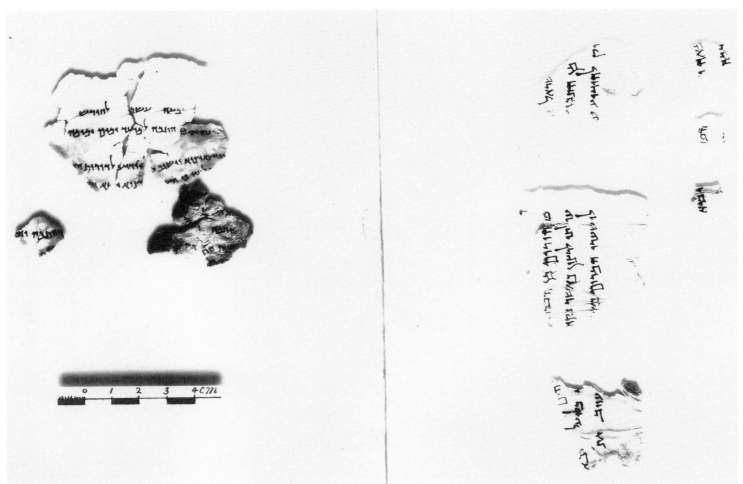

PLATE 785

PLATE 788

PLATE 787

PLATE 789

PLATE 790

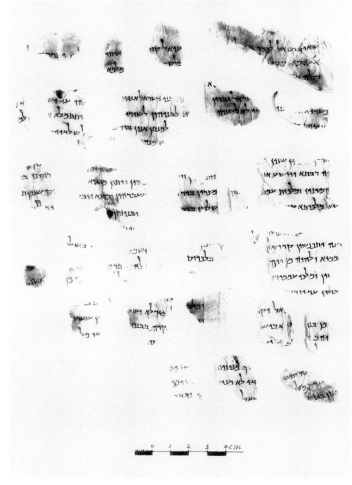

PLATE 791

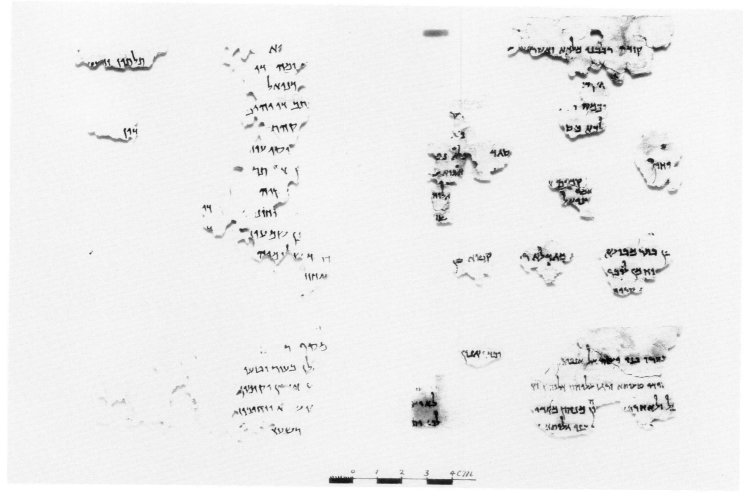

PLATE 792

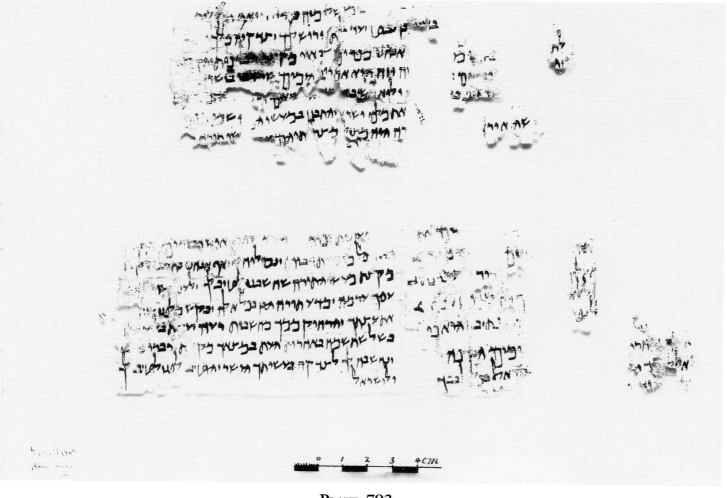

PLATE 793

PLATE 795

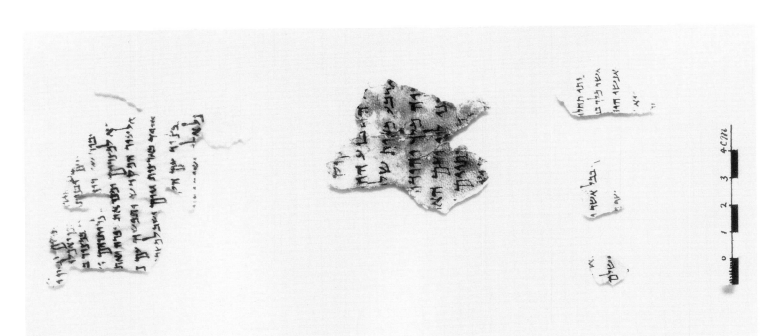

PLATE 794

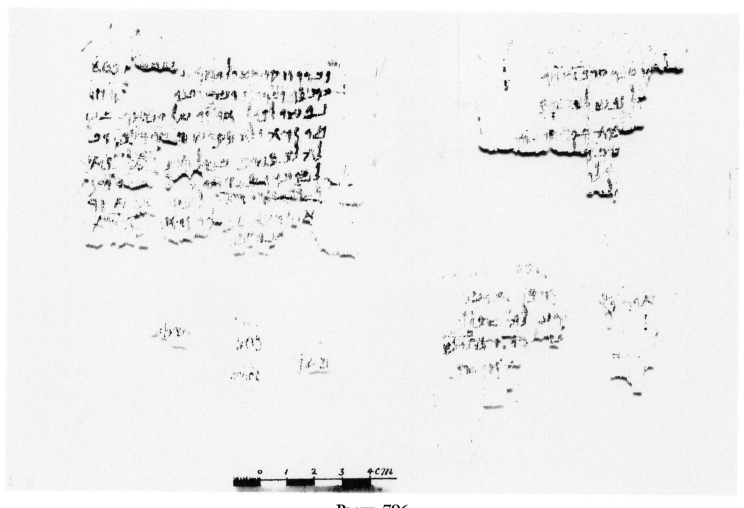

PLATE 796

PLATE 797

Plate 798

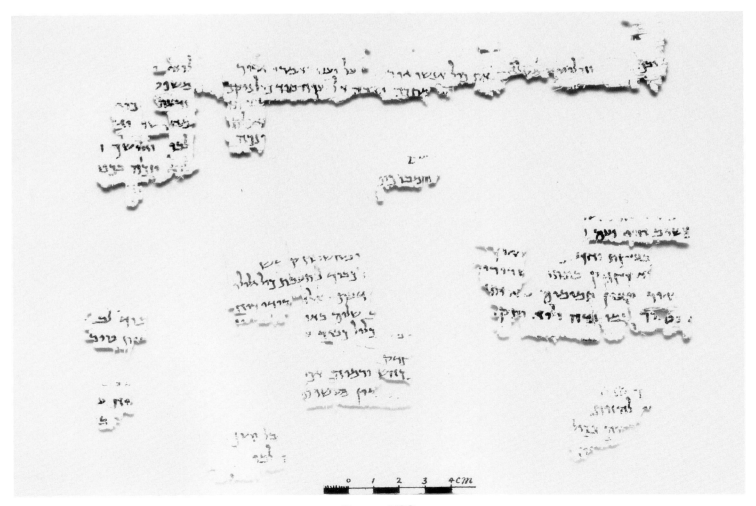

Plate 799

PLATE 800

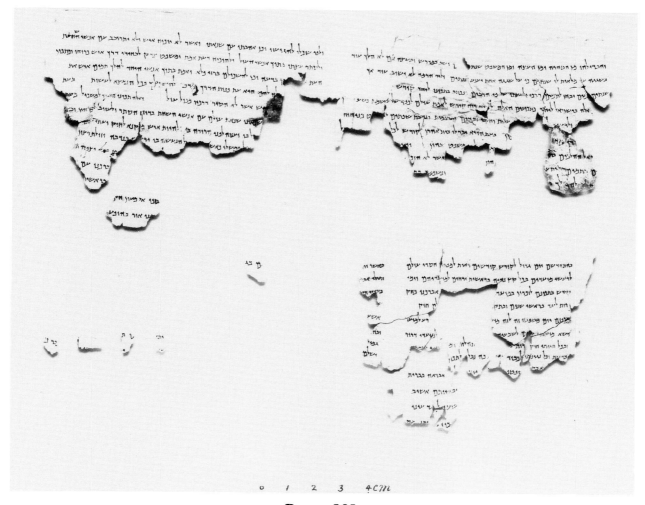

PLATE 801

PLATE 802

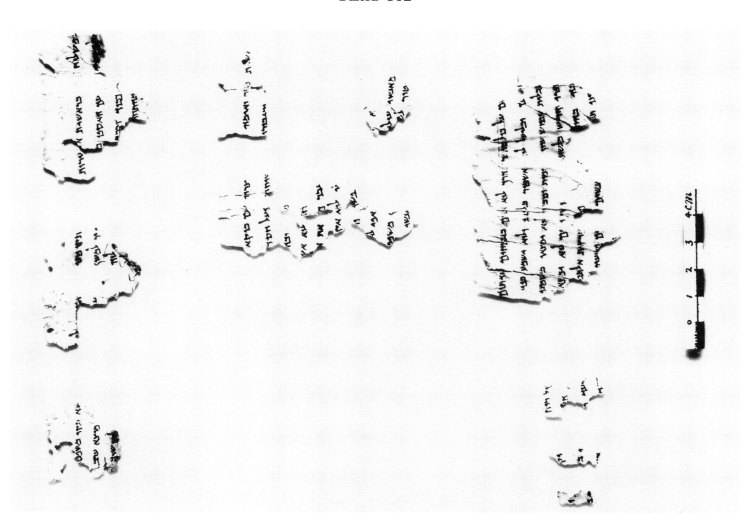

PLATE 803

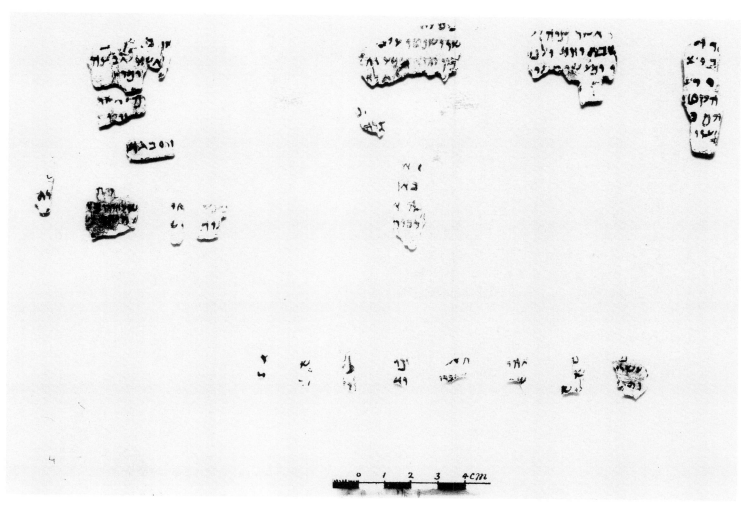

PLATE 804

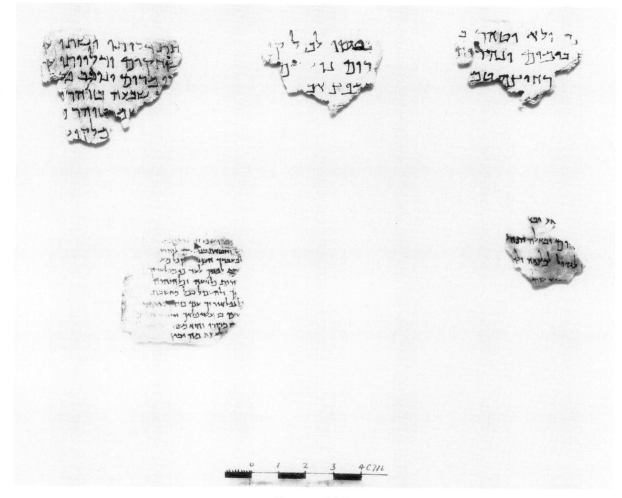

PLATE 805

Plate 806

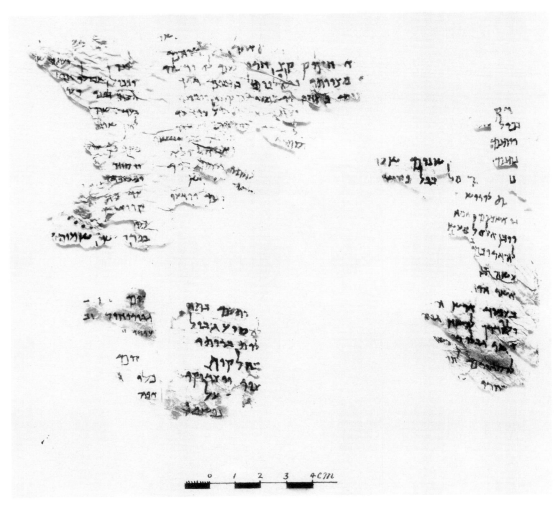

Plate 807

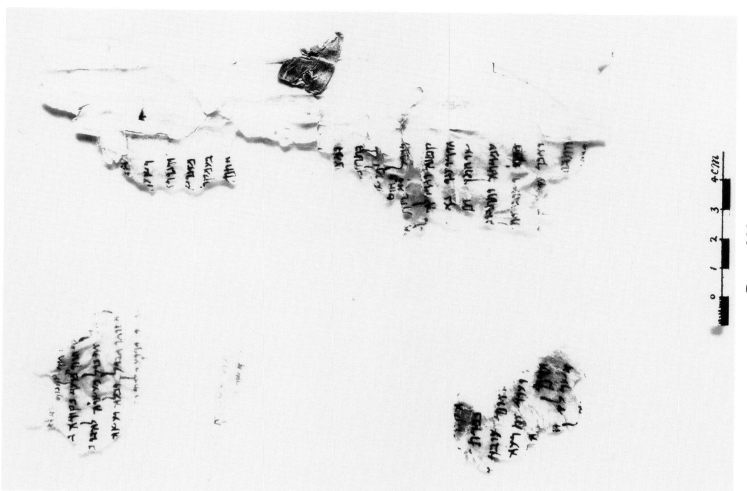

PLATE 808

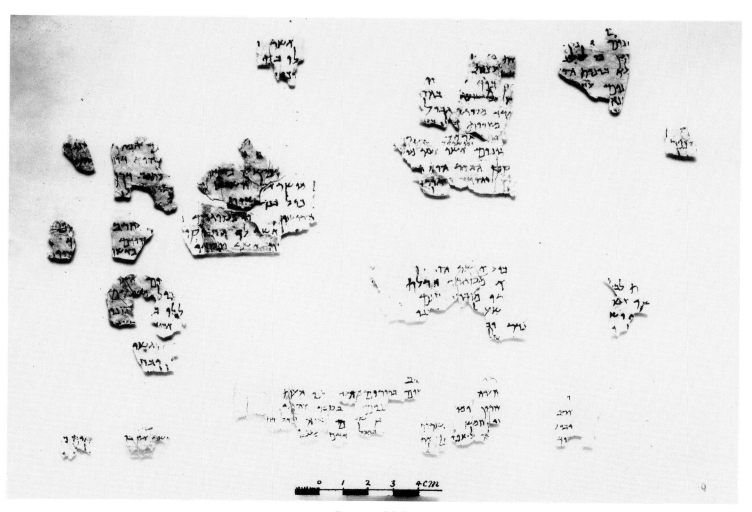

PLATE 809

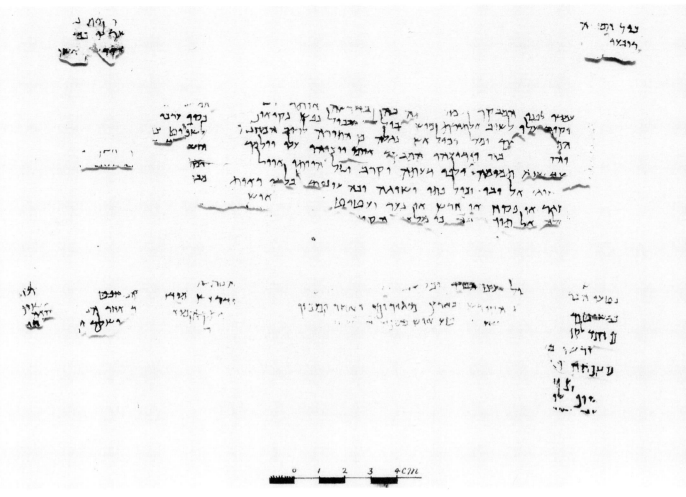

PLATE 810

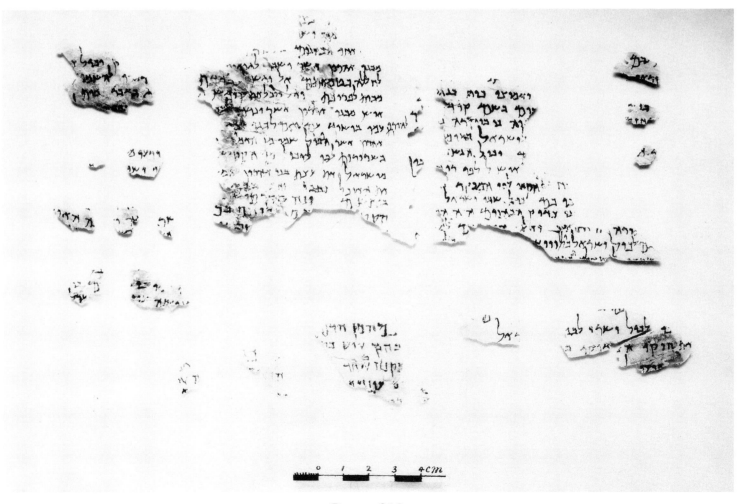

PLATE 811

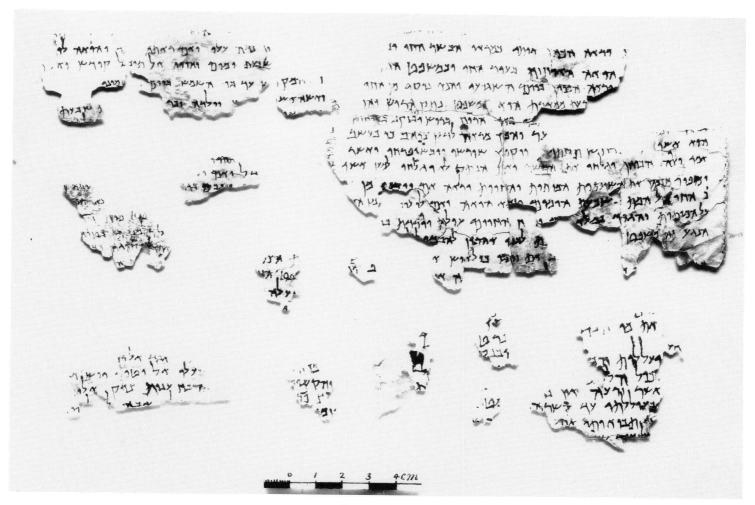

PLATE 812

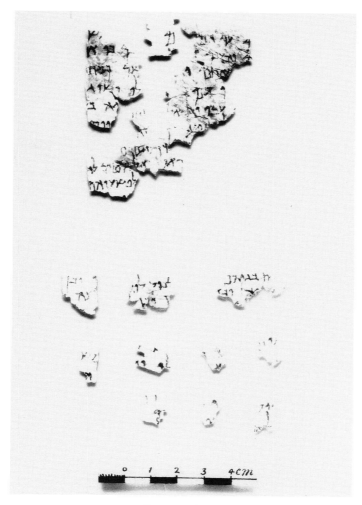

PLATE 813

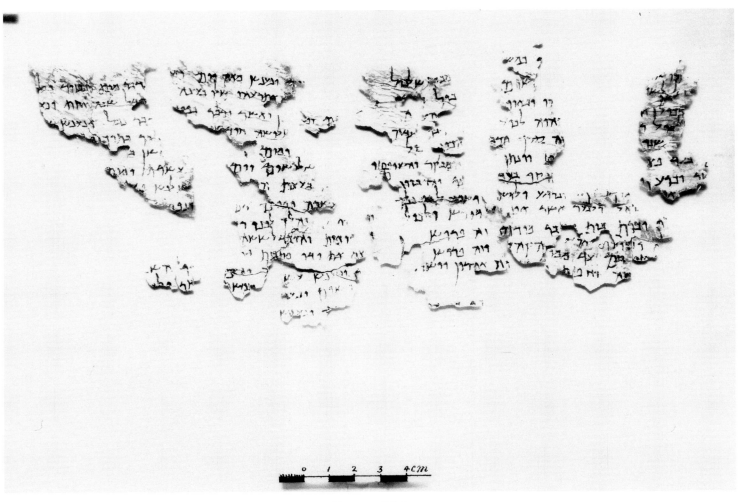

PLATE 814

PLATE 815

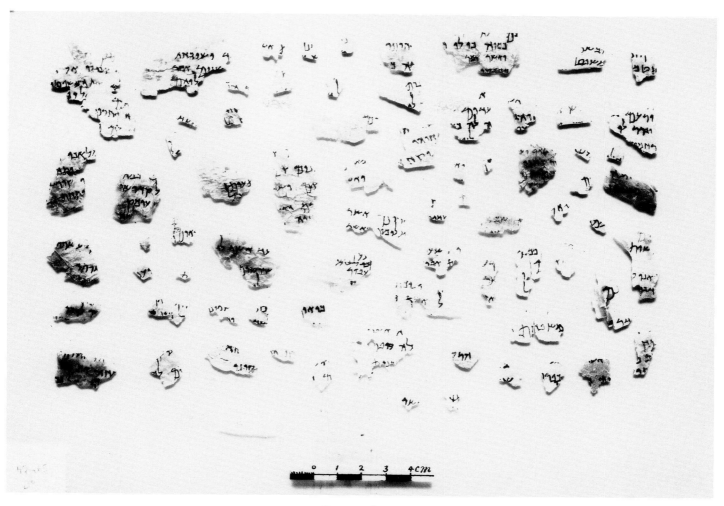

PLATE 816

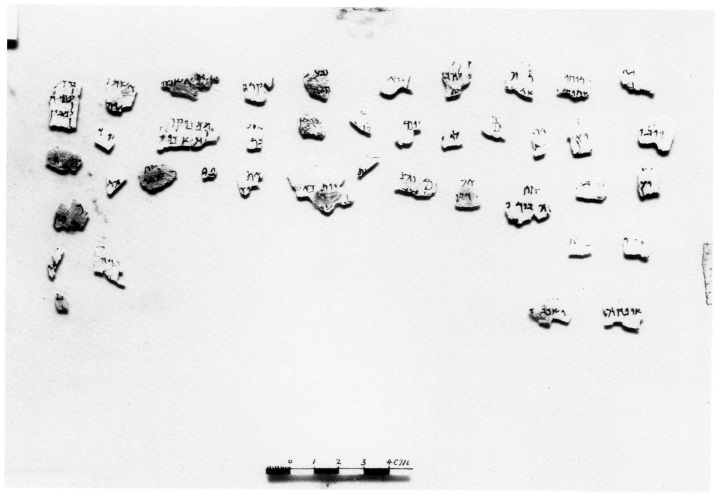

PLATE 817

PLATE 818

PLATE 819

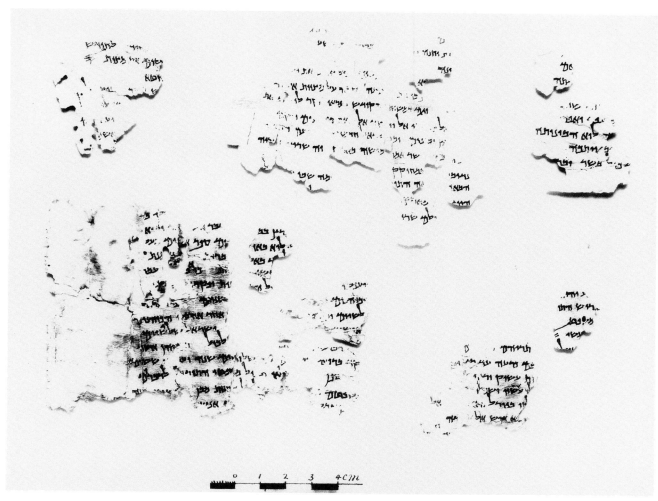

PLATE 820

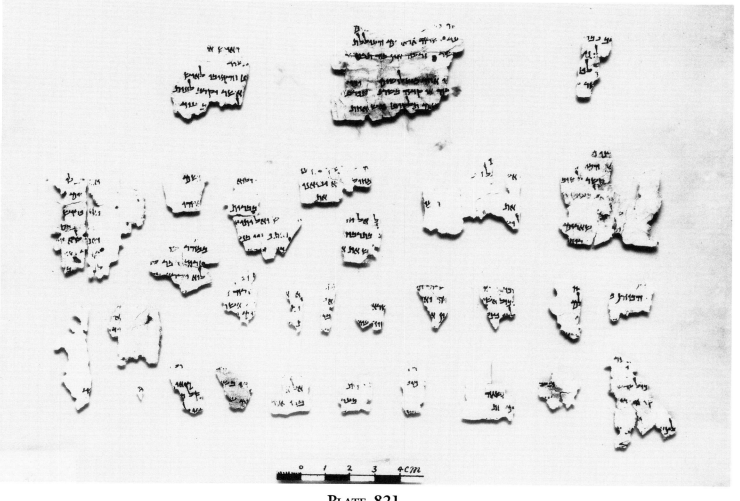

PLATE 821

PLATE 822

PLATE 823

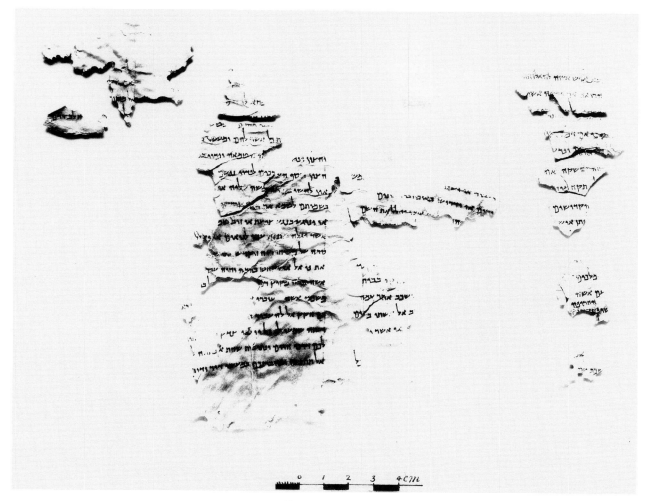

PLATE 824

PLATE 825

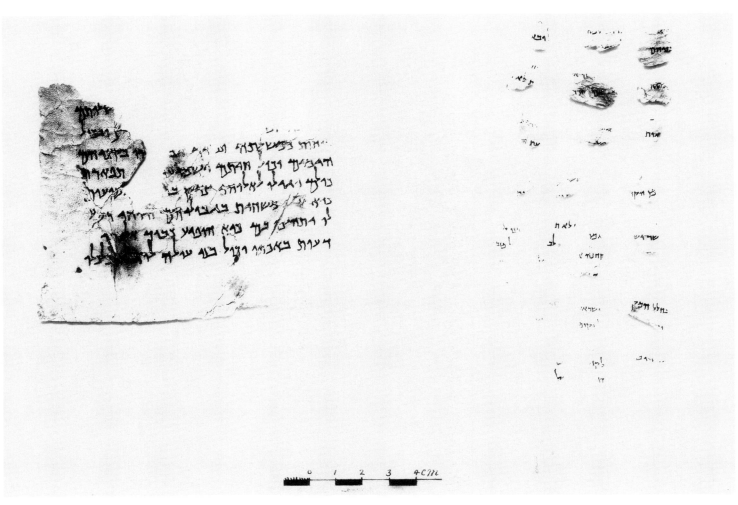

PLATE 826

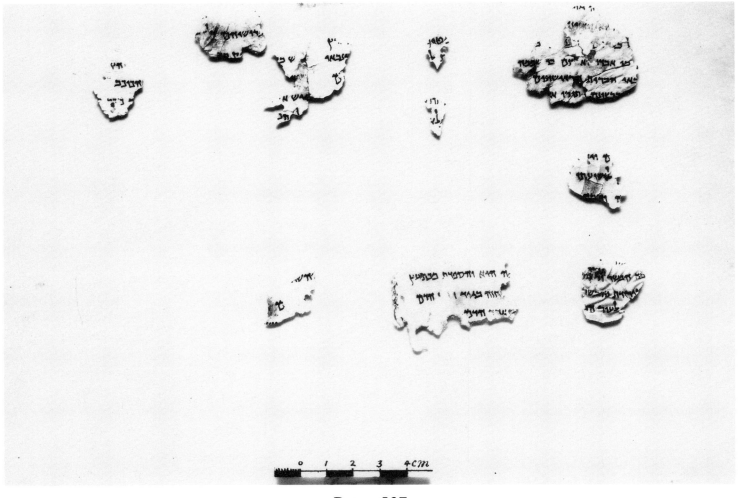

PLATE 827

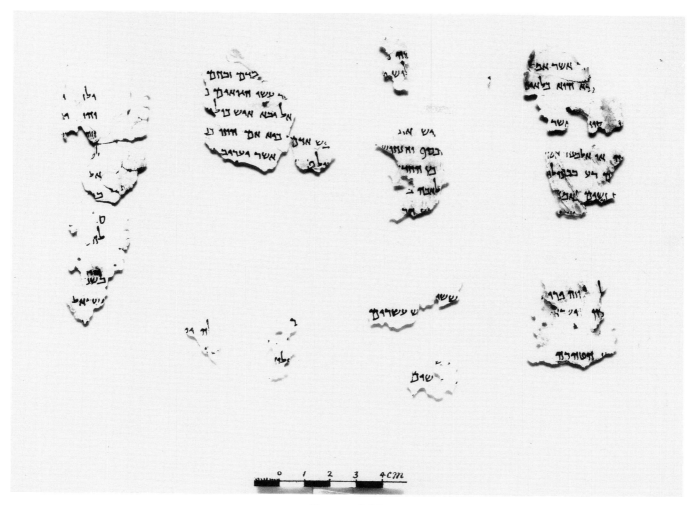

PLATE 828

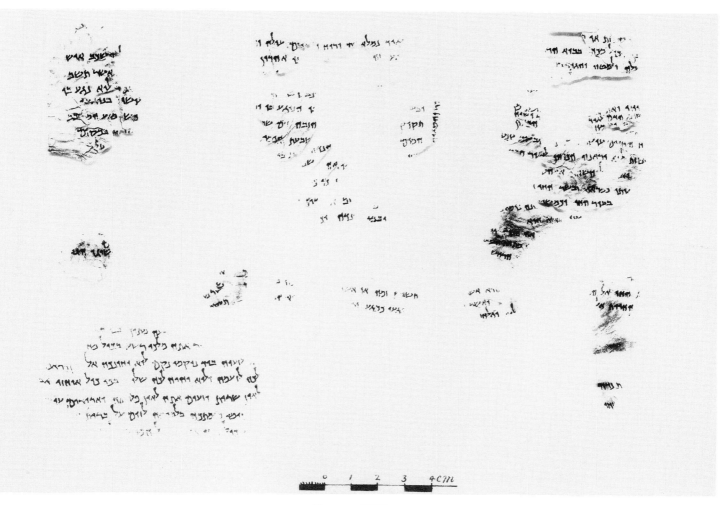

PLATE 829

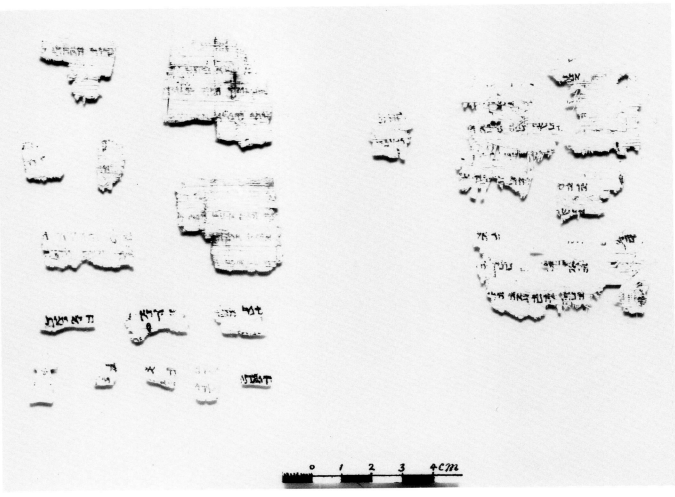

PLATE 830

PLATE 831

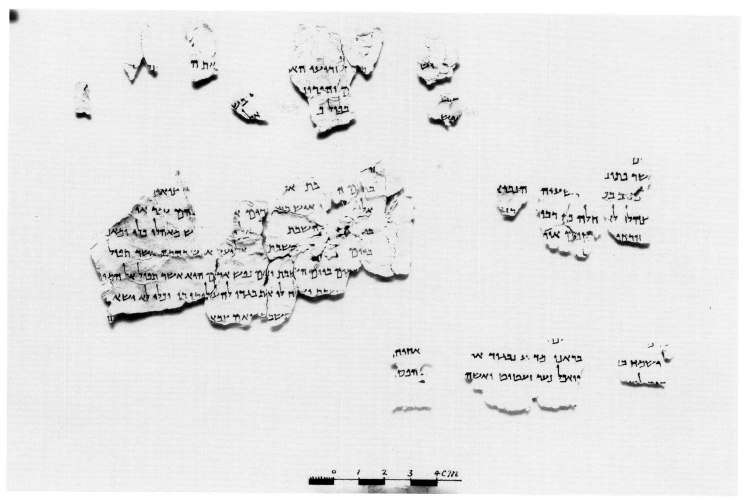

PLATE 832

PLATE 833

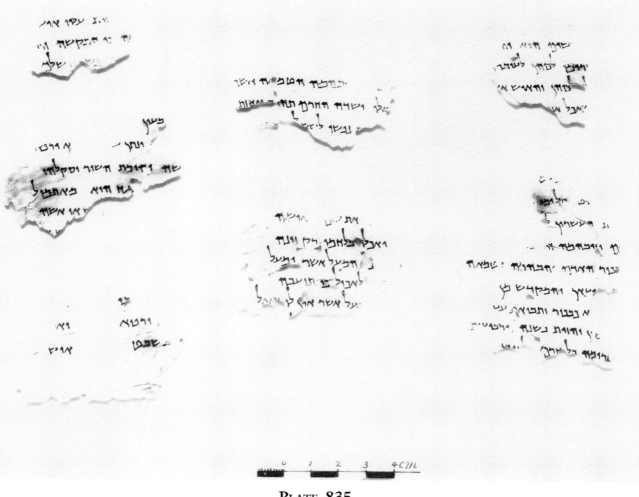

PLATE 834

PLATE 835

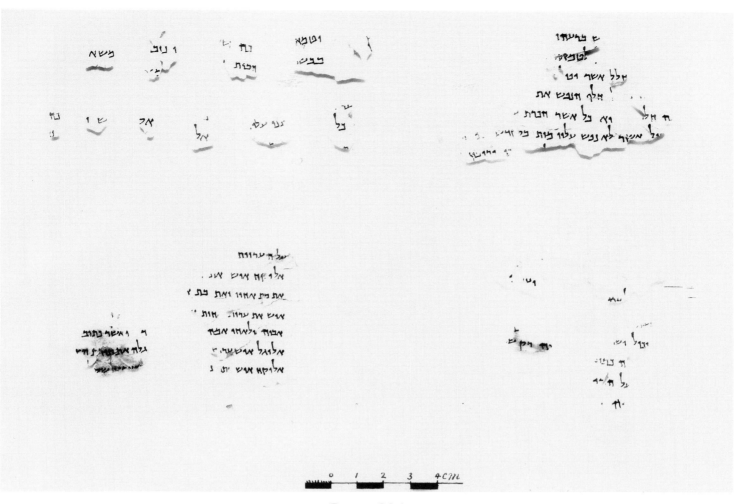

PLATE 836

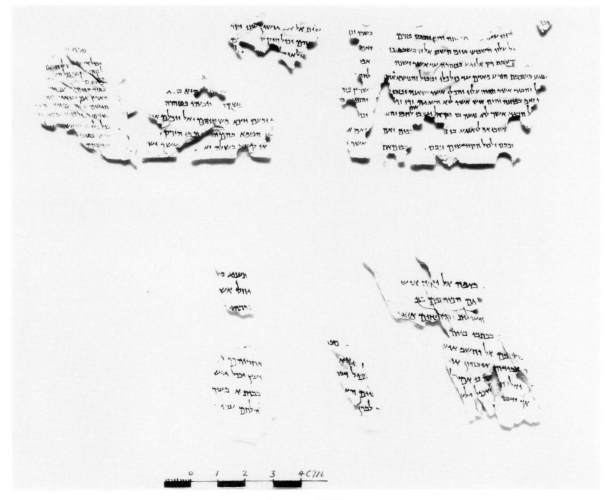

PLATE 837

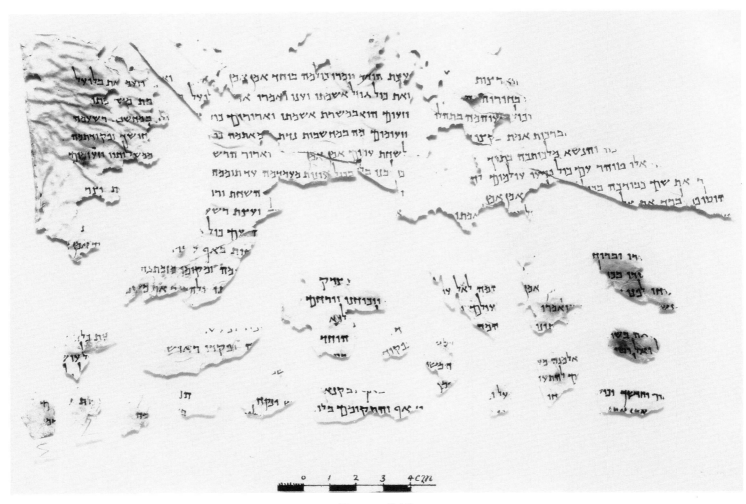

PLATE 842

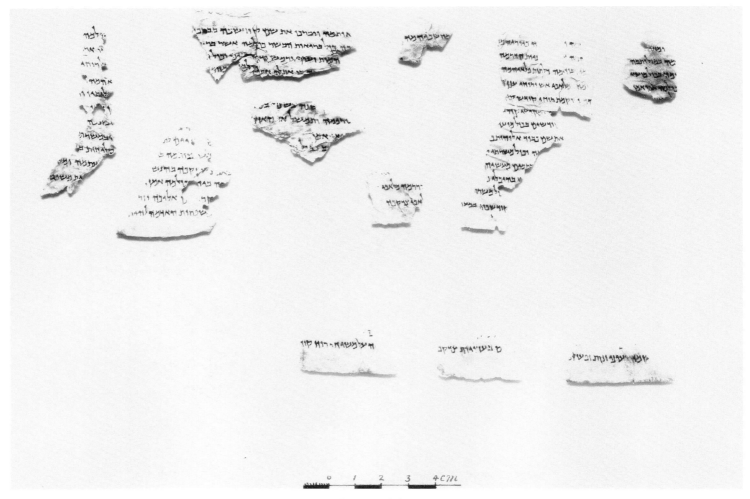

PLATE 843

PLATE 844

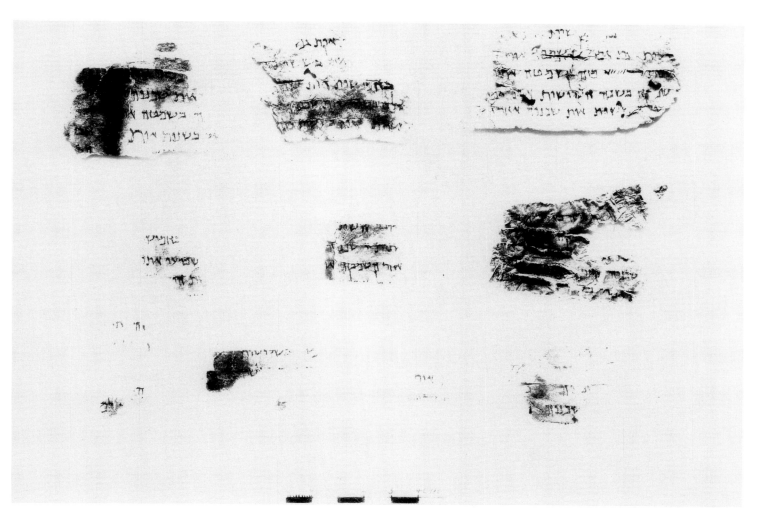

PLATE 845

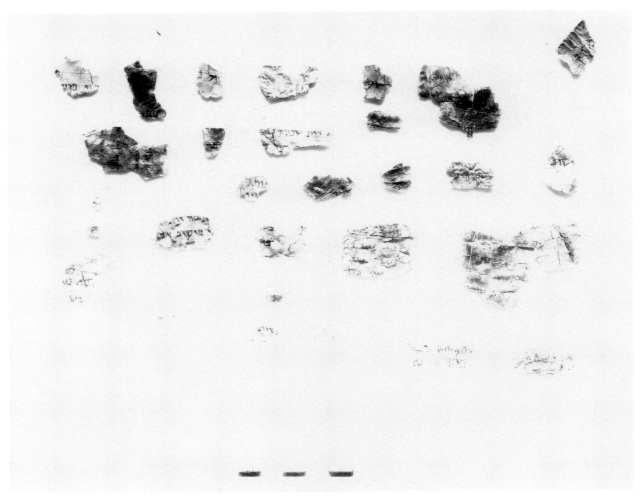

PLATE 846

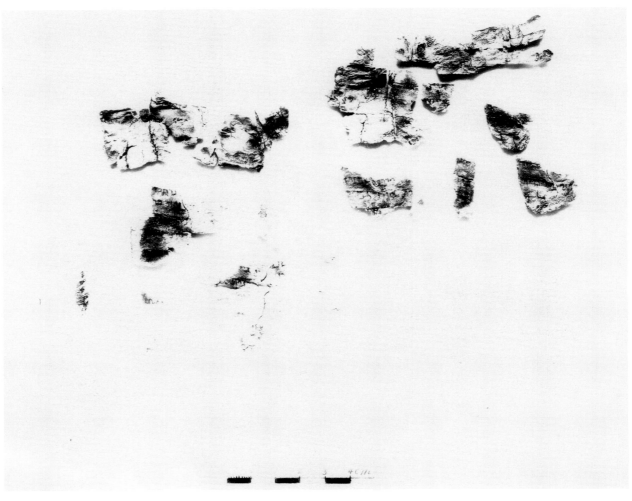

PLATE 847

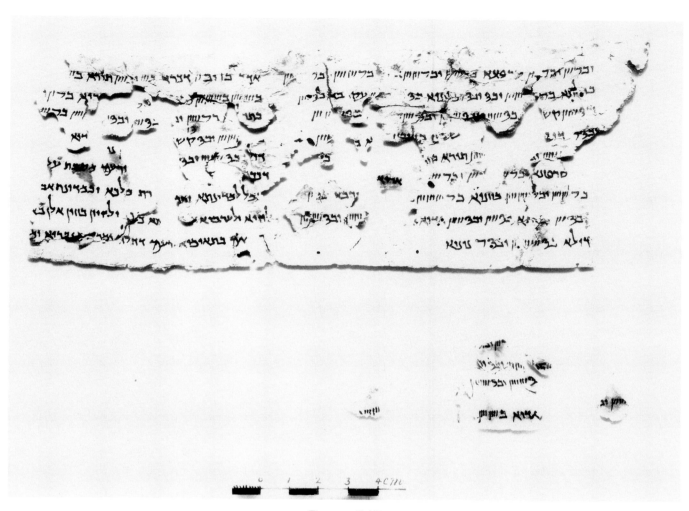

PLATE 848

PLATE 849

PLATE 850

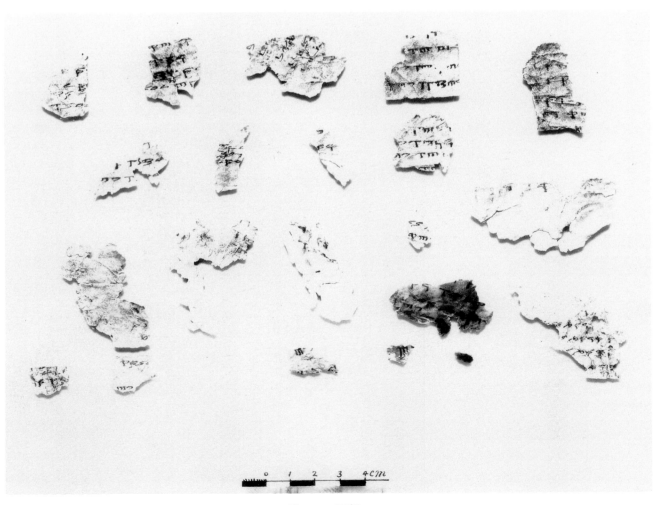

PLATE 851

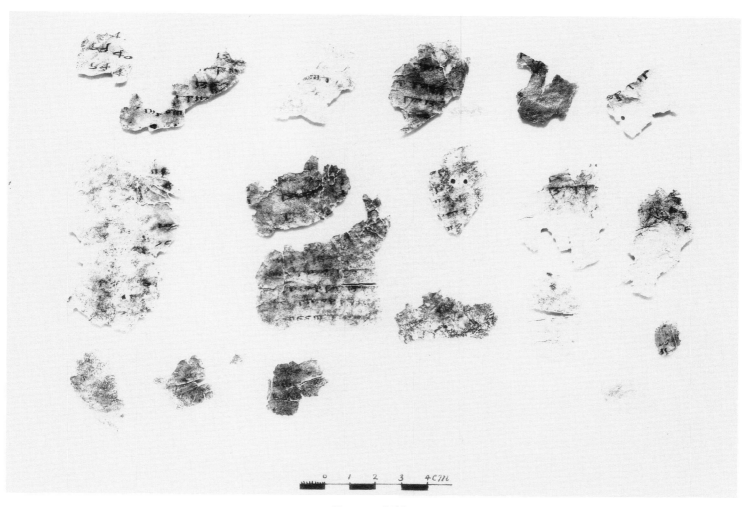

PLATE 852

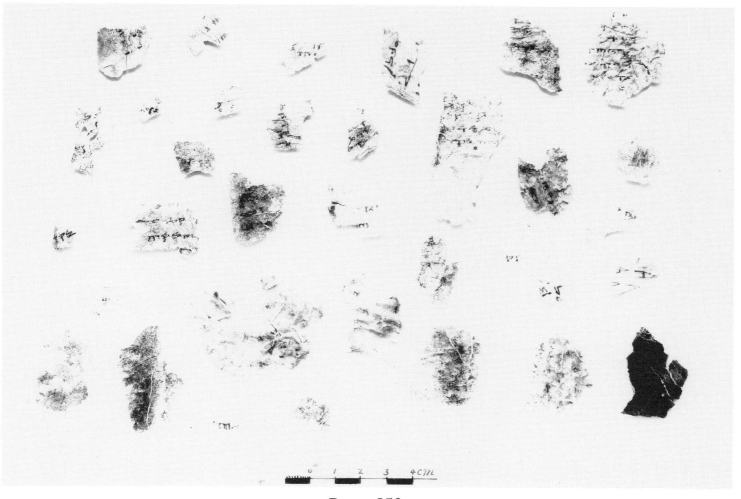

PLATE 853

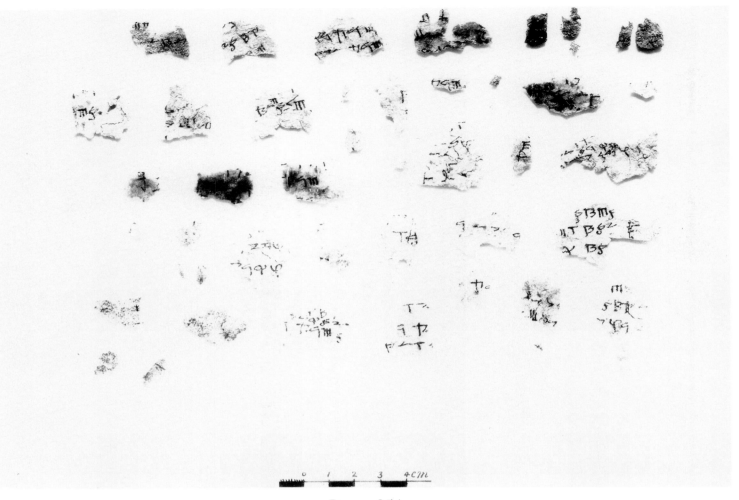

PLATE 854

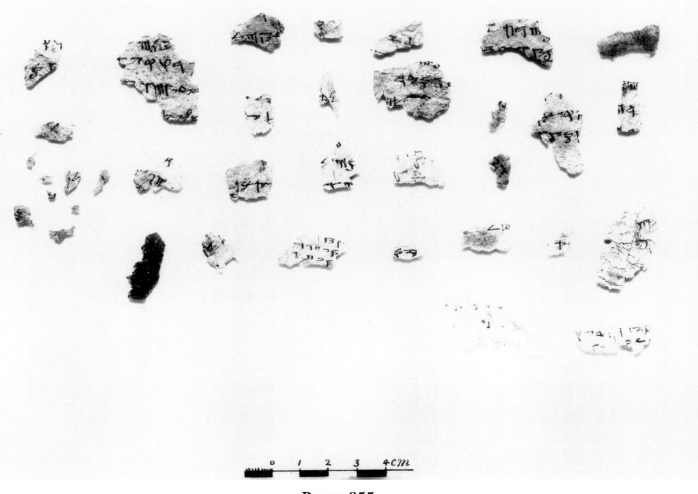

PLATE 855

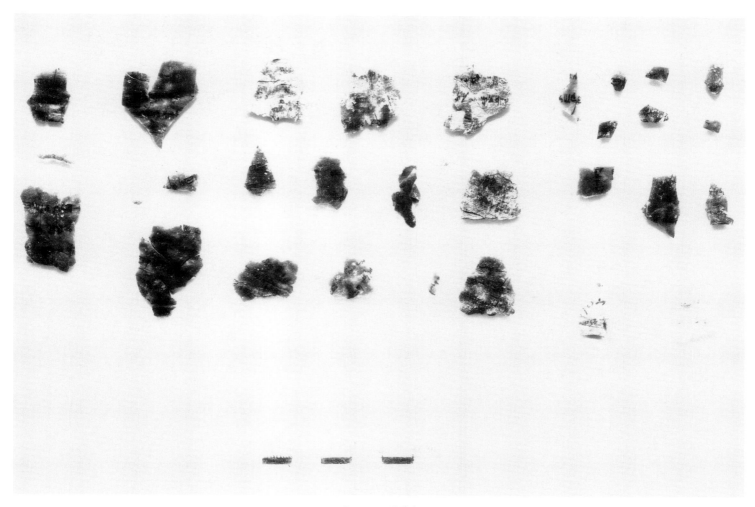

PLATE 856

PLATE 857

PLATE 858

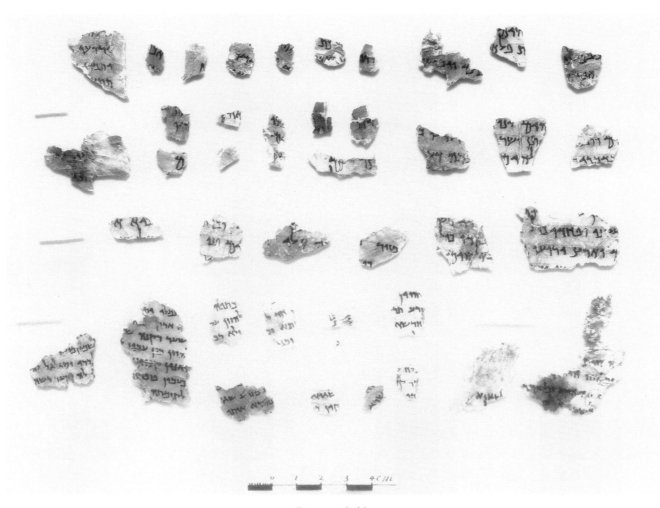

PLATE 859

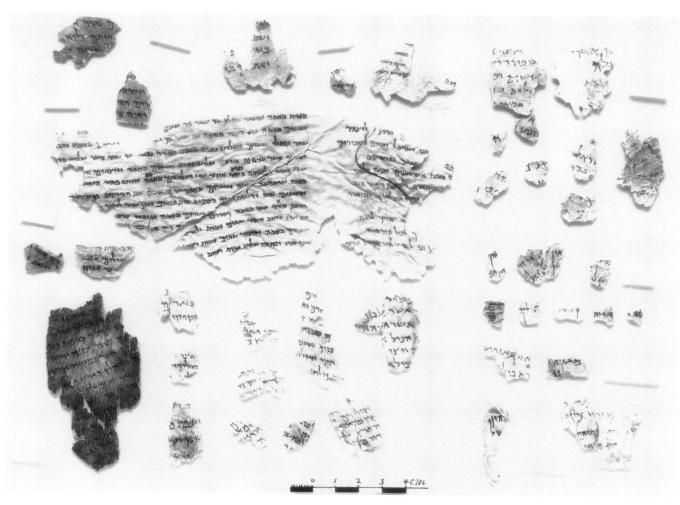

PLATE 860

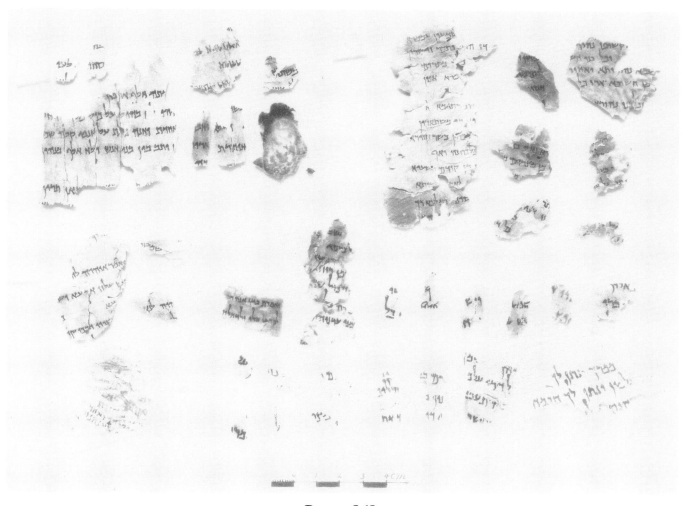

PLATE 861

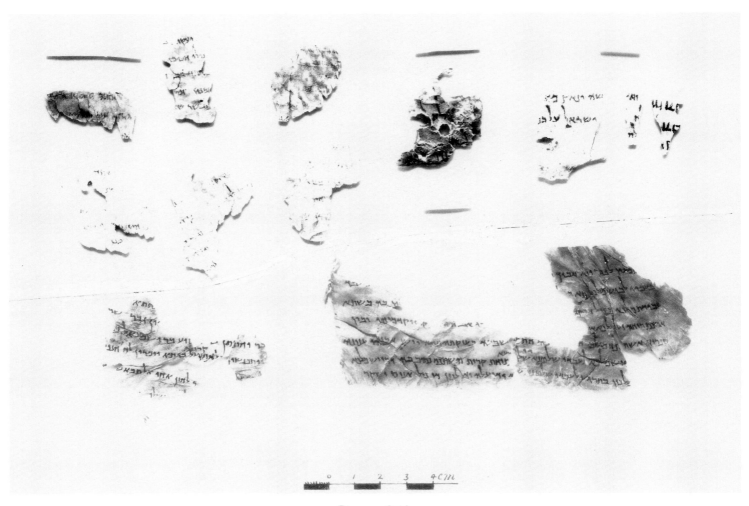

PLATE 862

PLATE 863

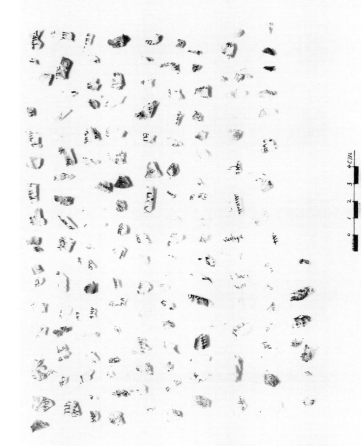

PLATE 864

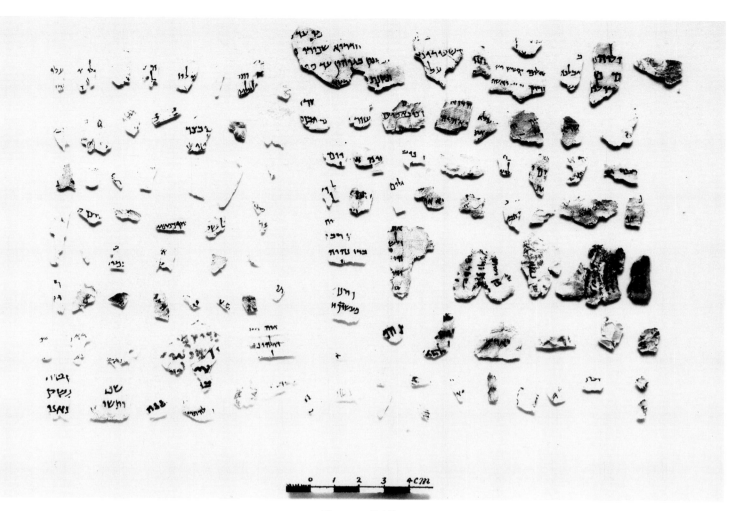

PLATE 865

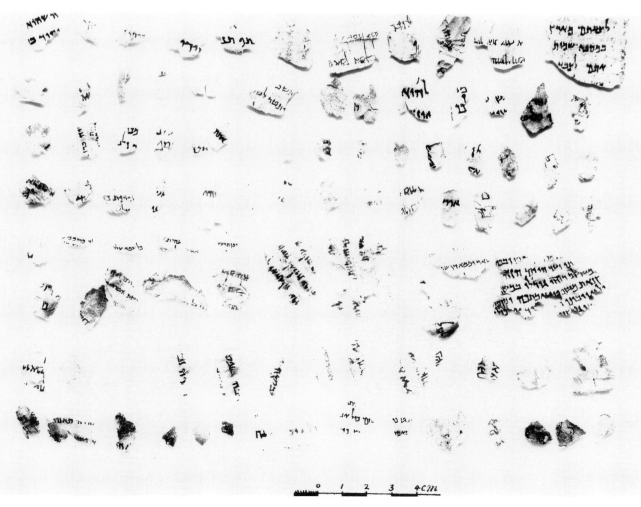

PLATE 866

PLATE 867A

PLATE 867B

PLATE 868

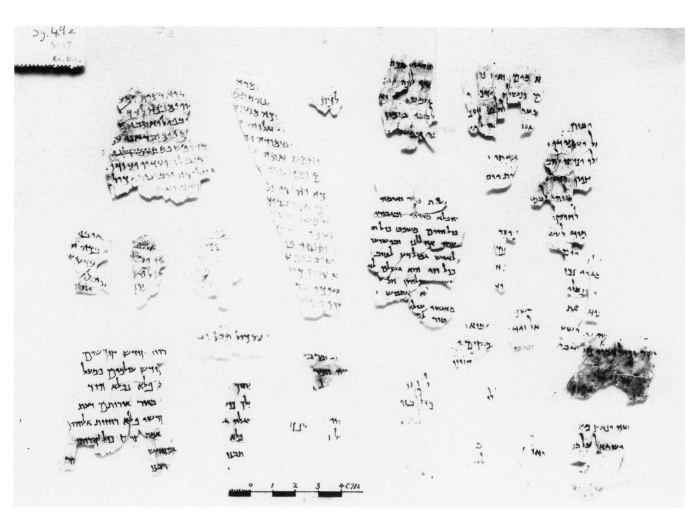

PLATE 869

PLATE 870

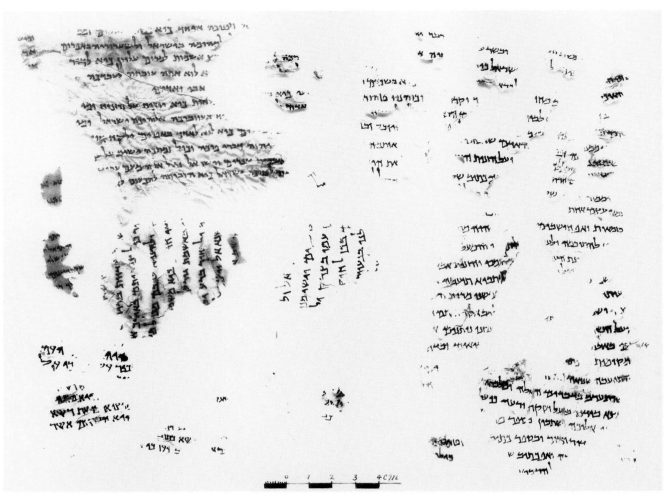

PLATE 871

PLATE 872

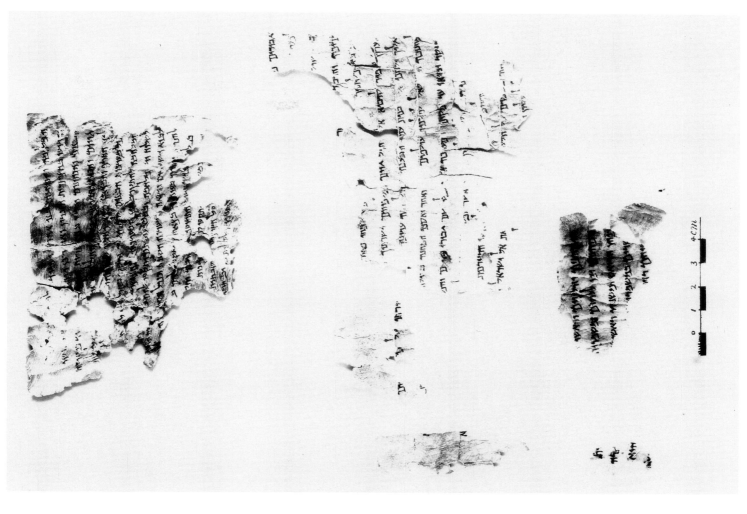

PLATE 874

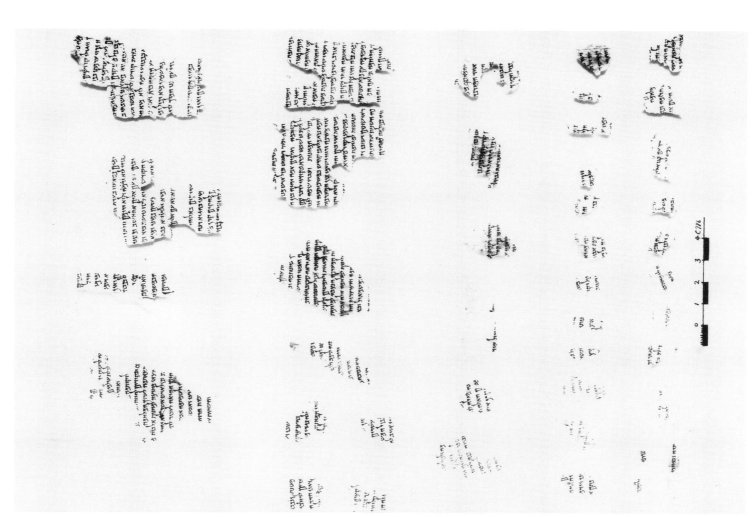

PLATE 873

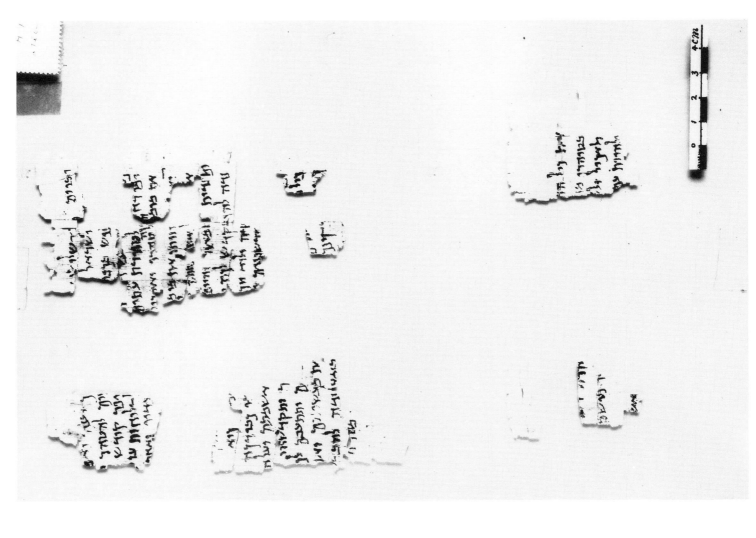

PLATE 876

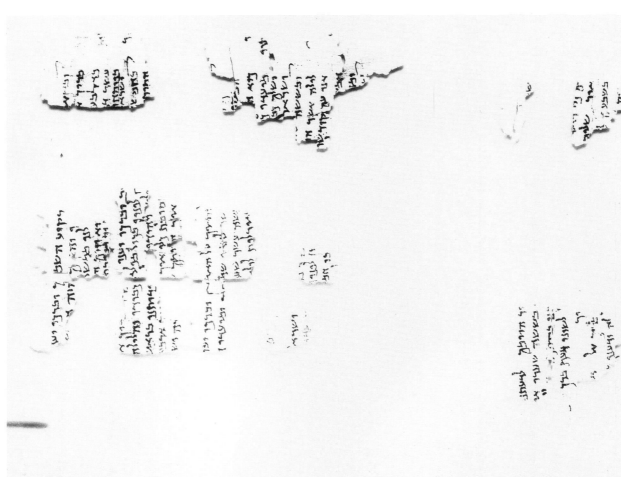

PLATE 875

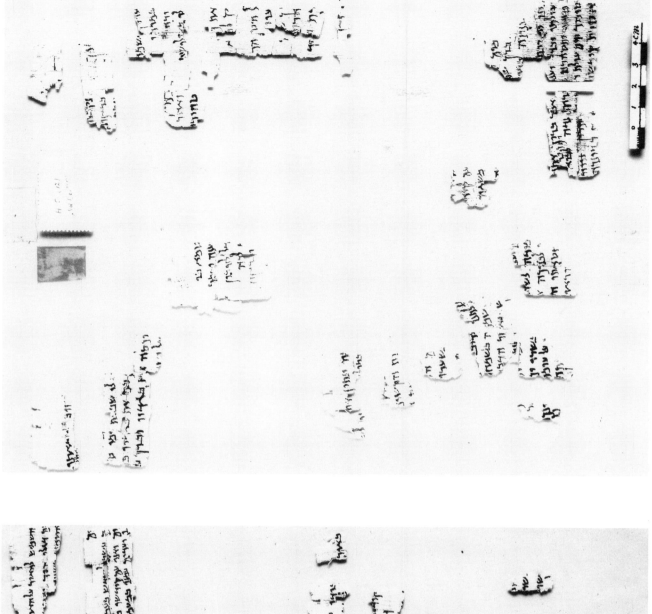

PLATE 878

PLATE 877

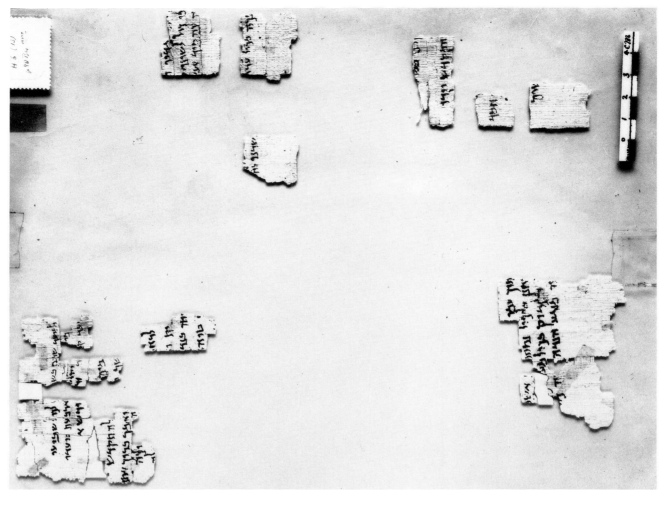

PLATE 880

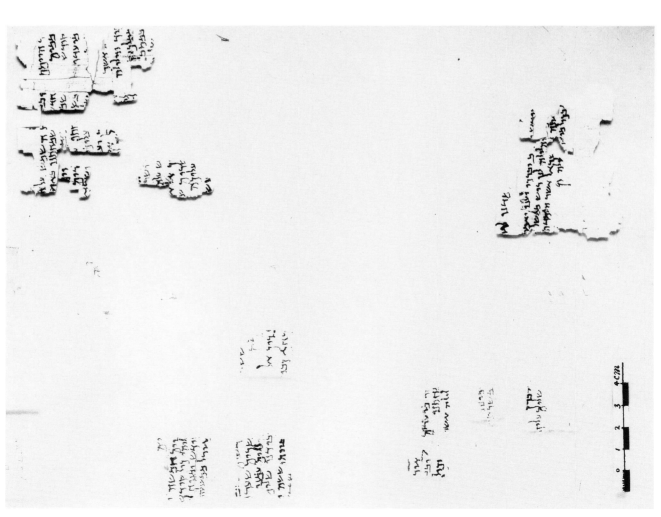

PLATE 879

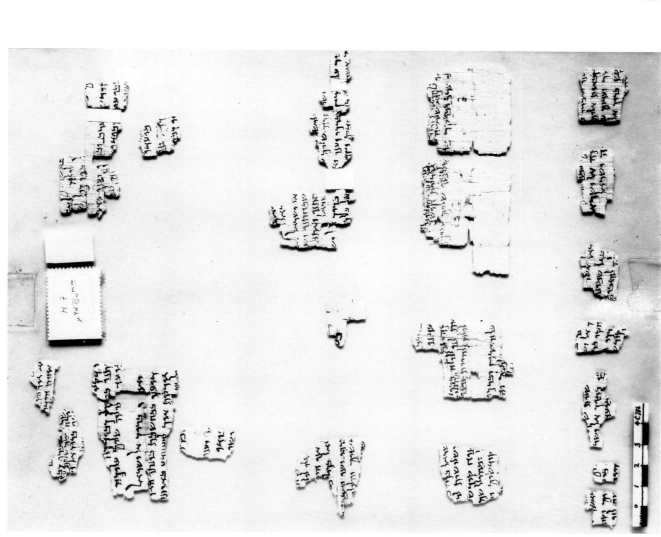

PLATE 882

PLATE 881

PLATE 883

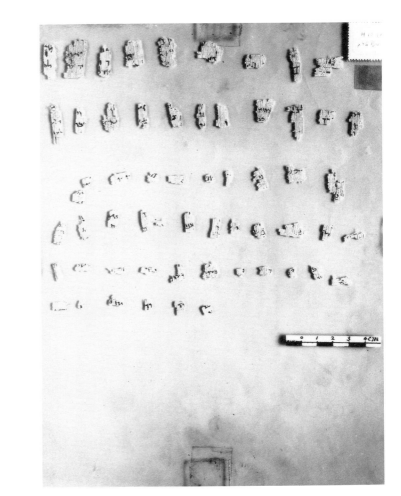

PLATE 884

PLATE 885

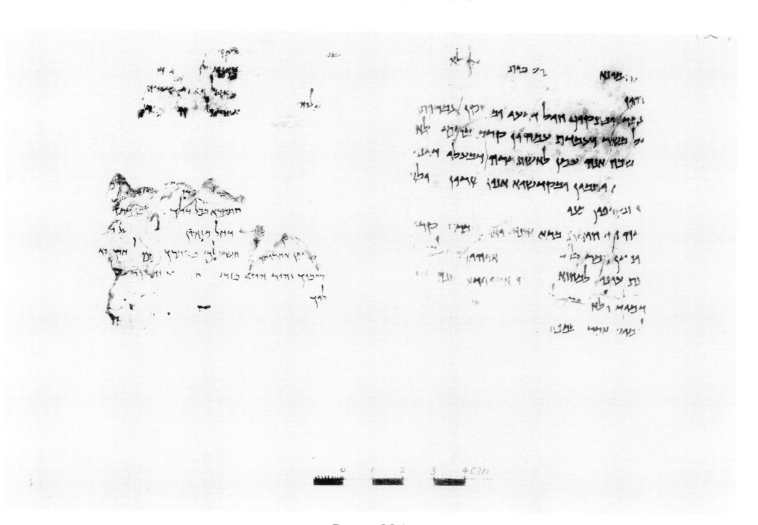

PLATE 886

PLATE 887

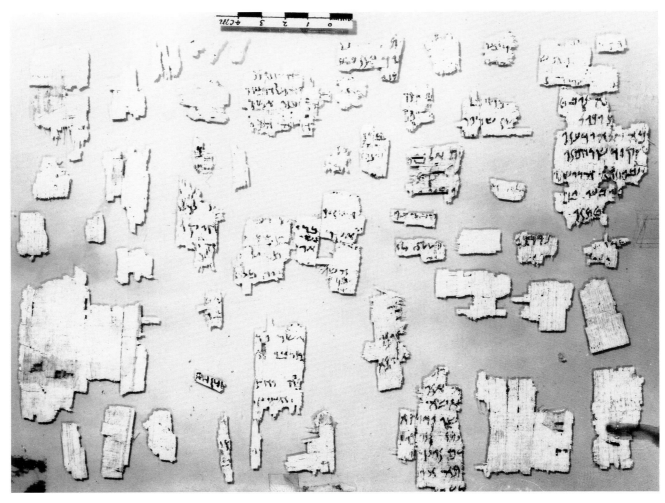

PLATE 888

PLATE 889

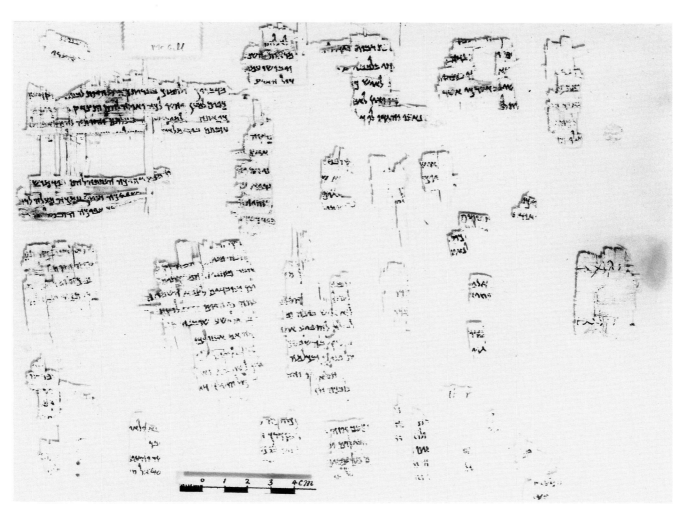

PLATE 890

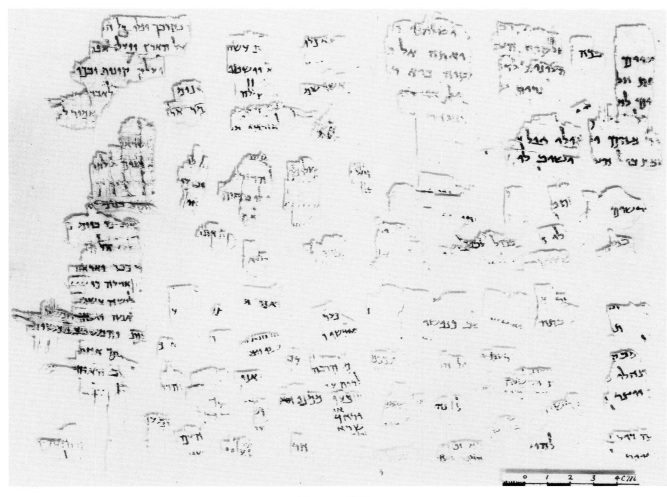

PLATE 891

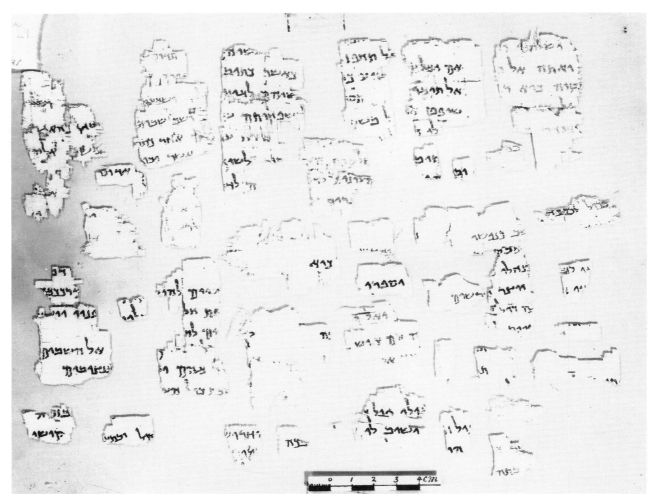

PLATE 892

PLATE 893

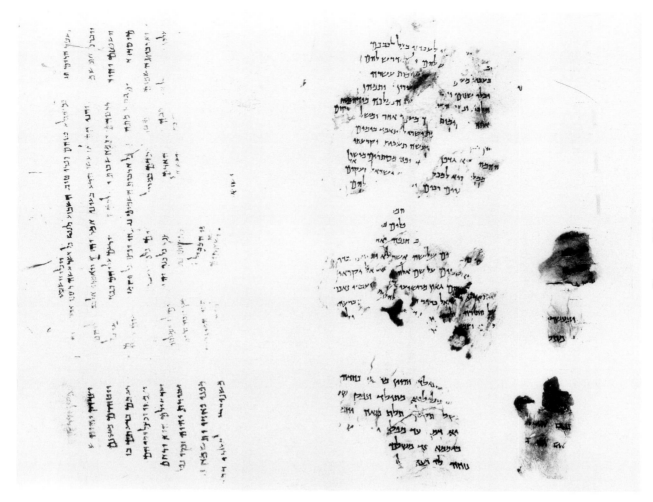

PLATE 894

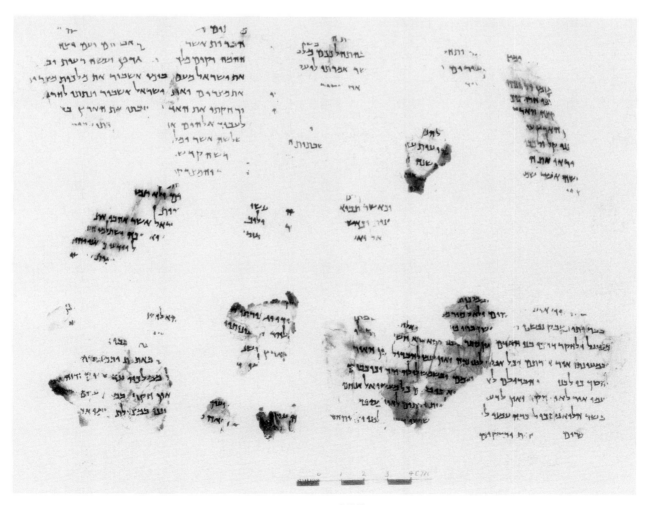

PLATE 895

PLATE 896

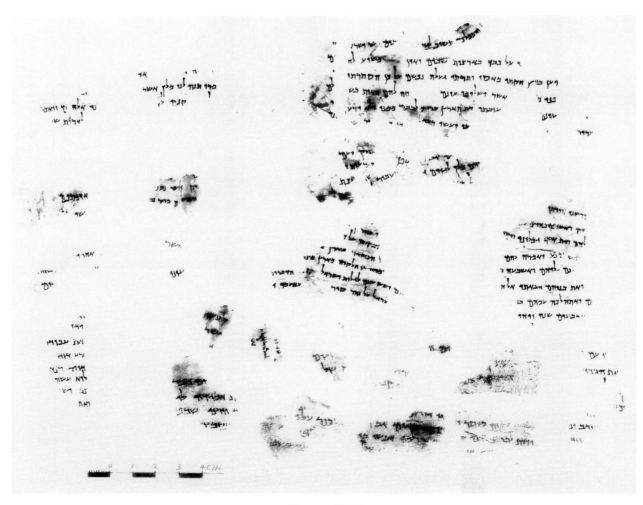

PLATE 897

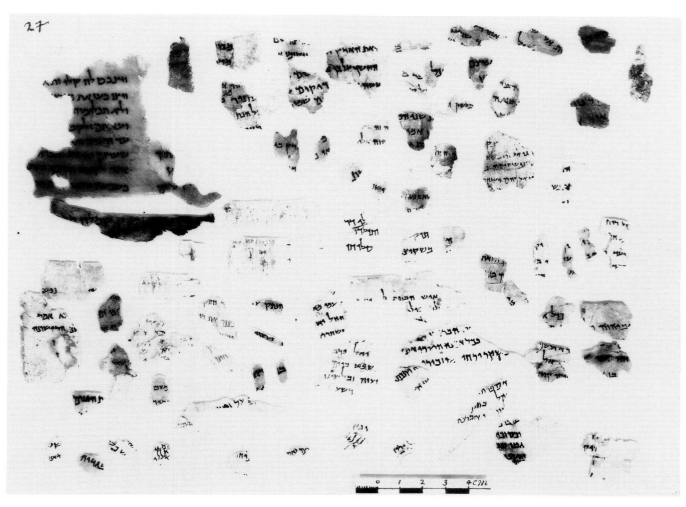

PLATE 898

PLATE 899

PLATE 900

PLATE 901

PLATE 902

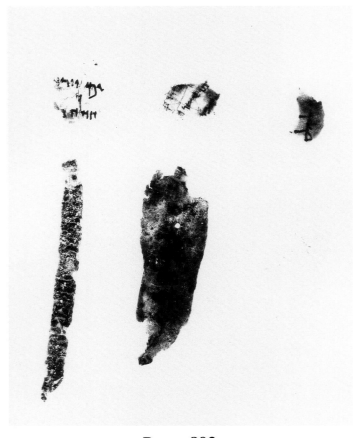

PLATE 903

PLATE 904

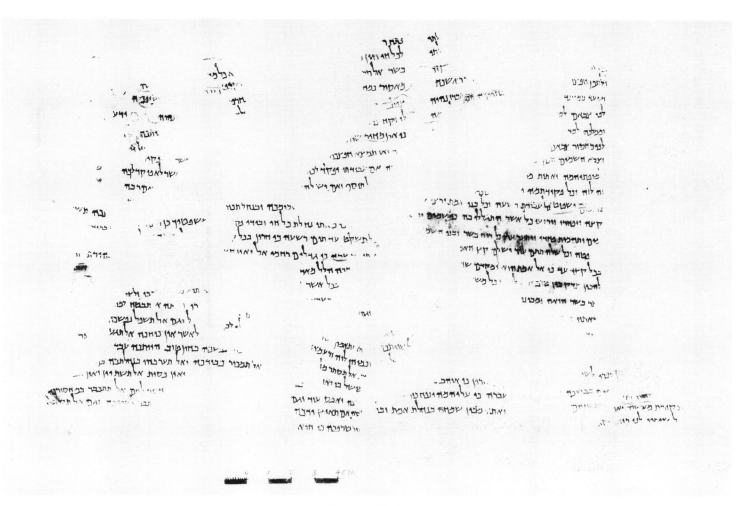

PLATE 905

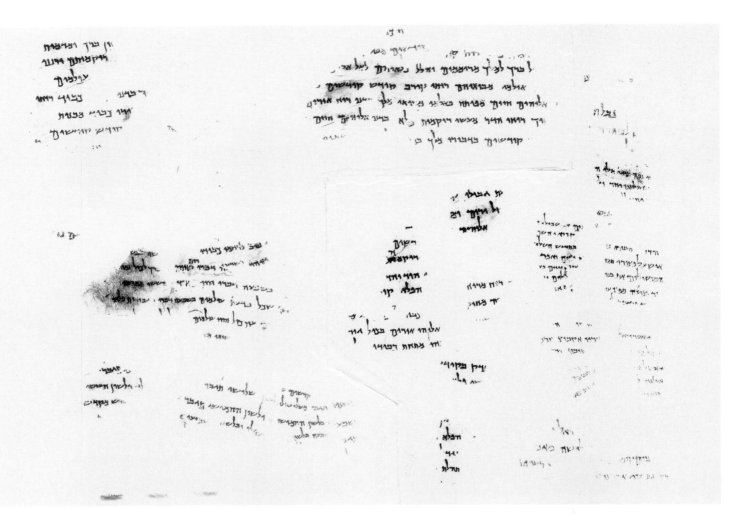

PLATE 906

PLATE 907